Rome and Parthia: Empires at War

Dedication

In loving memory of Geoff Sampson (1947–2019)

Rome and Parthia: Empires at War

Ventidius, Antony and the Second Romano-Parthian War, 40–20 BC

Gareth C Sampson

Pen & Sword
MILITARY

First published in Great Britain in 2020 by
Pen & Sword Military
An imprint of
Pen & Sword Books Ltd
Yorkshire – Philadelphia

ISBN 978 1 52671 013 0

A CIP catalogue record for this book is
available from the British Library.

Printed and bound in the UK by TJ International Ltd,
Padstow, Cornwall.

Pen & Sword Books Limited incorporates the imprints of Atlas,
Archaeology, Aviation, Discovery, Family History, Fiction, History,
Maritime, Military, Military Classics, Politics, Select, Transport,
True Crime, Air World, Frontline Publishing, Leo Cooper, Remember
When, Seaforth Publishing, The Praetorian Press, Wharncliffe
Local History, Wharncliffe Transport, Wharncliffe True Crime
and White Owl.

For a complete list of Pen & Sword titles please contact

PEN & SWORD BOOKS LIMITED
47 Church Street, Barnsley, South Yorkshire, S70 2AS, England
E-mail: enquiries@pen-and-sword.co.uk
Website: www.pen-and-sword.co.uk

Or

PEN AND SWORD BOOKS
1950 Lawrence Rd, Havertown, PA 19083, USA
E-mail: Uspen-and-sword@casematepublishers.com
Website: www.penandswordbooks.com

Contents

Acknowledgements

The first and greatest acknowledgement must go out to my wonderful wife Alex, without whose support none of this would be possible.

Special thanks go out to my parents, who always encouraged a love of books and learning (even if they did regret the house being filled with books).

There are a number of individuals who through the years have inspired in me the love of Roman history and mentored me along the way: Michael Gracey at William Hulme, David Shotter at Lancaster and Tim Cornell at Manchester. My heartfelt thanks go out to them all.

A shout goes out to the remaining members of the Manchester diaspora: Gary, Ian, Jason and Sam. Those were good days.

As always, my thanks go out to my editor, Phil Sidnell, for his patience and understanding.

It must also be said that as an independent academic, the job of researching these works is being made easier by the internet, so Alumnus access to JSTOR (Manchester and Lancaster) and Academia.edu must get a round of thanks also.

List of Illustrations

1. Bust of Cn. Pompeius Magnus
2. Bust of C. Iulius Caesar
3. Bust of M. Antonius
4. Bust of M. Vipsanius Agrippa
5. Prima Porta statue of Augustus
6. Coin of Orodes II
7. Coin of Pacorus
8. Coin of Antonius
9. Coin of Labienus
10. Coin of Antonius and Cleopatra
11. Coin of Artavasdes I of Media
12. Coin of Artavasdes II of Armenia
13. Coin of Augustus depicting the Parthian surrender of Roman standards
14. Coin of Augustus depicting the Parthian Triumphal arch

Maps & Diagrams

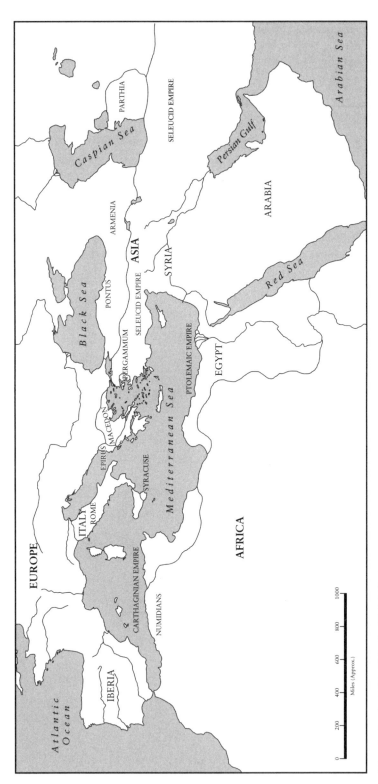

Map 1: Ancient World in the Third Century.

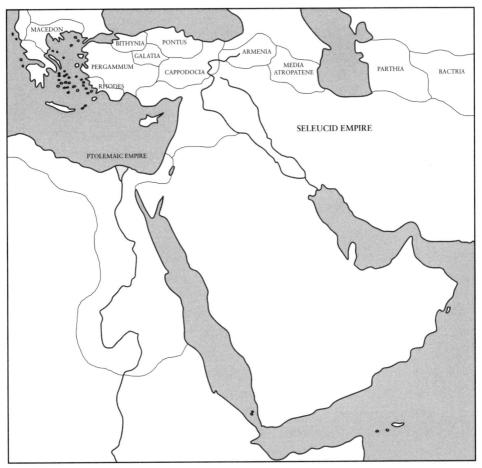

MACEDON

BITHYNIA   PONTUS

GALATIA

PERGAMMUM

CAPPODOCIA

ARMENIA

MEDIA
ATROPATENE

PARTHIA

BACTRIA

RHODES

SELEUCID EMPIRE

PTOLEMAIC EMPIRE

Map 2: Near East – Post Treaty of Apamea (188 BC).

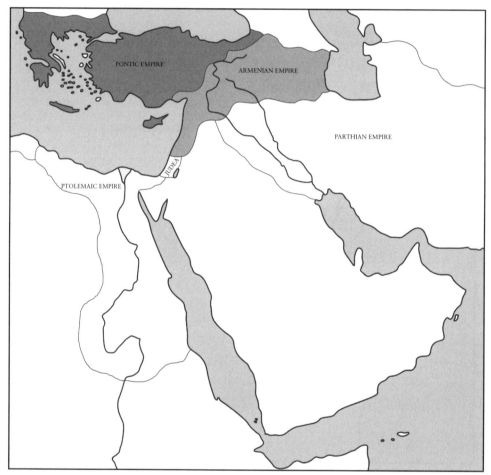

Map 3: Near East – Pontic & Armenian Empires (91–74 BC).

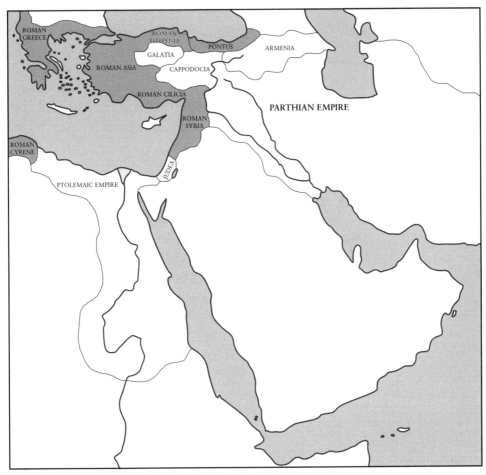

Map 4: Near East – End of Rome's Eastern War (63 BC).

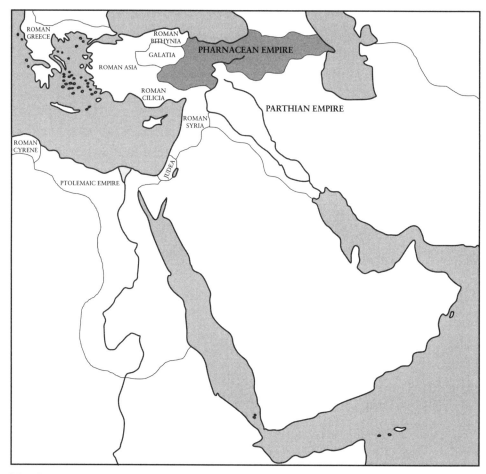

Map 5: Near East – Pharancean Empire (47 BC).

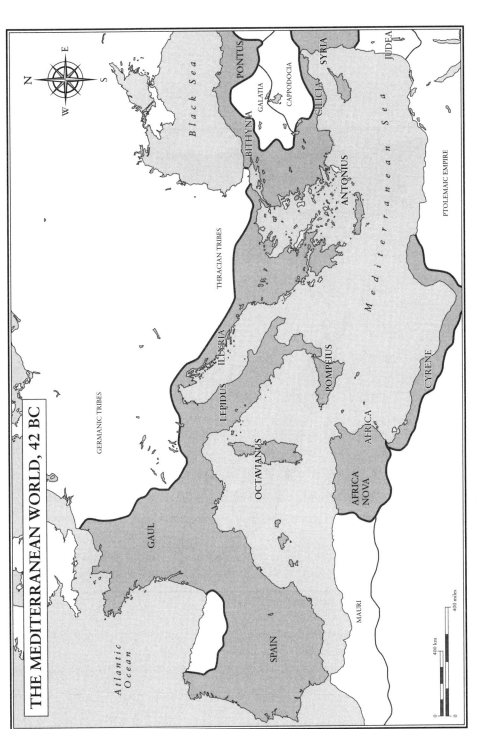

THE MEDITERRANEAN WORLD, 42 BC

GERMANIC TRIBES

Atlantic Ocean

GAUL

SPAIN

OCTAVIANUS

LEPIDUS

ILLYRIA

THRACIAN TRIBES

Black Sea

BITHYNIA

PONTUS

GALATIA

CAPPODOCIA

CILICIA

SYRIA

JUDEA

ANTONIUS

Mediterranean Sea

POMPEIUS

AFRICA

AFRICA NOVA

CYRENE

MAURI

PTOLEMAIC EMPIRE

N E S W

400 km

400 miles

0

0

Map 6: Ancient World – Roman Civil War (42 BC).

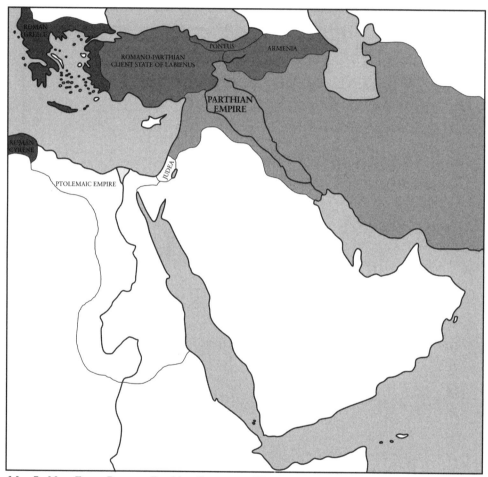

Map 7: Near East – Romano–Parthian Conquests (40 BC).

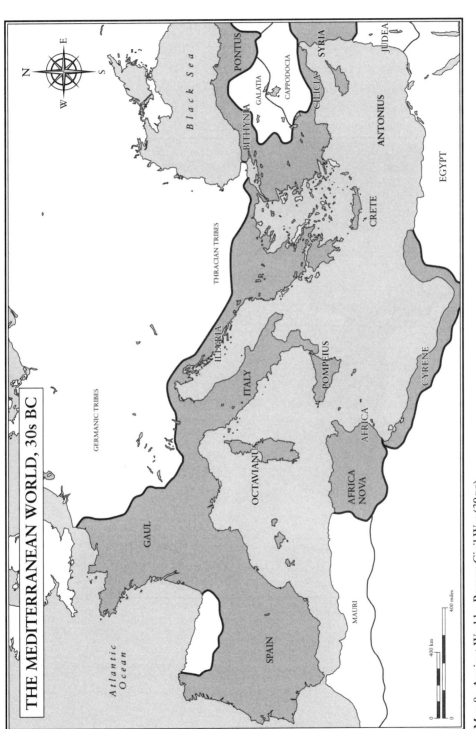

THE MEDITERRANEAN WORLD, 30s BC

Atlantic Ocean

Black Sea

GERMANIC TRIBES

THRACIAN TRIBES

GAUL

ILLYRIA

PONTUS

BITHYNIA

GALATIA

CAPPODOCIA

CILICIA

SYRIA

JUDEA

ANTONIUS

EGYPT

CRETE

ITALY

OCTAVIANUS

POMPEIUS

CYRENE

SPAIN

AFRICA

AFRICA NOVA

MAURI

N
E
S
W

400 km
400 miles

Map 8: Ancient World – Roman Civil War (39 BC).

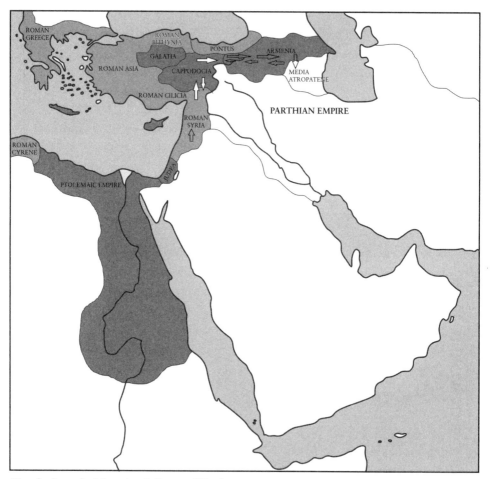

Map 9: Antonius' Invasion & Retreat (36 BC).

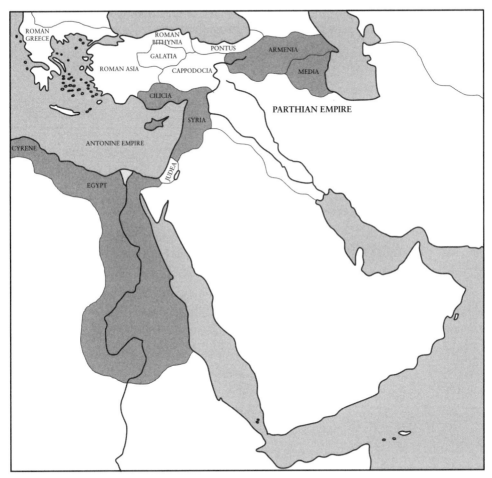

Map 10: Antonine Empire (34 BC).

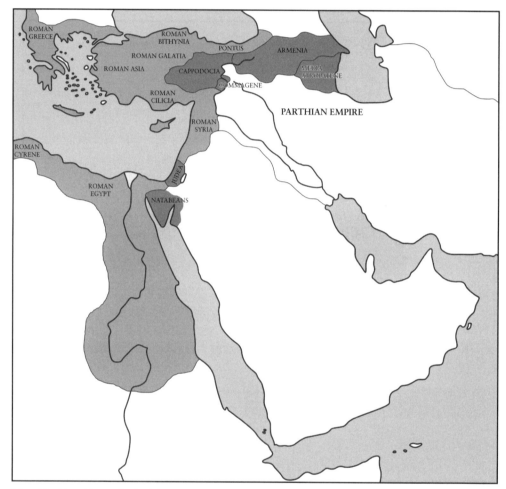

Map 11: Near East – End of the Romano–Parthian War (20 BC).

Introduction: Empires at War, with Each Other and Themselves

For over 600 years, the Middle East was defined by the division between the two superpowers of the ancient world: Rome and Parthia/Persia. Yet this division between two empires and two cultures, with either the Euphrates or the Tigris acting as the dividing line, was not inevitable and in fact flew in the face of the previous 500 years of history. Since the rise of the First Persian Empire under Cyrus the Great in the mid-sixth century BC, the Middle East was united, acting as the core of a universal empire, whose ruler claimed the title of 'King of Kings'. This concept survived the Persians and was adapted by Alexander the Great, who overthrew the Persian Empire and replaced it with one which unified Western and Eastern cultures, mixing Greek (Macedonian) with eastern customs (something the Persians had been trying by force for several centuries). Ever so briefly, one empire spanned from the Adriatic to the Indus. Yet even though Alexander's universal empire died with him, the dream did not, and the Hellenistic empires (Macedon, Seleucid and Ptolemaic) which rose from the ashes kept the dream alive between them.

Yet whilst the world was centred on these three empires and the Greco-Eastern culture they fostered, at the very far reaches of this civilization rose two states: one in the far west, on the edge of the (Greek) civilized world, and the other in the far east, on the edge of the Asian Steppes. From the mid-third century BC onwards, these two minor states began their journey into carving out huge empires at the expense of the triumvirate of Hellenistic empires. By the mid-second century BC, Macedon had been humbled by Rome and the Seleucids by Parthia, with the Ptolemies becoming more impotent and vulnerable as these new powers rose.

Thus, as the decades passed, these two new empires – one a republic, the other an oriental monarchy – began to move inexorably towards each other. By the first century BC, the two powers established first contract in Asia Minor, which was becoming something of the modern Balkans of its day. Yet it was at this point that both empires collapsed into civil war, within a year of each other, postponing the inevitable moment when they would clash. Both Rome and Parthia actually came close to being extinguished, with two new powers – the empires of Pontus and Armenia – taking advantage of their weakness to carve out empires of their own.

Yet whilst the Parthian Empire was seemingly paralyzed by its civil war, Rome rose to the occasion and simultaneously fought both external wars and a bloody internal one. When the dust had settled, Rome had conquered both of the new empires and taken a bold imperial leap into dominating the Near East. With Pontus and Armenia having fallen, Rome soon set its sights on what was believed to be an ailing Parthia. The result was the Battle of Carrhae, one of the most important battles in the history of the Middle East, stopping Rome's eastward expansion in its tracks.

The conflict soon fizzled out when a half-hearted Parthian raid on Roman Syria was defeated and both sides allowed the conflict to abate, each preferring to concentrate on internal political matters. Rome's attention was focussed on the bloody degeneration of the Republican system and a potential clash between two of the three leading oligarchs, Caesar and Pompeius (with Crassus having been killed in the aftermath of Carrhae). In Parthia, the focus was on the new King Orodes II, who had come to the throne in a double coup (against first his father and then his brother), and his need to secure his throne and prevent a further collapse of royal power that had dominated the previous two generations.

Thus matters in the East were left unresolved. Both empires were built on expansion (eastwards and westwards respectively), and neither had ever tolerated a rival. Furthermore, both were fuelled by a cultural legacy of the previous universal empires, and the desire to recreate either the Alexandrian Empire or the Persian one. For either to be achieved, their rival must fall.

Thus we come to the Second Romano-Parthian War, perhaps less well known than its predecessor, but whose implications were far more lasting. This work will analyse the conflict between these two great powers, and especially focus on the unusual phenomenon that both were conducted against the background of multiple civil wars on each side. This presented opportunities and weaknesses for the conduct of both campaigns, and ultimately meant that neither could wholeheartedly commit to the war, always fighting with one eye on events at home.

This volume will focus on the activities of some of history's most famous figures, certainly on the Roman side: most notably M. Antonius, his Egyptian wife, the Pharaoh Cleopatra, and C. Iulius Caesar Octavianus, who would become Augustus, the First Citizen (now viewed as Emperor) of Rome. However, just as importantly, if not more so, it will focus on the figures who have been neglected by subsequent history, such as the noted Roman general P. Ventidius, who became the most decorated Roman general against the Parthians. It will also highlight the rise of various Roman warlords in the East, who tried to carve out their own fiefdoms in the region, most notably Q. Caecilius Bassus, C. Cassius and Q. Labienus 'Parthicus'.

However, this volume will not simply focus on the Roman aspect of these clashes, but will also analyze these conflicts from the Parthian side, wherever possible. Thus we will encounter the talented and ambitious Parthian Prince Pacorus, whose campaigns came so close to destroying the power of Rome in the East and expanding the Parthian Empire to the Mediterranean and beyond, as well as his more machiavellian brother Phraates IV, whose strategies did so much to preserve Parthian power.

The war fought between 40 and 20 BC fluctuated between periods of intense military campaigning and years of plots and counter-plots and proxy wars, as both sides not only had to negotiate fighting wars of conquest against their powerful neighbour but balance this against ongoing civil wars at home. Thus, in many ways, this period was as much about empires being at war with themselves as being at war with each other. The results of these two decades of on-and-off warfare were to shape the ancient world for the next 600 years and prove to be the death of the dream of a universal civilization stretching from east to west.

Timeline of the Key Events
of the Period 40–20 BC

49–27 BC	Third Roman Civil War.
40–20 BC	Second Romano Parthian War.
40 BC	Romano-Parthian invasion of Roman East, led by Parthian prince Pacorus and Roman general Q. Labienus.
	Pact of Brundisium between Antonius and Octavianus ends another round of Roman Civil War.
39 BC	Roman invasion of Romano-Parthian Asia Minor by P. Ventidius.
	Roman victories at the Battles of Mount Amanus and Cilician Gates.
	Reconquest of Roman Near East.
38 BC	Second Parthian invasion led by Pacorus.
	Roman victory at the Battle of Gindarus, Parthian army destroyed, Pacorus killed.
	Antonius returns to the East. Triumph of Ventidius.
	Palace coup puts Phraates on Parthian throne.
37 BC	Pact of Tarentum between Antonius and Octavianus renews the Triumvirate.
	Romano-Judean War. Roman capture of Jerusalem.
	Roman victories in Armenia and Caucasus.
36 BC	Roman defeat.
	Roman invasion of Media-Atropatené (part of the Parthian Empire).
	Antonius forced to retreat back to Armenia by Parthians.
	Roman Civil War between Octavianus and Sex. Pompeius.
35 BC	Antonine reorganization of the East.
	Defection of Artavasdes of Media.
	Roman Civil War between Antonius and Sex. Pompeius.
	Death of Sex. Pompeius.

34 BC	Romano–Armenian War.
	Founding of Antonine Empire.
32 BC	Romano–Median army invades Parthian Empire.
	Roman Civil War between Antonius and Octavianus.
31 BC	Romano–Median army defeated by Parthians.
	Parthians overrun Media and Armenia.
	Battle of Actium – Antonius and Cleopatra defeated.
	Parthian Civil War between Phraates IV and Tiridates II.
30 BC	Roman invasion and conquest of Egypt.
	End of the Ptolemaic and Antonine dynasties.
	Death of Antonius, Cleopatra and Ptolemy Caesarion.
29 BC	Tiridates defeated by Phraates and escapes to Roman Syria.
	Octavianus returns to Rome.
26 BC	Tiridates invades Parthia from Roman territory, renews Parthian Civil War.
27 BC	Octavianus establishes his sole rule of the Republic and becomes Augustus.
	End of the Third Roman Civil War.
	Augustus launches attack on southern Arabia.
	Indian (Sakan) embassies reach Augustus in Spain.
25 BC	Tiridates defeated by Phraates once more and again flees to Roman territory.
	Kingdom of Galatia annexed by Rome.
	Arabian campaign ends in disaster and retreat.
	Kushite (Nubians) invasion of Roman Egypt.
24 BC	Romano–Nubian War in southern Egypt.
23 BC	Agrippa sent to command in Syria, possibly opens negotiations with Phraates.
	Augustus falls dangerously ill, sparking succession crisis.
	Second Constitutional Settlement by Augustus, cementing his rule.
	Death of Marcellus, heir to Augustus.
	End of Romano–Kushite War.
22 BC	Augustus tours Rome's eastern provinces.
	Second Indian (Sakan) embassies reach Augustus in the East.
21 BC	Augustus reaches Roman Near East, negotiations with Phraates.

20 BC   Return of the Roman standards (and prisoners) lost by Crassus
and Antonius
Roman invasion of Armenia, pro-Roman client king crowned
by Tiberius.
Pro-Roman client king of Media-Atropatené crowned.
End of the Second Romano-Parthian War.

Notes on Roman Names

All Roman names in the following text will be given in their traditional form, including the abbreviated first name. Below is a list of the Roman first names referred to in the text and their abbreviations:

A.	Aulus.
Ap.	Appius
C.	Caius
Cn.	Cnaeus
D.	Decimus
K.	Kaeso
L.	Lucius
M.	Marcus
Mam.	Mamercus
P.	Publius
Q.	Quintus
Ser.	Servius
Sex.	Sextus
Sp.	Spurius
T.	Titus
Ti.	Tiberius

Part I

The Rise of the New World Order (to 44 BC)

Chapter One

The Rise of the New World Order; Rome and Parthia (to 50 BC)

The Second Romano–Parthian War was not just a clash between two mighty empires, but the culmination of a near 300-year process which began with the destruction of the Persian Empire at the hands of Alexander the Great. It was the decisive collision between the two great new powers that had emerged on the peripheries of the Hellenistic world order – one in the west, the other in the east – yet had overthrown their more established rivals. For several centuries these two emerging world powers had steadily been advancing towards each other, crushing and absorbing the states that lay between them, until they finally met in the Near East in the mid-first century BC. These new powers were led by men who wanted to lay claim to inherit the mantle of the two great universal empires that had gone before them, those of Persia and Alexander, which made a clash between them inevitable, with the lands of the Middle East their prize. Therefore, to understand fully the clash between these two new empires, we must briefly acquaint ourselves with their individual histories and the wider context that joined them together.

1. The Hellenistic World and the Rise of the New Powers (fourth to third century BC)

At first glance there seems to be little that links the two states of Rome and Parthia: one a city-state republic based in Italy, the other an oriental monarchy whose heartland lay on the eastern shores of the Caspian Sea. Yet both shared the same status, being on the fringes of the 'civilized' world or, more importantly, the fringes of the great empires that occupied the 'civilized' world. This otherness and distance from the centres of power allowed them to grow, almost unnoticed, by the major powers of the ancient world. Thus, whilst the great powers of the ancient world warred with each other, they ignored these rising threats until it was too late, and each grew stronger by exploiting the weaknesses of the great powers.

The era that these burgeoning new powers grew in had been shaped by the momentous events that had taken place in the fourth century BC. Up until that point, the ancient world had been dominated by the great Persian Empire, the largest empire that the world had seen, stretching from Greece to India. It had been forged by Cyrus the Great, the Persian king who had annexed the Median, Lydian and Babylonian kingdoms and forged them into one universal empire. The empire continued its expansion in all directions, ultimately absorbing the Parthian region, annexing Egypt and Asia Minor and crossing into Greece, occupying Macedonia. It was in Greece that the most famous (at least in the West) wars were fought when the Greek states, led by Athens and Sparta, defeated the Persian invasion of Xerxes, stopping Persia's western expansion. Had this not occurred, then it is more than likely that Italy would have soon followed, extinguishing Rome before it had begun its journey to empire.

Though the Persian Wars are greatly mythologized in the West, the Persian Empire itself was not significantly affected and continued to be the leading power of the ancient world over the next 150 years, helped to a great extent by the ongoing warfare between the Greek states. Yet by the 340s BC a new power had emerged in Greece, namely the Kingdom of Macedon, which benefited from the exhaustion of the major Greek city-states of Athens, Sparta and Thebes, each of which had been able to gain only a temporary dominance over the others. It was Macedon, under King Philip II, that was able to control all of Greece, enabling him to turn his attention to Persia. An untimely assassination robbed Philip of his chance, but his son and successor seized the moment, attacked and incredibly overthrew the Persian Empire, going on to be known to history as Alexander the Great.

In terms of Rome and Parthia, again they lay on the peripheries of these great conquests. As a province of the Persian Empire, Parthia became part of the Alexandrian Empire, whilst Rome sat uncomfortably close, separated only by the Adriatic. Livy famously took time out of his Roman history to consider what would have happened if Alexander had survived and turned his attention westwards to Italy, one of the world's earliest counterfactual histories.[1]

Yet Alexander died aged only 32, and with him expired the dreams of a universal empire, his generals ripping the empire apart in a series of wars. Again, both Rome and Parthia lay on the outskirts of this warfare and were little affected. By the early third century, Alexander's empire had been replaced by three great Hellenistic powers: Macedon (who also controlled Greece), the Ptolemaic Empire, centred on Egypt, and the Seleucid Empire, which stretched from Asia Minor to India, incorporating the region of Parthia in its far north-eastern border, along with Bactria (see Map 1). Naturally enough, these three powers then engaged in periods of warfare between themselves, with a series of Syrian Wars between the Ptolemaic and Seleucid Empires raging across the Near East.[2]

2. The Growth of Rome in the Third Century BC

By the time of Alexander's death in 323 BC, Rome was emerging as a regional power in Italy. For four centuries (if we are to believe the Roman traditions on their origins and early chronology) Rome had been a minor city-state, overshadowed by the great Etruscan civilization to the north and the Greek city-states to the south.[3] The city itself came close to extinction when it was sacked (c.390–386 BC) by invading Gauls, who occupied northern Italy. Having rebuilt their city and reorganized their army in the wake of this setback, the Romans then spent the next sixty years engaged in warfare with their neighbours, slowly expanding their zone of control in western central Italy. Victory at the Battle of Antium in 338 BC brought Rome control of the Latin states of central Italy. The settlement that followed laid the foundations for Rome's supremacy in Italy and the wider Mediterranean, and incorporated four key strands: autonomy, land, citizenship and manpower.

Each defeated state retained their autonomy, with their own languages, customs and ruling elites, albeit with each city being bound to Rome separately by treaty, accompanied by the loss of an independent foreign policy. These cities also lost land to Rome, which became Roman public land (*ager publicus*) used to plant Roman colonies, to ease social pressure in Rome and act as watch posts in former enemy territory. A new graded citizenship system was expanded to these defeated cities, with some receiving full Roman citizenship and others a lesser Latin status, thus absorbing the local elites into the Roman system and letting them rule their cities on Rome's behalf. Finally, each of the individual treaties made provision for the defeated cities to send men to fight in Rome's armies, the foundation of the manpower system which allowed Rome to field armies far bigger than its own resources allowed and ultimately to tap into the entire manpower of Italy.

The next sixty years saw an intensity in Roman warfare which culminated in victories over an alliance of Samnites, Etruscans and Gauls in the Third Samnite War and ultimately, by 280 BC, saw the whole of central Italy controlled by Rome. The next decade witnessed a Roman war with the Greek general Pyrrhus, who was attempting to forge his own Adriatic empire from Sicily to southern Italy and western Greece. Victory in this war brought Rome control of southern Greece and thus into contact with the Carthaginian Empire, which partially controlled Sicily. Naturally the two expanding powers (one southwards, the other northwards) came into conflict, sparking the First Punic War, a conflict that ended with Rome in partial control of Sicily, followed shortly afterwards by Sardinia and Corsica.

With the Roman sphere of influence expanding, attention soon turned to the east and mainland Greece. In 229 BC Rome took advantage of a power vacuum in mainland Greece caused both by the collapse of the ruling dynasty in Epirus and the death of the Macedonian King Demetrius II in battle against invading Thracian tribes. The decline of Epirote power had led to the rise of a new Illyrian kingdom, that of the Ardiaei, whose ships increased their piratical attacks on Roman interests. Determined to protect their trade and their eastern flank, Rome launched an invasion of Illyria, quickly establishing a protectorate over the coastal cities. Thus Rome, for the first time, had crossed the Adriatic and established a presence in mainland Greece, an act that was bound to lead to tensions with a recovering Macedon, which for over 100 years had been the hegemon of Greece. A Second Illyrian War soon followed in 219 BC, further entrenching Rome's position.[4]

A clash with Macedon was postponed when the Second Punic War broke out, a war which nearly destroyed the Roman state. Sensing his opportunity, the new Macedonian king, Philip V, allied with the Carthaginians, hoping to profit from Rome's defeat and remove its influence from mainland Greece. The First Macedonian War (214–205 BC) had no major battles between Rome and Macedon, but Rome constructed an alliance of Greek states who fought Philip in mainland Greece. The war ended in stalemate but saw a Roman fleet operating in the Aegean for the first time, in alliance with the city-state of Pergammum on the coast of Asia Minor, an enemy of the Seleucid Empire, from which it had seceded. A peace treaty between the two powers formally ended the war in 205 BC but left matters between them unresolved. Four years later Rome completed its victory over Carthage, giving it control of the western Mediterranean and all of its resources.

3. The Growth of Parthia in the Third Century BC

The history of Parthia, by contrast, is little-known for the early part of this period, it being on the edge of first the Persian, then the Alexandrian and finally the Seleucid Empire. The region itself was on the edge of the wide Eurasian Steppes, which gave the inhabitants a semi-nomadic lifestyle. References to the region can be found as far back as the early seventh century, and we certainly find 'Parthian' troops as part of the Persian army which invaded Greece. The key problem we have is that prior to 247 BC we simply have no clear records for what occurred in Parthia, or even who the inhabitants were. Being on the edge of the steppes meant that regular migrations of tribes would have taken place, and we have no clear concept of the identity of a 'Parthian' people until they gained their independence.[5]

Key to the rise of Parthia was the weakness of the Seleucid Empire. Unlike the Persian Empire that it sought to emulate, the Seleucids struggled to maintain the internal cohesion of their vast territories, especially given ongoing warfare, particularly in the west of the empire against the other Hellenistic powers. By 247 BC the governor of the neighbouring province of Bactria used the inattention of the Seleucid government to declare independence. In the struggle that followed (which is poorly recorded), Parthia too gained its independence from the Seleucid Empire and avoided being added to the new Bactrian Kingdom.[6]

Central to this process was the shadowy figure of Arsaces, the legendary first king of Parthia and founder of the Arsacid dynasty. In many ways Arsaces is a shadowy figure, comparable to that of Romulus in Roman history. If the Parthians wrote any histories of their own, then they do not survive, and even if they did it is unlikely that any were contemporaneous. This leaves us relying on external Greco-Roman sources for his life, of which the surviving ones preserve differing versions (see Appendix Two). Thus we have a wide range of possibilities, from him being a tribal chieftain of a nomadic tribe who either invaded Parthia or were invited in by the Bactrian rebels, to him being a Bactrian nobleman himself.

Furthermore, there is no certainty that there even was an Arsaces, similarly to questions that have been levelled at Romulus. It may well have been an assumed title, linking the rulers of Parthia to a legendary ancestor, a descendant of the Persian Emperor Artaxerxes II (404–358 BC). Furthermore, one story of the history of the early Parthian push for independence has a pair of brothers, Arsaces and Tiridates, mirroring Rome's Romulus and Remus. Just as in Roman history, one brother disappears from history, and in the Parthian case one version has Arsaces dying soon afterwards and Tiridates ruling in his stead. There is much scholarship on this issue, but this work is not the place to go into detail on this fascinating subject.[7] The key points for this study are that Parthia was able to break away from the Seleucid Empire, at the same time as Bactria, and formed an independent kingdom under a new Arsacid dynasty.

Not long after their independence, the Parthians invaded and annexed the Seleucid province of Hyrcania on the coast of the Caspian Sea, expanding their growing kingdom. Parthia clearly benefited from the ongoing Syrian War between the Seleucids and the Ptolemies in the Near East, which meant that Seleucus II could not break away and deal with the rebellious provinces in the east.[8] This gave both Parthia and Bactria time to become established. Again, the sources are poor and confused on Seleucid history in this period. Nevertheless, it seems that, having settled the wars in the west, Seleucus did indeed turn his attention to his rebellious provinces in the east and launched an expedition to recapture them (c.236 BC). Despite his initial successes, Seleucus either withdrew or was defeated and captured, depending on the ancient source,[9] and thus left Parthia and Bactria independent. The withdrawal and subsequent death of Seleucus II (c.225 BC) gave the Parthians further time to consolidate their new kingdom. Regardless of the identity of the first Parthian kings, we do know that c.211 BC the old king died, and the succession fell to his son Arsaces II.[10]

This change of monarch seemed to prompt the new Seleucid Emperor, Antiochus III, to take action. Antiochus had come to power in 223 BC and had reforged the Seleucid Empire, enabling him to turn his focus on recovering the lost eastern provinces.[11] The Parthians were defeated in battle and Antiochus took Hyrcania. We are not clear on what happened next, but it seems that Arsaces and Antiochus reached terms, with Antiochus acknowledging the rule of the Arsacid dynasty in Parthia, but Arsaces acknowledging Antiochus as his overlord. Thus Parthia returned to the Seleucid Empire, but this time as a client kingdom, with the Arsacid dynasty remaining as its rulers. Antiochus then moved onto defeating and reabsorbing Bactria on much the same terms, before annexing swathes of territory in the East, bringing the empire once more to the borders of India.

The fortunes of Rome and Parthia therefore diverged wildly in this period, with Rome establishing itself as the dominant power in the western Mediterranean, albeit having come close to destruction at the hands of Carthage, whilst Parthia managed to gain independence from the Seleucid Empire, only to fall back to the status of a client kingdom.

4. Overthrowing the Hellenistic World Order (200s–140s BC)

It was with Antiochus that the fates of the two states became interlinked. Clearly the Parthian state would not flourish in the face of a strong Seleucid Empire, but it was not yet powerful enough to defeat the Seleucids. However, within a decade Antiochus would face the Romans as the First Romano-Seleucid War broke out (192–189 BC). In the aftermath of the Second Punic War, and flushed by their victory and control of the western Mediterranean, the Roman Senate determined that their security could not be guaranteed as long as Macedon remained on their eastern flank. Thus Rome went to war with Macedon and, in a result that heralded the dawn of a new age, the Romans defeated the Macedonians at the Battle of Cynoscephalae in 197 BC. For the first time since the breakup of the Alexandrian Empire there was a new power in the ancient world.

Rome took no territory in Greece, but famously declared the Greek states and Federations were to be 'free', albeit under Roman protection.[12] Macedon remained intact, but in a much-diminished position. This gave Antiochus the opportunity to further expand the Seleucid Empire and replace Macedon as the premier power in Greece. He was aided in this by the presence at the Seleucid court of none other than Hannibal, the Carthaginian general who had led the Second Punic War against Rome. Antiochus, the leading Hellenistic general, then invaded Greece, whose independence had been guaranteed by Rome.

Unfortunately for Antiochus, his forces fared no better against the Roman legions than those of Philip V of Macedon, and he was defeated at the Battle of Thermopylae (191 BC). Having driven Antiochus from Greece, the Romans continued their eastward expansion and crossed into Asia Minor for the first time to confront the Seleucids on their own territory. The resulting Battle of Magnesia (190 BC) was another Roman victory, meaning that three great powers of the ancient world had been defeated in less than ten years.[13]

It is no exaggeration to say that this was a blow from which the Seleucid Empire never recovered. The subsequent Treaty of Apamea (188 BC) reduced the Seleucid army and navy and stripped them of all territories in Asia Minor, which now became a buffer zone between the two powers (see Map 2).[14] The states of Pergamum and Rhodes were both enlarged and tasked with keeping Seleucid power in the region under observation. Antiochus himself was killed in a minor skirmish just a year later in 187 BC.

Whilst Rome was concerned with destroying Seleucid power in its western territories, this obviously had an impact in weakening it in the east. Arsaces II seems to have played the role of dutiful client king for the rest of his reign (c.210–185 BC), as does his successor Phriapatius (c.185–170 BC). Interestingly, it has been argued that Phriapatius was not the son of Arsaces II but a cousin and descended from Tiridates, the shadowy brother of Arsaces, and thus a second branch of the Arsacid dynasty took the throne.[15] This switching of branches, between the descendants of Arsaces and those of his brother Tiridates, seems to have been a feature of the Arsacid dynasty and one which may not have been as peaceful as we imagine. Yet the next generation of Parthian monarchs – two brothers, Phraates I (c.168–165 BC)[16] and Mithradates I (c.165–132 BC) – came to power when the Seleucid Empire was crumbling, thanks to its humiliation by Rome, and did not seem to share their predecessors' reticence.

Though Phraates only reigned for five years, we have sources that show that the Parthians were militarily active in the Caspian Sea region, defeating a tribe known as the Mardi, and thus the Parthians had once again started to expand regionally. Yet it was under his brother Mithradates I that the Parthians truly began to take advantage of Seleucid weakness. His initial thrust, however, was against his neighbour Bactria, whose rulers were distracted by wars with their eastern neighbours. If Bactria was not completely overrun, then it was reduced in power with Parthia annexing territory.

At the same time, the new Seleucid ruler, Antiochus IV (son of Antiochus III), was busy shoring up Seleucid power in the west, in which he met with some success. In 170 BC he launched a successful attack on Egypt, asserting Seleucid dominance, but was unable to annex the country, with Rome monitoring his actions. A second attempt at invasion in 168 BC was prevented by a single Roman ambassador, C. Popillius Laenas (consul In 172 and 158 BC), who informed Antiochus that if he invaded Egypt then he would be at war with Rome. This was a point emphasized by the famous story of Popillius drawing a circle around the king in the dust and not allowing him to leave until he had responded to the ultimatum, thus showing where the power lay in the West.

Rome was then fighting Macedon for a third time (172–167 BC), with the new Macedonian King Perseus attempting to reassert Macedon as the main power in Greece. The war ended with the destruction of the Macedonian army at the Battle of Pydna (168 BC). The following year saw the destruction of the Kingdom of Macedon, carved up into four separate republics, all under the protection of Rome. Illyria and Epirus fared no better; Epirus especially was devastated by Roman armies for supporting Perseus. Illyria also saw the end of its power and independence. Though Rome took no actual territory in Greece, the destruction of Macedon and

Epirus, along with Illyria, made it clear that they were all client states of Rome.

Thus by 167 BC Rome had achieved a clear domination over the Hellenistic powers. Macedon had been destroyed, the Seleucid Empire humbled and the Ptolemaic Empire of Egypt was now under Roman protection. Nevertheless, Antiochus attempted to consolidate his potion in the west of his empire. Armenia fell in 165 BC, but an attempt to reassert his control of Judea led to the revolt of the Maccabees. Yet Antiochus had avoided another war with Rome, which had showed no interest in crossing beyond the Aegean in force.

Unfortunately for Antiochus, the existential threat to his empire came not from the west, but from the east. Having successfully expanded the Parthian state at Bactria's expense, Mithradates turned his attentions eastwards, towards the Seleucids. Again, details are scant, but Antiochus left the quelling of the Judean revolt to a general and marched towards the east, most probably in response to a Parthian thrust. Unfortunately for the Seleucids, Antiochus died in 164 BC. The throne should have gone to his eldest son, Demetrius, but he was a hostage in Rome at the time and the Senate refused to release him.[17] So the Seleucid throne fell to a 9-year-old boy, Antiochus V, and once again Rome had weakened the Seleucid Empire, this time with severe consequences. Seizing his opportunity, Mithradates launched an invasion of the core Seleucid territory of Media, finally annexing it c.155 BC.

By this time Demetrius had escaped from Rome, murdered his younger brother and been appointed Seleucid Emperor in his place, and was successfully crushing the Judean revolt. Unfortunately for him, the fall of Media opened up the route to the Seleucid heartland of Mesopotamia, including its capital Seleucia. By the 140s BC, Mithradates had invaded Mesopotamia, defeated Demetrius and in c.141 BC was crowned King of Kings (the Persian and Seleucid title) in Seleucia.[18] A total Seleucid collapse was only avoided when Parthia's eastern borders were attacked by migrating tribes of Saka, forcing Mithradates to return to the east. This allowed Demetrius time to recover and launch a counter invasion, reoccupying Mesopotamia. This resurgence proved to be short-lived, as Demetrius was defeated, captured and sent to the Parthian east as a prisoner.

Rome, meanwhile, had not been idle either, and a Fourth Macedonian War, against the Macedonian usurper Andriscus, ended in 148 BC. Despite a poor start, the Romans soon destroyed the Macedonian army and in 147 BC ended their experiment with client republics, making Macedon a Roman province. Matters in Greece took a turn for the worse when the Achaean League, which had unwisely thrown in its lot with Andriscus, went to war with Rome. Rome defeated the Achaeans in 146 BC, obliterated the city of Corinth and annexed the rest of mainland Greece to its Macedonian province.

By 140 BC the Romans had advanced to the Aegean and the Parthians to the Euphrates. Between them lay the rump of the Seleucid Empire – sandwiched between two aggressive powers – an ailing Ptolemaic Egypt and a host of smaller kingdoms. The new world order of Rome and Parthia had been established

6. Crisis, Collapse and Recovery (140s–90s BC)

Clearly the Parthian conquest of Mesopotamia would have been noted in the Senate at Rome. Unfortunately, we have no detailed record of Roman history in this period, due to the loss of the annalist historians (especially Livy). The earliest surviving 'Roman' source to mention the Parthians is Polybius (see Appendix Two).[19] Thus we have no record of the Roman reaction to the Parthian annexation of Mesopotamia. We have to assume that the Roman oligarchy saw no cause for alarm and would probably have welcomed the defeat of the Seleucid Empire, viewing the Parthians as a useful counterweight to Seleucid power, keeping them focused on the east of their empire and not the west, where Rome had its influence.

Yet it is probable that the Romans did not realize the potential danger. Had the Seleucid Empire collapsed, and the Parthians crossed the Euphrates, then the obvious next target would have been the other surviving Hellenistic power, the Ptolemaic Kingdom of Egypt, then a friend and ally of the Roman People (the Centuriate and Tribal assemblies). Furthermore, the Senate extended its involvement in the Near East by supporting the Maccabean revolt in Judea, which led to Judea gaining autonomy from the Seleucid Empire.[20] Rome therefore had a clear stake in the Near East should the Parthians cross the Euphrates and attack Rome's allies.

As it was, the Seleucid Empire was able to stabilize, aided greatly by the Parthians having to focus on their eastern steppe borders and the change of king. Mithradates I was succeeded by his son, Phraates II (c.132–126 BC). Phraates seems to have been too occupied with defending Parthia's eastern borders to have been able to exploit the chaos in the Seleucid Empire. With Demetrius a captive, a civil war broke out in the remnants of the Seleucid Empire, meaning that no immediate attempt was made to profit from Parthia's distraction in the east and recover their Mesopotamian heartland. However, the victor of the civil war, Antiochus VII (brother of Demetrius), was able to muster one final attempt at reversing the Parthian conquests, and in 130 BC launched a major invasion force, which surviving sources place at 80,000–100,00-strong, clearly an exaggerated figure, but which nonetheless shows the seriousness of the Seleucid campaign.[21]

In one campaign Antiochus was able to defeat the Parthians on multiple occasions and recover Mesopotamia, encouraging the local rulers and population to rise up against the 'foreign' invader. It was the winter of 130/129 BC that undermined Antiochus' position, for having billeted his men in the Mesopotamian cities, their behaviour and demands for supplies turned the locals against the Seleucids. Furthermore, Phraates released the 'rightful' Seleucid king, Demetrius, and sent him back to Syria, clearly aiming to undermine Antiochus and perhaps rule the Seleucid Empire as a Parthian client.[22]

The Parthians were able to successfully engineer uprisings against the Seleucid garrisons, and then Phraates marched on Antiochus, the bulk of whose army was scattered in winter quarters. Despite being outnumbered, Antiochus gave battle; the result was the complete destruction of the Seleucid Army. Antiochus himself was killed and his son and successor, Seleucus, was taken hostage. However, upon his release, Demetrius immediately installed himself as Seleucid Emperor once more and prepared to fight his old captors.

Phraates moved westwards to prepare for an invasion of Syria. Had he been successful he would have overrun Syria and taken the Parthian Empire to the Mediterranean and into Rome's orbit of influence. Such an outcome was averted when Phraates had to abandon his Syrian campaign to once more repel a tribal invasion of Saka on Parthia's eastern borders. Thus a new status quo was established, with the Euphrates as the dividing line between the Seleucid and Parthian Empires. The destruction of Antiochus' army drained the Seleucids of the last of their offensive capabilities, whilst the Parthian Empire's eastern troubles prevented an attack on Seleucid Syria.

The situation for Parthia became much worse when Phraates himself was defeated and killed in battle (c.126 BC) against the invading Saka tribes. It is reported that the Saka overran the whole of the Parthian Empire up to Mesopotamia.[23] He was succeeded by his uncle, Artabanus I,[24] who seems to have bought the Parthians some breathing space by paying off the Saka, albeit temporarily. However, in c.122 BC he too took up arms against the tribes, which had seemingly overrun Parthia's eastern borders, but was injured in battle and died from an infection or poisoned wound.

It seems that the Seleucids were in no position to take advantage of this Parthian weakness, but another power was. The Arab Hyspaosines, who ruled the city of Alexandria-Antioch on the Persian Gulf, founded his own kingdom, Characene, and utilized existing dissatisfaction amongst the Mesopotamian cities against Parthian rule to annex much of Mesopotamia, including Babylon and Seleucia. However, this new power proved to be short-lived and the Parthian governor, Himerus, was able to recover the Mesopotamian cities, though Characene retained its independence.

In the meantime, the Roman Republic was steadily expanding eastwards. In 133 BC the Romans gained their first territory in Asia Minor when the Kingdom of Pergammum was bequeathed to the Roman People by its last king, Attalus III. This unusual move was seemingly borne out of the desire to stop his kingdom, one of the richest in Asia Minor, being carved up by his neighbours and rivals, also ensuring that he spited them by bringing Rome directly into Asia Minor. The Romans did not spurn this bequest, given the wealth it would bring, and annexed it to their empire, albeit after having to suppress a rebellion from Attalus' none-too-happy subjects. Rome thereby gained a chunk of territory in Asia Minor, a clear threat to the other kingdoms of the region.

The imminent collapse of the Parthian Empire was prevented by the accession to the throne of Mithradates II (also known as the Great), who may have been the son or brother of Artabanus.[25] He seems to have started by ensuring the security of the new Mesopotamian heartlands by defeating the Kingdom of Characene (c.121 BC) before moving eastwards to reclaim the eastern provinces overrun by the Saka tribes.[26] Under Mithradates, not only were the eastern lands recovered but the Parthian Empire became stable and prosperous, with peace and security in the east allowing a flourishing of trade links to China. Chinese records reveal an official embassy to the Parthian court in this period, establishing diplomatic ties.

In the west, Mithradates does not seem to have considered an invasion of Seleucid Syria, perhaps concerned by the possible reaction of Rome, but did expand Parthian influence by attacking and defeating the Kingdom of Armenia, which now became a Parthian client. The empires of Rome and Parthia thereby edged ever closer, with only a handful of minor kingdoms between them: Bithynia, Cappadocia, Commagene, Galatia and Pontus.

Rome, meanwhile, had not expanded further eastwards and seemed to be content to live in peace with the neighbouring kingdoms of Asia Minor. Furthermore, Rome's military attention was concentrated on its European borders (Gaul and Macedon), which brought it into contact with the native tribes of the region. Much as Parthia's borders had collapsed under the weight of tribal migration/invasion in the 120s BC, Rome experienced similar in the 110s and 100s BC when migrating Germanic tribes, notably the Cimbri and Teutones, pushed southwards and defeated the Romans in a number of set-piece battles, culminating in one of Rome's greatest ever defeats at the Battle of Arausio in 105 BC.[27] By 102 BC, the tribes turned to the invasion of Italy and the destruction of the Roman system, which was only averted by the Roman general C. Marius, who won two crushing victories at the Battles of Aquae Sextiae (102 BC) and the Raudine Plain (101 BC), destroying the migrating tribes.

In the meantime, Rome had found the time to try to address a growing pirate problem in the Mediterranean, dispatching M. Antonius (grandfather of the Triumvir) to Cilicia on the southern coast of Asia Minor to stem the attacks. From 102 BC onwards, Cilicia became a Roman protectorate, bringing Rome's influence to the borders of Seleucid Syria whilst continuing the encirclement of the kingdoms of Asia Minor.

Thus, by 100 BC the three great empires of Rome, the Seleucids and Parthians had all faced total collapse, yet had recovered, to some extent. Of the three it was the Seleucids who were looking the most vulnerable, reduced to a rump of just Syria – with Judea having gained independence – and sandwiched between the two larger, aggressive empires. Many must have assumed that it was only a matter of time before one or the other empire annexed Syria, bringing the two powers face to face. As it happened, Seleucid Syria did fall, though to neither Rome nor Parthia, but a third power, the alliance of the kingdoms of Pontus and Armenia, which were to humble all three of the great empires.

8. Instability in Asia Minor and the Meeting of Empires

The rise of these two allied powers, both swift and unexpected, was centred on two men: Mithridates VI, King of Pontus, and Tigranes II, King of Armenia. Pontus was a coastal kingdom on the southern shore of the Black Sea which had been in existence since the late third century BC. Under the rule of Mithridates VI (from 120 BC), however, it had expanded to become the dominant power in the Black Sea region, having annexed the Crimean Kingdom and much of the eastern Black Sea coastline. It had clearly benefited from Rome's removal of the Seleucid Empire from the region.[28] Furthermore, Mithridates also seemed to benefit from Rome's lack of attention to eastern matters whilst they were busy fighting wars on their northern borders and in North Africa.

Unfortunately for Mithridates however, the Roman province of Asia sat to his west, and Rome clearly saw Asia Minor as its sphere of influence. In 98 BC the Roman general C. Marius, who had left Rome and was touring the East, visited Mithridates and warned him that his ambitions would bring him into conflict with Rome.[29] This brought home to Mithridates that Rome, having overcome its conflicts in the north, was now prepared to turn its attention eastward once more.

Furthermore, to the east lay the expanding Parthian Empire of Mithradates II, who had recently defeated Armenia and brought that kingdom into its orbit and thus onto his borders. Thus, like the

Seleucids, Mithridates found himself sandwiched between the two expanding empires.[30] Unlike the Seleucids, however, Mithridates had both the desire and the resources to avoid becoming a victim to either of these two aggressive empires. Having determined on this path, he looked for regional allies to support him and increase his resources. His initial ally was Nicomedes III, King of Bithynia (another kingdom of Asia Minor), who married Mithridates' sister. Between them they invaded and partitioned the region of Paphlagonia, which lay between their two kingdoms, followed by the Kingdom of Galatia.

By c.96 BC[31] the pair turned their attention to Cappadocia, driving out King Ariarathes VIII, who died soon afterwards, ending the ruling dynasty. In his place Mithridates put his own son on the Cappadocian throne, ruling as Ariarathes IX, a client king, and bringing Cappadocia into the growing Pontic Empire.

Yet whilst Rome had not intervened in any of his previous empire-building, on this occasion two factors had changed. Firstly, Rome's attention was now no longer focussed on its European borders or North Africa, meaning the Senate and its leading generals would be on the lookout for fresh challenges, especially in the lucrative East.[32] Secondly, Mithridates' move to put his son on the Cappadocian throne alienated his ally Nicomedes, who appealed to Rome. In a perhaps telling move, the Senate dispatched a Praetor to investigate the matter, none other than Marius' protégé L. Cornelius Sulla.[33]

Sulla quickly ruled against Mithridates and allowed the Cappadocians to choose a new native king, Ariobarzanes I.[34] Having no wish to be goaded into a war with Rome, and at their time of choosing, Mithridates accepted the decision and withdrew. However, with Rome now clearly extending a de facto protectorate over Cappadocia and placing a client king on the throne, this did not only alarm Mithridates but also the Parthians. Having expanded into Armenia, which bordered Cappadocia, the two empires effectively met, albeit through their respective client kingdoms, if not declared territory. Thus Mithradates II of Parthia dispatched an emissary (Orobazus) to Cappadocia to meet with Rome and determine its intentions, the first formal meeting between representatives of the two empires.[35]

The meeting ended with Sulla famously sitting between the Parthian emissary and the Cappadocian king, a piece of theatre that cost the

Parthian emissary his life. No formal treaty seems to have been agreed at this point, but Sulla (and Marius) seem to have clearly laid down a marker that Cappadocia (and Asia Minor) lay within Rome's sphere of influence. Thus the matter was left, but Asia Minor was now a powderkeg, with Roman, Parthian and Pontic ambitions in place.

9. Civil War, Collapse and the Rise of the New Powers (80s BC)

Soon after this meeting, the Armenian King Tigranes I, who had been defeated by the Parthians, died and his son Tigranes II, who had been a hostage at the Parthian court, was installed as the new Parthian-appointed King of Armenia. The price of the throne was a significant portion of the region of Atropatené, which was added to the Parthian Empire. Despite his years at the Parthian court, Tigranes clearly had no wish to act as a Parthian puppet, which can be seen by a marriage alliance to a daughter of none other than Mithridates VI himself. Thus was forged a new alliance between the Kingdoms of Pontus and Armenia, who between them ruled from the Black Sea to the Caspian.

Marriage alliances were common enough, and without a change in external circumstances perhaps nothing would have come of it. Yet both men were suddenly presented with the most fortuitous set of circumstances, namely the collapse of the three great empires of Rome, the Seleucids and the Parthians into their own civil wars. In 91 BC the Roman Republic began its First Civil War, with Rome at war with two confederacies of Italian peoples who rose up in rebellion. Wasting no time, Mithridates and Tigranes made their move and attempted to annex Bithynia and Cappadocia respectively.[36] Mithridates removed Nicomedes IV of Bithynia, son of Mithridates' old ally Nicomedes III, who had acceded to the throne in c.94 BC, whilst Tigranes invaded Cappadocia and removed Ariobarzanes.

Despite the war in Italy, the Senate saw the danger and dispatched a three-man commission to Bithynia, headed by another Marian ally, M. Aquilius (Consul in 101 BC). The commission again ordered the restoration of both kings, backed up by Roman forces from Greece and Asia, and again Mithridates (and Tigranes) obeyed. Unfortunately, the commission, perhaps guided by Marius' instructions, ordered the two newly restored kings to provoke Mithridates by invading Pontus. If this was the Roman (Marian) intention, then it worked all too well as Mithridates took the offensive and declared war on Rome, initiating the First Romano-Pontic or Mithridatic War. The Roman position in Asia Minor collapsed in the face of the onslaught, with the Romano-Allied armies being defeated and Bithynia and Asia overrun. Aquillius was captured on the island of Mytilene, returned to Pergamum and publicly executed by Mithridates by having gold poured down his throat.

By 88 BC the Roman position in the civil war was much improved and L. Cornelius Sulla, the newly elected Consul, had been chosen to lead the war on Mithridates. However, the political legacy of the war against the Italians spilled over into violence and led to Marius double-crossing his protege and seizing the command for himself.[37] This in turn led Sulla, and his fellow Consul Q. Pompeius Rufus, to march their army on Rome itself and seize control of the Republic, rekindling the civil war. Mithridates seized on this opportunity and invaded mainland Greece, reversing over 100 years of Roman dominance and taking the Pontic Empire from the Black Sea to the Adriatic (see Map 3).[38]

In just two years Rome's entire eastern empire had been conquered by Mithridates, overturning more than a century of eastward expansions. Yet Parthia was in no position to exploit its rivals' weakness as it too collapsed into civil war. Unlike Rome, the details are only sketchy, but it seems to have been caused by the ill-health (and subsequent death) of Mithradates II and a struggle for the succession amongst the various branches of the Arsacid dynasty.[39] Again seizing the opportunity, and perhaps freed of any personal obligation to his former captor, Tigranes invaded western Parthia. With the absence of a strong central ruler, Tigranes retook Atropatené and conquered Media, northern Mesopotamia (Gordiene, Adiabene, Osrhoene and Mygdonia) and possibly Cappadocia once more.

Tigranes was able to take further advantage of a third civil war in the region, one between rival claimants to the Seleucid throne. Having the largest army in the region and having defeated Parthia, he was 'invited' to take the Seleucid throne and thus invaded and annexed Syria, Cilicia, Commagene and Phoenicia in 83 BC, expanding the Armenian Empire from the Caspian Sea to the Mediterranean and to the borders of Judea. Tigranes crowned this achievement by creating a new imperial capital, Tigranocerta,[40] and seizing the title of King of Kings from the Parthians.

Thus the Seleucid Empire finally fell, not to the Parthians or the Romans, but to the Armenians. This Pontic-Armenian alliance achieved spectacular success, having, in less than a decade, overturned a century of Roman and Parthian expansion. The responses of these two great empires differed. In Parthia's case, we can reconstruct a series of overlapping rival claimants to the throne, which seem to have spanned two generations, all vying for sole rule. Like Rome, this civil war seems to have been conducted in different phases, between different claimants, fought between 92 and 61 BC.

Unlike the Roman Civil War, however, we have no narrative sources for the war, and thus no clear detail, which has led this period to be known as a Parthian Dark Age. The rival claimants and how long they were fighting for, or even who they were fighting, has to be reconstructed from various fragmentary sources, such as Babylonian astronomical calendars and surviving coin hoards. We have evidence of a number of rival Parthian kings in this period: Sinatruces (c.92–68/67 BC), Gotarzes I (c.91–87 BC), Mithradates III (c.87–80 BC), Orodes I (c.80–75 BC) and even an unknown Arsaces XVI (c.78/77–62/61 BC),[41] all seemingly from rival branches of the Arsacid dynasty.

By the mid to late 70s BC the Parthian King Sinatruces, who appears to have been involved in the outbreak of the civil war, seems to have defeated the majority of his rivals and secured the throne (although there may have been one rival, Arsaces XVI, still fighting). He seems to have brought a degree of stability to the Parthian Empire. In c.69/68 BC he was succeeded by his son Phraates III, whom it has been argued continued to fight this mysterious challenger, the unknown Arsaces XVI, and it was only by c.61 BC that the Parthian Civil War had been brought to a conclusion.[42]

Thus, throughout this period, Parthia was restricted to southern Mesopotamia and its old Parthian homelands to the east of the Caspian Sea. Rome, by contrast, although it continued with its civil war – which lasted until 70 BC – was still able to field large armies and had commanders who realized that the struggle for power in Rome had to be tempered with defending their empire. With only superficial control of Rome and Italy, Sulla left in 88 BC and invaded Pontic-controlled Greece. The full details of the Mithridatic Wars sit outside this work, but by 86 BC Rome had two separate armies fighting Mithridates in Greece under two antagonistic Roman commanders, L. Cornelius Sulla and L. Valerius Flaccus (Cos. 87 BC), representing the new anti-Sullan government in Rome. Defeated first at the Battle of Chaeronea and then at Orchomenus, Mithridates was driven from Greece and followed into Asia by both Roman armies.

In 85 BC, with Greece and Asia restored to Roman control, Sulla brokered a peace with Mithridates (the Treaty of Dardanus), which allowed him to retain his throne and his original empire in return for an indemnity, which Sulla would use to fund his own invasion of Italy and prosecute the ongoing Roman Civil War. Sulla then seized control of the second Roman army and returned to Greece, leaving a legate, L. Licinius Murena, in Asia to defend Rome's eastern borders whilst he invaded Italy. Thus in Asia Minor the status quo was restored. Murena soon launched another war against Mithridates, but was defeated and ordered by Sulla to desist and observe the treaty. By 81 BC Sulla had control of most of the Western Republic, making his treaty with Mithridates official Roman policy. Though Sulla resigned and died soon after (78 BC), the Senate maintained the peace with Mithridates, distracted by a further outbreak of civil war in Italy and an ongoing civil war in Spain.

By the time of Sulla's death, Roman rule had been restored to Greece and Asia, but Mithridates still maintained his Pontic Empire and there was a new power in the form of the Armenian Empire, which dominated the Near and Middle East.[43]

8. Rome's Great Eastern War (74–62 BC)[44]

Civil war or no civil war, it is not surprising that the Roman oligarchy soon found an excuse to go to war with the two new emergent empires. They had not forgotten that Mithridates had annexed a whole swathe of their empire, nor the butchery that accompanied it. Nor would they allow a new empire to emerge in the Near East that so clearly threatened their interests. It was only four years after the death of Sulla, and three after the latest civil war in Italy (between M. Aemilius Lepidus and Q. Lutatius

Catulus & Pompeius), that Rome was given the perfect excuse to go to war once more in the East.

In 74 BC, the King of Bithynia, Nicomedes IV, a staunch Roman ally and enemy of Mithridates, died. Realizing that his kingdom would be annexed by either Rome or Pontus, he chose the former and spited his old enemy from the grave by bequeathing his kingdom to Rome, an act he suspected would draw Rome and Pontus into conflict once more. Naturally the Senate accepted such a gift and moved to annex Bithynia, and Mithridates again found himself on the backfoot. If he did nothing, then Rome would annex more territory in Asia Minor, bringing Rome's empire to his borders, and the inevitable clash one step closer. Yet Rome was in far stronger shape than at any time in the previous twenty years, despite the ongoing war in the Western Republic.

Seeing little choice but an inevitable conflict with Rome, Mithridates made the best of the situation and again attacked first before Rome had time to gather its forces.[45] Bithynia was overrun, as was the Roman province of Asia once more. Furthermore, Mithridates had in his army a number of Roman noble exiles from the ongoing civil war, which allowed him to portray this campaign as part of the Roman civil war rather than an external invasion. He even made contact with the Roman general Q. Sertorius in Spain, who was fighting a civil war against the Sullan regime in Rome. Sertorius in turn sent over the Roman general M. Marius (a kinsman of the famous civil war general) to act as a figurehead for Mithridates' campaign.[46]

Nevertheless, despite early successes the Roman forces gathered under the leadership of the two Consuls, M. Aurelius Cotta and one of Sulla's proteges, L. Licinius Lucullus.[47] Despite the war ostensibly being about the Kingdom of Bithynia, Lucullus was clear in his objective that this war was the time that Rome would stamp its dominance on Asia Minor and the Near East. When Mithridates was driven out of Asia and Bithynia, Lucullus pushed on into Pontus. By 70 BC Mithridates had been defeated by Lucullus and seen Pontus overrun by Rome, and he had no choice but to flee. He chose to seek sanctuary with his old ally Tigranes of Armenia.

This was the last thing Tigranes needed, as he had been studiously neutral in the war between his old ally Mithridates and Rome. Having forged a new eastern empire, he did not desire a war with Rome. Yet by 71/70 BC the buffer between the Armenian Empire and Rome had been lost, and Rome was now on the borders of the Armenian Empire. The decision was taken away from him in 69 BC when Lucullus crossed the upper Euphrates and invaded Armenia, signalling war between the Roman Republic and the Armenian Empire, without referring the matter to the Senate. Here we can clearly see that Lucullus was not bothered about the niceties of needing a reason to go to war with a neighbouring state, saw the Armenian Empire as a strategic threat to Rome's interests and acted accordingly.

Despite being heavily outnumbered, Lucullus pushed immediately for the new Armenian capital of Tigranocerta and there met the Armenian king in battle. The Battle of Tigranocerta was a decisive Roman victory, with the Armenian army collapsing and being routed. Yet this proved to be the apogee of Lucullus' campaign. Mithridates and Tigranes retreated into the Armenian heartland, and in 68 BC Lucullus' army mutinied and refused to go any further.

Whilst Lucullus had not been defeated militarily, he had been left exposed politically and it was events at Rome that proved his undoing. When he left Rome, the civil war was raging in the Western Republic, with a Senatorially sponsored Pompeius (another protege of Sulla) fighting against the Roman general Sertorius in Spain. By 71 BC Sertorius had been murdered and his successor (and assassin) M. Perperna quickly defeated. Meanwhile, back in Italy, a small slave rebellion in Capua in 73 BC had snowballed into a full-scale Slave War in the heartlands of Italy, building on the devastation and disruption caused by nearly two decades of civil war. By 72 BC this slave rebellion, led by a Thracian named Spartacus, threatened the very existence of the Republic.

With Pompeius in Spain and Lucullus in the East, it was another of Sulla's proteges who stepped up to the mark, M. Licinius Crassus. Crassus was the son of a civil war general, who had been murdered when Rome fell to a siege in 87 BC, and had subsequently raised an army and joined Sulla's invasion of Italy. It was his generalship that won the final battle of that phase of the civil war in Italy, the Battle of the Colline Gate (82 BC), which had put Sulla in control of Rome. Whilst Pompeius had taken a command in the West and Lucullus in the East, Crassus had bided his time and used his vast fortune to build up his political power in

Rome. Thus when Spartacus threatened Rome he was appointed to take command of the Republic's armies and soon destroyed the slave rebellion in 71 BC. By late 71 BC Rome was faced with two victorious generals, Pompeius and Crassus, and their armies approaching Rome. Yet rather than renew the First Civil War, the two men put their differences to one side and united their efforts to gain dominance of the Republic, which they used to reshape the constitution.[48]

When Lucullus left Rome in 74 BC, it was as the duly appointed proconsul of the Sullan regime in Rome. By 70 BC, however, the Sullan faction was no longer in control of the Republic, usurped by the alliance of Pompeius and Crassus. Pompeius received an extraordinary command over the whole Mediterranean in 67 BC, in order to end the pirate problem that had been plaguing Rome. By 66 BC, with this task accomplished, Pompeius had the command of the 'Great Eastern War' transferred from Lucullus to himself. Pompeius thus took command of a war of conquest across the Near East, the aim of which had far outstripped the recovery of the Kingdom of Bithynia and was now nothing less than the destruction of the Pontic and Armenian Empire and the establishment of Roman dominance in the East (see Map 4).

9. From the Spoils – Rome and Parthia (60s BC)

The fourth power in this equation was Parthia, which may still have been fighting a civil war, between Phraates III and Arsaces XVI. The Roman destruction of the Armenian Empire was more than Phraates could have hoped for. Seemingly too weak to challenge Tigranes themselves, the Parthians sat back and watched their enemy be destroyed by a rival power. In 69 BC both Mithridates and Tigranes appealed to the Parthians to aid them in fighting Lucullus, but Phraates had nothing to gain by supporting his enemies and everything to gain by watching them collapse. Lucullus subsequently opened negotiation with Phraates to ensure Parthian neutrality.

With the Armenian Empire collapsing, Phraates and the Parthians could reoccupy their lost territories. Yet the defeat of the Armenian Empire brought Roman forces to the borders of Parthia and also weakened Parthia. The arrival of Pompeius in Armenia ended Mithridates' and

Tigranes' attempts at a revival of their fortunes, with Mithridates fleeing to the Bosphorus and Tigranes seeking terms with Rome. The defeat of Tigranes led to an Armenian Civil War, with his son, also Tigranes, attacking his father. It was at this point that Phraates intervened and attempted to restore Parthian fortunes by backing the younger Tigranes, installing him as a Parthian client on the throne of Armenia. Unfortunately for Phraates, the younger Tigranes was defeated by the elder.

Pompeius then oversaw the dismemberment to the Armenian Empire. Tigranes the elder retained a much-reduced Kingdom of Armenia, the Seleucid Empire was briefly restored in Syria and Ariobarzanes was again restored to the throne of Cappadocia. Yet there were Parthian territories that had fallen to Tigranes which Phraates wanted restored, notably Sophene and Gordiene. Initially these were granted to Parthia's ally, the younger Tigranes, but were soon annexed and passed to the restored Kingdom of Cappadocia.

Pompeius was revelling in his victories and the expansion of Roman power, and marched Roman armies across the Middle East, including a campaign that reached to within. He marched Roman armies to within three days of the Caspian Sea, fighting campaigns against the Iberians and Albanians. Phraates seemingly used this Roman diversion to invade Armenia and seize the province of Gordiene. Pompeius, however, had moved southwards, invading Media and defeating the Median king. Tigranes, now a Roman ally, appealed to Pompeius about the Parthian invasion.[49]

It was at this point that the two empires came close to war, with Phraates attacking a Roman ally, Armenia, and the Romans in an expansive mood. As it was, Pompeius pulled back from attacking the Parthian Empire, which was clearly beyond the remit granted by the Senate and People of Rome, nor did he wish to become embroiled in a long drawn-out eastern war, leaving him vulnerable in Rome and thus liable to suffer a similar fate to Lucullus. His erstwhile ally Crassus would have had no compunction about betraying him, nor would the Sullan faction think twice about undermining him, especially with Lucullus back in Rome. Thus Pompeius opted for diplomacy, backed by a show of force. The question of the Armenian/Parthian border was referred to a commission of senators, who ruled that Gordiene should remain with Armenia, whilst Parthia received Adiabene.

Pompeius also ordered two of his legates, A. Gabinius and L. Afranius, to cross into Parthian Mesopotamia, with Gabinius reaching the Tigris and Afranius crossing back into Syria from the north. The warning to the Parthians was clear: the Romans could pass where they chose in the Middle East. Nevertheless, war was averted and friendly, albeit one-sided, relations were established between the two powers, though no formal treaty or boundaries were ever agreed.

If the Parthians were hoping that after defeating Mithridates VI (who committed suicide in 63 BC) and Tigranes II, now a staunch Roman ally who needed Roman assistance to defend himself from Parthia, Rome would return to its Asian provinces, they were sadly mistaken. Pompeius had clearly learned the lesson of the rise of the Armenian Empire and the danger that a rival power dominating the Near East would spell to Rome. With Pontus and Armenia destroyed, the clear beneficiary would be Parthia, as Phraates' attack on a weakened Armenia had shown.

Pompeius took steps to protect Roman interests in the East with the largest imperial expansion since the annexation of Greece. Pontus had been conquered and turned into a Roman province, Cappadocia restored as an ally, Media and Commagene defeated and Armenia turned into a Roman ally. Pompeius then turned southwards, where the newly restored Seleucid Kingdom of Syria was annexed, as was Phoenicia.[50] The long-standing Roman ally of Judea was attacked, with Jerusalem taken by force. Pompeius even attacked the Nabatean Arab Kingdom, extending Roman territory around the Mediterranean coast up to the borders of Ptolemaic Egypt. Egypt only retained its independence due to the fact that the rest of the Roman oligarchy would not stand for Pompeius conquering it – and its fortunes – himself. In 65 BC Crassus himself had attempted to annex Egypt by Censorial decree, without even leaving the comforts of Rome, but had been blocked by his colleague.

Whilst the Parthians saw their new enemy Armenia destroyed and regained some of the territories they had lost, they were now ringed with Roman provinces and allies right up to their borders. Their long-term ambition of annexing the last of the Seleucid Empire and taking Parthian territory up to the Mediterranean, thereby recreating the great Persian Empire, had, at least in the short term, been dashed.

By 63 BC the Pontic and Armenian Empires, which so briefly had eclipsed both the Roman and Parthian Empires, had been destroyed. In their place stood the enhanced empire of Rome, with provinces scattered around the Mediterranean, supported by allied kingdoms. The two great empires had finally reached each other and shared a border: the Euphrates. Rome was in the ascendant, yet it was far from clear that a recovering Parthian Empire would take this subordinate role without a fight.

10. Interlude – Paralysis and Bloodshed at Rome (63–55 BC)[51]

Rome's victory in the Great Eastern War had destroyed the empires of Pontus and Armenia and annexed the remnants of the once great Seleucid Empire. There now essentially only existed the two powers of Rome and Parthia. Although the Ptolemaic Empire was still in existence, it held only the Kingdom of Egypt and had only retained its independence due to Rome's protection and the fact that no Roman oligarch would trust one of his colleagues not to profit from overseeing its annexation. In many ways, Ptolemaic Egypt, the last of the Hellenistic successors to Alexander the Great, was the one great prize which remained.

War between the two great empires was inevitable. Both had been expanding in opposite directions, towards each other, and neither would brook a rival in their quest for domination in the Near East. In the short term though, the Parthian Empire was recovering from its civil war, an unstable monarchy and being dominated first by Armenia and then Rome, and thus was in no condition to launch a war against its new neighbour. Although Rome was militarily stronger, military campaigns on the edge of the empire took second place to matters of politics in Rome. Pompeius may well have been the leading oligarch of the Republic at this time, but he still had to answer to the Senate and People. More importantly, his very success – and the political methods he had used to achieve them – ensured that he would be opposed by a number of factions within the Roman oligarchy, who between them could successfully confront him. Thus, unlike Alexander, Pompeius could not turn his attention to conquering whomever he liked, but had to return to Rome to defend his very position.

Pompeius had overseen the greatest reorganization of the Near East since the breaking up of Alexander's empire, yet his military supremacy counted for nought in the Senate and he spent the next few years back in Rome in fruitless effort to get this reorganization ratified by the Senate and People. Despite placing one of his supporters in the Consulship for both 61 BC (M. Pupius Piso Frugi Calpurnianus) and 60 BC (L. Afranius), his opponents, including his old rival Crassus, united to successfully oppose him. Pompeius changed tactics in 59 BC and employed a new agent to do his bidding, an up-and-coming Roman statesman named C. Iulius Caesar. Pompeius also turned to his old rival Crassus, and between them, using Caesar as an agent, Pompeius' eastern settlement was ratified in 59 BC.[52]

Yet the years that followed saw the Republic collapse into further political violence. Caesar got his reward and was appointed to a Gallic command, whilst Pompeius and Crassus remained in Rome to guard their political position, ensuring that any Parthian campaign was put on hold. To secure their position they chose a new agent to be elected as Tribune, P. Clodius Pulcher. Clodius unleashed a wave of violence in Rome, aided by the splitting of Pompeius and Crassus into rivals once more. By 56 BC the Republic was nearly paralyzed with violence, so much so that the three men – Pompeius, Crassus and Caesar – formed a temporary political faction, the Triumvirate, with the intention of temporarily seizing control of the Republic and ending the chaos. Only with political control of the Republic could the Triumvirs fully turn their attentions to matters in the empire. Caesar received another five years to conquer Gaul, Pompeius determined to rule in Rome and Crassus received command of a war against Parthia.

11. The First Romano-Parthian War (55–50 BC)

The full details of the First Romano-Parthian War have been explored elsewhere, but we can present the outline here.[53] Despite the attention of Rome's oligarchs being distracted by the chaos in Rome itself, Parthia under Phraates III had been steadily recovering, with his last rival being eliminated c.61 BC. Yet by c.58/57 BC the Parthians once more collapsed into turmoil, presenting their rivals with a perfect opportunity. Phraates was overthrown and murdered in a coup led by his two sons, Mithradates IV[54] and Orodes II. The two brothers promptly fell out and Mithradates, who had been installed as the new king, was in turn overthrown by his brother Orodes.

Mithradates fled to Roman Syria, then commanded by Pompeius' lieutenant A. Gabinius, the man who had led a Roman army to the Tigris during the last war. At the time Gabinius (Cos. 58 BC) had a special command in the Roman East, by Tribunician law (*plebiscitum*), passed by none other than Clodius himself, clearly at the behest of the Triumvirate (especially Pompeius). Thus we can see Pompeius ensured he retained control of the East, even if he could not be present in person. Ostensibly Gabinius was in the East to put down a revolt in Judea, but when Mithradates arrived (in 56 BC) a new opportunity presented itself. Thus Gabinius, no doubt with Pompeius' backing, prepared a Parthian expedition to restore Mithradates as a client king on the Parthian throne.

In late 56 BC the Triumvirs' plans changed. Following the reformation of their alliance, Pompeius and Crassus agreed to rule Rome jointly as the Consuls for 55 BC. Part of this agreement extended to a division of labour after their year in office. Despite his conquests in the East, Pompeius had a greater desire to dominate the Republic as its Princeps, or First Citizen, much as his mentor Sulla had intended, to ensure it did not collapse into bloody chaos. By contrast Crassus, after spending the last fifteen years at Rome in the political arena, wanted one last military campaign. Though his generalship was beyond doubt, his victories to date had been over fellow Romans in the Civil War (notably the Colline Gate) and the slave army of Spartacus. An eastern war of conquest would have been the prefect pinnacle of his career.

Furthermore, another civil war in Egypt meant that there was an opportunity to restore the deposed Ptolemaic Pharaoh Ptolemy XII Auletes to his throne, with all the opportunities for wealth and patronage that entailed. Thus the Triumvirs changed their plans, with Gabinius being diverted from restoring Mithradates to restoring Ptolemy XII. Interestingly, one of the junior officers in Gabinius' army was a young M. Antonius.[55] Mithradates himself was dispatched back to Parthia to stir up civil war and await the Roman army under the command of Crassus.

We will never know the full intention of Crassus' (and the Triumvir's) campaign goals. Certainly installing a puppet king on the Parthian throne would have brought Parthia under Rome's patronage, but as Mithradates' power lay in Iran, perhaps Crassus intended the annexation of Mesopotamia, thus opening up access to the Persian Gulf and the Indian trade routes to Rome. In the short term, Crassus and the Triumvirate received a setback, however, as Orodes, clearly sensing the danger, went on the offensive against his brother, who had established himself in the key Mesopotamian cities of Babylon and Seleucia. Mithradates was clearly not a skilled general, both cities soon fell, and he surrendered to Orodes in 55 BC and was promptly put to death. Orodes consolidated his position as sole ruler of the Parthian Empire, the decades-long era of civil wars seemingly having come to an end.

In the grand scheme of things the loss of Mithradates was nothing more than a temporary setback and, if anything, removed the urgency of the Roman campaign. Crassus left Rome in late 55 BC and spent the following year preparing his army with minor campaigns in the region. Certainly a new figurehead or puppet ruler could be found from within the fragmented Arsacid dynasty. By 53 BC Crassus deemed his army to be ready and launched a full-scale invasion of the Parthian Empire, aiming a decisive strike at the important Mesopotamian region, containing the key cities of Babylon, Seleucia and Ctesiphon (the Parthian summer capital). A number of factors led to this decision: the region lay at the very western reach of the Parthian Empire, but contained the former Seleucid heartlands, an urbanized region, and was at the centre of the opposition to Orodes. It also occupied a key river network and the key trading routes, whose annexation must have been the primary objective for Crassus.[56]

Opposing Crassus was not Orodes himself, but his key general Surenas, most likely a title rather than a name, for the head of the influential Suren clan, who had backed Orodes' recent bid for the throne. As such he was both the key lieutenant and an expendable commodity for Orodes. Though clearly given a poisoned chalice of a command, Surenas prepared a Parthian army which played to their strengths and Roman weaknesses. Parthian forces had recently been defeated by the Armenians, who in turn had been crushed by the power of the Roman legions.

Surenas eschewed a mixed force containing lightly armed infantry and concentrated upon cavalry, both the heavily armoured cataphracts and, more importantly, thousands of mounted archers. The two armies met at Carrhae in May 53 BC, which resulted in the greatest Roman defeat since the Battle of Arausio (105 BC), with seven legions surrounded, pinned down and cut to pieces by an endless barrage of arrows. The only possible Roman salvation was a cavalry breakout led by Crassus' son Publius, but that ended in Publius' death and the destruction of the outnumbered cavalry. The battle only ended at nightfall as Crassus and the survivors retreated from the battlefield.

What followed was a long retreat back to Roman Syria, with the remnants of the Roman legions being pursued by the Parthian cavalry. Crassus himself fell soon afterwards in a parlay which turned into a fight, his head being dispatched to the Parthian capital, having been filled with molten gold (the second Roman general to suffer that fate[57]). The Roman survivors, commanded by C. Cassius Longinus, reached Syria, though they left behind thousands of Roman prisoners, who were transported to the east of the Parthian Empire along with the legionary eagles, the very public sign of the Roman defeat.

In the aftermath, Orodes entrenched his position on the Parthian throne by claiming the victory over Rome for himself, executing Surenas into the bargain. The key Parthian objective was not Roman territory, but the regions they had lost to Armenia in the aftermath of the Romano-Armenian War. Thus Armenia was brought back into the Parthian fold as a client. Orodes and the Armenian King Artavasdes II were celebrating a marriage alliance between the two – with Orodes' son Pacorus marrying Artavasdes' sister – when the news of Carrhae arrived, along with Crassus' head.

Thus by 52 BC the Parthian Empire had once more re-established itself as the leading empire in the Near East and was confident enough to start raiding Roman Syria, though not invading in force. Rome itself was slow to respond, its attention more focussed on domestic politics, notably the rivalry between Pompeius and Caesar and the consequences of the removal of the third Triumvir, Crassus, from this equation. Defence of the region thus fell to C. Cassius Longinus, who amongst his other accomplishments was able to crush a Judean rebellion.

In 51 BC the Parthians felt secure enough to launch an invasion of Syria led by the Parthian prince Pacorus, pinning the Romans back into

Antioch. A further thrust was made into Commagene and Cappadocia, and then Cilicia, defended as it was by the noted Roman writer Cicero. This seems to have taken the form of a large raid rather than an army of occupation. The defence of Cilicia held, and Cassius was able to score Rome's first victory over the Parthians by destroying a force led by the general Osaces.

Summary

By the end of 51 BC the status quo had seemingly been restored, with the Romans defending the province of Syria and driving the Parthians back, albeit temporarily. Yet the Parthian victory at Carrhae had swung the balance of power back in their favour once more and allowed them to restore a hegemony over much of the Near East, notably Armenia and Commagene. Most importantly, Carrhae shattered the myth of Roman invincibility in the East and undid much of the momentum gained by Lucullus and Pompeius in the Great Eastern War.

Chapter Two

The Cold War: Parthia and the Roman Civil War (50–44 BC)

T he First Romano-Parthian War rather fizzled out, but saw the two great powers' fortunes reversed. The war had started with Rome on the offensive, invading the Parthian Empire with an eye to annexing territory and reaching the Persian Gulf. It ended with Parthia on the offensive, invading Rome's empire with an eye to annexing territory and reaching the Mediterranean. Despite the war ending in stalemate, with both empires neither losing nor gaining any territory, there was one clear winner: the Parthian Empire. Seven Roman legions had been destroyed, one of Rome's leading oligarchs killed and the Parthian court decorated with Roman legionary eagles and the head of Crassus.

Naturally, all involved assumed that the war would continue, with either a renewed Roman onslaught, to recover lost pride and avenge Carrhae, or a further Parthian onslaught to take Syria and inherit the mantle of the great Persian Empire. In the end the repulsed Parthian invasion of 51 BC was followed by a ten-year lull in the fighting.

1. The Winners – Orodes Ascendant

As always, without any native primary sources, analysing the Parthian Empire after their victory in the First Romano-Parthian War is an incredibly difficult task.[1] Yet we must endeavour to give the Parthians a voice or we relegate them to the role of faceless villain; Rome's latest enemy, rather than a strong civilization and expanding empire in their own right. What little we do know of the Parthians in this period confirms the Roman impression that their empire was weak and vulnerable. Up until the death of the Parthian King Mithradates II (c.91 BC) the Parthian Empire was on a seemingly unstoppable western expansion, determined to recreate the great Persian Empire of old. The death of Mithradates seems to have brought about a civil war amongst the Arsacid dynasty, out of which the empire, and its monarchy, emerged far weaker (see Chapter One).

As always, the more powerful neighbouring states sensed this weakness, with first the Armenians and then the Romans invading. Yet whereas the Armenian Empire had succeeded in humbling the Parthians, the Romans only made them stronger. It is probably not too much of an exaggeration to say that the victory at Carrhae saved the Parthian Empire. At a stroke, a generation of decline was overturned, with pride in Parthian military ability and the role of the monarchy restored. Just as his ancestors had done, Orodes II could claim a great victory over a western military power. Furthermore, he had won a victory not over a declining Seleucid Empire, but a rising Roman one.

It is notable that Orodes himself went from gaining the throne through two successive coups – firstly against his father and then against his brother – to enjoying the longest reign of any Parthian monarch since Mithradates II himself. Yet this accomplishment was clearly built on the work of others. Aside from organizing palace coups, Orodes seems to have steered clear of any fighting, preferring to leave that to others, notably Surenas and Orodes' own son Pacorus.

Naturally, as King of Kings, the Parthian monarch would take all the glory of the victories, but away from the imperial propaganda those at court knew the truth and the real architects of this victory. Yet whilst the battlefield may not have been familiar territory for Orodes, the palace and court politics clearly were, and Surenas – famed for his total victory over Rome on the battlefield – soon found himself removed from the picture (and the world). An absolute monarch, though perhaps in name only, could brook no rivals.

With Surenas out of the way, there remained the matter of Orodes' own son and possible heir, Pacorus. Having just seized the throne from his father, and then elder brother, clearly Orodes had to be worried about his own son, especially one who had spearheaded the first Parthian invasion of Syria and who must have been popular with the army. This all lay in contrast to Orodes, who seemed to have preferred palace life. Thus, not long after the return of the Parthian forces, and perhaps with Roman influence detected (see below), Pacorus too fell from grace (though not from life).

Again, we may only speculate about events taking place in the Parthian court and wider empire, but it becomes clear that renewing the war on Rome was not Orodes' priority. The war had given him more than he could ever have hoped for: a clear and comprehensive victory over the Romans, coming, as it did, during the turbulent early years of his reign. This victory and the accompanying prestige would have allowed him the chance to cement his rule within Parthia, both at court and within the wider empire, which to Orodes would have been far more important than adding new territories to the western edge of the empire.

We have no knowledge of other events, either in the Parthian court or taking place in the wider empire, but history has shown us numerous occasions where new monarchs who rise to the throne via a palace coup had to fight to consolidate their position. Victory at Carrhae not only gave Orodes the breathing space he required to do so, but an unparalleled piece of propaganda. We must assume that the wider empire was told of Orodes' great victory at Carrhae, not Surenas'.

In terms of fighting Rome, it was clear that the conquest of Syria would take a major invasion force, and Orodes could and probably did expect a renewed Roman invasion, headed no doubt by one of the two remaining Triumvirs: either Caesar, fresh from his Gallic conquests, or Pompeius, the architect of Rome's growing eastern empire. The order of the day for Orodes would therefore have been to consolidate his grip on power and wait for Rome.

2. The Losers – Crassus Unmourned and Unavenged

Yet the expected Roman response did not materialize. Whilst the Senatorial nobility was clearly alarmed by such a blow to Roman martial prowess, in what was clearly the greatest Roman defeat in a generation,[2] their attention was firmly focussed on domestic politics. Whilst in hindsight such a response seems short-sighted, there were several factors at play here. Firstly, the whole campaign was seen by many as a vanity project for Crassus and his fellow Triumvirs, and retrospectively a number of bad omens and portents were found which justified the failure of the campaign in religious terms, rather than military ones.[3]

Aside from religion, in terms of 'realpolitik', the campaign was part of the Triumvirs' aggressive plan of expansion, rather than Senatorial policy. In 56 BC three of Rome's leading men banded together to form a cabal to dominate the Republic, seizing control of the bulk of Rome's armies and with it control of foreign policy. Thus, to the opponents of the Triumvirate, Crassus' failure was the failure of the Triumvirate, and could be privately celebrated. Furthermore, in Roman terms, this was a clash on the eastern fringe of their empire, far away from Rome, against a foreign foe that few in Rome knew anything about, and which many must have assumed was due to Crassus' own failings (he had not fought a campaign since the defeat of Spartacus in 71 BC) rather than Parthian strength, an attitude which unfortunately still prevails today.

Yet whilst all these factors were in play, the key to Rome's inactivity lay in the crisis that was affecting Roman domestic politics and a breakdown in Republican government. The Triumvirs had temporarily seized power in 55 BC when Pompeius and Crassus were elected as Consuls. Yet even the combined power of these men and Caesar was not enough to stop the Republic from descending into bloody chaos. The years 53 and 52 BC opened in Rome with no curule magistrates having been elected due to the ongoing violent disorder on the streets of Rome, with armed gangs of supporters of the leading politicians clashing with each other. Matters came to a head in January 52 BC with the murder of P. Clodius Pulcher, one of the leading architects of this violence. Pompeius seized this opportunity and was appointed by a reluctant Senate to be sole Consul for 52 BC, with a mandate to restore the Republic.[4]

We can see that events in Rome again mirrored those in Parthia to some extent. In both cases, domestic political consideration far outweighed the renewal of the war between them. Orodes was fighting to secure his throne, whilst Pompeius was struggling to secure his dominant position in the Republic. The other surviving member of the Triumvirate, C. Iulius Caesar, was in Gaul fighting a war of conquest which had been ongoing since 58 BC. Furthermore, Crassus' death followed that of Caesar's daughter (and Pompeius' wife) Iulia, which had already weakened ties between the two surviving Triumvirs.

Within the Triumvirate there was a balance of power. Pompeius and Crassus were contemporaries, both having fought under Sulla in

Rome's First Civil War and both having joined forces in 71–70 BC to reforge the Republican system. Caesar, very much the junior member of the cabal, had acted as an agent to both men. Furthermore, whilst Caesar's political profile was ascending, the two most powerful men in Roman politics were still Pompeius and Crassus, with both men wielding considerable political power and armed force in the tumult of the 50s BC. For Pompeius, Crassus' death in the East in 53 BC was a stroke of luck, further strengthening his political position as the dominant man in the Republic. This can be seen by Pompeius' rapid marriage to Cornelia, the widow of P. Licinius Crassus (son of the Triumvir) and daughter of Q. Caecilius Metellus Scipio, who soon became Pompeius' fellow Consul. Thus Pompeius married into both the Metellan-Scipio and the Crassan families.[5]

When events at Rome had stabilized, under the rule of Pompeius, the Senate took two actions with regard to the situation in Syria, both of which we can see were tainted by the ongoing political feud between the remaining Triumvirs. In 52 BC the Senate appointed a new Proconsular commander in Syria to replace Crassus, yet their choice was hardly an inspiring one: M. Calpurnius Bibulus. Bibulus is most known to us as Caesar's fellow Consul from 59 BC, who spend a fruitless year opposing Caesar and the Triumvirate and eventually retired to his house searching for ill omens which would invalidate Caesar's legislation. Prior to his Consulship he had been involved in the Second Civil War in 62 BC, subduing the Paeligni in Italy, but seems to have no other military experience. It was probably not a coincidence that a Pompeian-dominated Senate sent a well-known opponent of Caesar to this command. In the long term it was clear that a new eastern campaign would be not only required, but desirable for one of Rome's leading generals. In the meantime, however, the Senate dispatched a competent non-entity. More importantly, it seems that the Senate did not furnish Bibulus with any additional forces: he was to make do with the remnants of the seven legions which were defeated at Carrhae.

The issue of reinforcements surfaced again in 50 BC, and was once more subject to partisan politicking. Following the Parthian invasion of 51 BC, it seems the Senate finally decided to reinforce Syria, but combined this with an attempt to defuse the escalating political clash between Pompeius and Caesar:

'Then a decree of the Senate was made that for the Parthian campaign one legion should be sent by Cnaeus Pompeius, a second by Caius Caesar, and it was clear enough that the two legions were to be withdrawn from one man.'[6]

'He [Pompeius] represented that Bibulus required soldiers against the Parthians; and in order that no new levies should be made, since the matter was urgent, as he claimed, and they had an abundance of legions, he got it voted that each of them, himself and Caesar, must send one to him. Thereupon he failed to send any of his own soldiers but ordered those whose business it was to demand that legion which he had given to Caesar. So nominally both of them contributed, but in reality, Caesar alone sent the two.

'These legions, therefore, were apparently made ready to be sent against the Parthians, but when there proved to be no need of them, there being really no use to which they could be put, Marcellus, fearing that they might be restored to Caesar, at first declared that they must remain in Italy, and then, as I have said, gave them into Pompeius' charge.'[7]

Thus, depending upon which bias you wish to use, it was either the Senate that organised for two legions of battle-hardened veterans to be sent to Bibulus – but the whole scheme was highjacked by Pompeius – or it was all Pompeius' ruse to deprive Caesar of a legion. In any event the net effect was the same, as Bibulus received no further legions in his defence of the East. The Parthian War was being used as just another political weapon in the ongoing clashes between the various factions of the Senatorial order.

In practical terms this meant that no reinforcements were sent to Roman Syria, and C. Cassius Longinus, the de-facto commander in the Roman east (until Bibulus' arrival), was left on his own to face the Parthian invasion. Fortunately for the Senate, he proved to be more than capable and was to defeat the Parthian invasion of Syria (see Chapter One).

3. Calpurnius Bibulus and the 'War' in Syria (51–50 BC)

Although appointed in 52 BC to take up his post in 51 BC, it seems that
M. Calpurnius Bibulus was in no hurry to reach Syria to take up his
command and face the Parthians. Whether by design or good fortune,
Dio tells us that Bibulus arrived in Syria only after Cassius' victory
and the Parthian withdrawal: 'He [Pacorus] had scarcely retired when
Bibulus arrived to govern Syria.'[8]

The loss of the relevant sources deprives us of a chance to study
Bibulus' actions in detail, but the *Periochae* of Livy does preserve the
following note: 'The book also contains an account of the war conducted
by Marcus Bibulus in Syria.'[9]

We only have two other brief notices on Bibulus' actions, both of which
indicate that there were still Parthian forces in Syria, after the defeat of
Pacorus' general, perhaps the signs of a very slow withdrawal of Parthian
forces or Pacorus having left raiding parties in the province:

> 'Do not forget to follow the policy of M. Bibulus, who kept himself
> shut up in a very strongly fortified and well-supplied town, as long
> as the Parthians were in the province.'[10]
>
> 'But as it is, that he [Bibulus] who never set foot outside the city
> gate as long as the enemy was west of the Euphrates, should be
> specially honoured, and that I, on whose army he depended entirely,
> should not be able to obtain a similar honour, is an insult to us.
>
> 'Cato, too, who votes twenty days' supplicatio to Bibulus! Pardon
> me, I cannot and will not put up with this.
>
> 'But the Parthians prevent my being much afraid, who suddenly
> retreated, leaving Bibulus half dead with fright.'[11]

The letters of Cicero, our only contemporary source, do not paint
Bibulus or his activities in a positive light. However, as the letter above
shows, Cicero had had his nose put out of joint by the Senate honouring
Bibulus' actions rather than Cicero's own (in the East). Cicero at this time
was far too close to the war for his own liking, having been dispatched to
be governor of the neighbouring province of Cilicia.

Nevertheless, given the resources he had at his command, the remnants
of Crassus' army and any local levies he could muster, and given that

Bibulus must have expected a fresh Parthian invasion at any point, his cautious strategy seems to have been justified. The Parthian invasion of Syria had shown that whilst they were masters of open warfare, they were not so adept at siege warfare and had issues when faced with a well-defended city. So Bibulus sat back in a well-fortified position and waited for the next Parthian onslaught. Dio, a much later source, provides us with further details on Bibulus' activities:

> 'He [Bibulus] administered the subject territory in peace and turned the Parthians against one another. For after winning the friendship of Ornodapates, a satrap, who had a grudge against Orodes, he persuaded him through messengers to set up Pacorus as king, and with him to conduct a campaign against the other.
> 'So, this war between the Romans and Parthians came to an end in the fourth year after it had begun, and while Marcus Marcellus and Sulpicius Rufus were Consuls.'[12]

It seems that Bibulus exploited the one obvious Parthian weakness, which was political rather than military, centred on the weak grip on the throne held by Orodes himself. As always with rumours of coups and plots, especially in another empire, the truth is impossible to determine. It certainly seems that prior to the Battle of Carrhae, Orodes' position was precarious and that even with this great victory, he had significant work to do to cement his position, even without the Romans stirring up further trouble for him. Bibulus, despite Cicero's envious comments, was awarded a *supplicatio* (a public vote of thanks) by the Senate, more in relief that the situation in Syria had stabilised, and returned to Rome in 49 BC, taking a command with the Pompeian/Senatorial forces in the Third Civil War.[13]

The First Romano-Parthian War ended not with a bang, but with a whimper, and the expected retaliations from both sides never materialized, as they turned their attention internally, onto domestic politics, rather than externally, to war with their rivals. For the Parthians, it was a case of Orodes cementing his grip on the throne and preventing any further coups. For the Romans, it was the sudden collapse of the relationship between Caesar and Pompeius and the Senate, and the outbreak of the Third Civil War.[14]

3. The Roman Civil War and the Eastern Powers (49–48 BC)

It is one of the great coincidences that in this period, the internal politics of both empires, despite being such different systems, mirrored each other when it came to collapsing into civil war and the weaknesses that this caused. A generation earlier, Rome fought the First Civil War (91–70 BC) at the same time as Parthia did its (c.91–61 BC). The internal collapse of both of the great powers allowed, albeit temporarily, the rise of two new empires in the Near East: the Pontic (which at its height encompassed all of Greece and Asia Minor) and the Armenian (which encompassed Syria and stretched from the Caspian Sea to the Mediterranean). It was Rome which recovered first and destroyed both the rising powers of the Pontic and Armenian empires in the Great Eastern War (74–63 BC), a war which not only expanded Rome's empire into the Middle East but paradoxically also strengthened the Parthian Empire.

Yet Parthia collapsed into another round of instability which saw Orodes seize the throne, giving Rome both the opportunity and the excuse to intervene. Now at its moment of greatest weakness in the Middle East, following Carrhae, the Republic once more imploded into another devastating civil war. The details of this war fall outside of the remit of this work and have been covered elsewhere.[15] Yet the Third Civil War, between Caesar and Pompeius and their respective factions, divided the Roman world, with the Eastern Republic falling under the control of Pompeius.

Whilst Rome's eastern provinces were spared any actual combat between the opposing factions, which was mainly concentrated in Spain, Africa and Greece, they did suffer at the hands of the Roman commanders. Naturally enough, Pompeius dispatched emissaries to the provinces and kingdoms of the East, seeking men and money to support his war in the West, regardless of how much that would weaken them, especially in the light of the Parthian threat. This task fell to Pompeius' father in law, Q. Caecilius Metellus Pius Scipio Nasica:

> '[Scipio] had requisitioned large sums of money from the communities and the despots, and had also exacted from the tax-farmers of his province the amount owing for two years, and had borrowed in advance from the same persons the amount due for the

following year, and had levied horsemen from the whole province. When these were collected, leaving in his rear the neighbouring Parthian enemy who a little before had slain the commander, M. Crassus, and had kept M. Bibulus closely invested, he had withdrawn his legions and cavalry from Syria. And as the province had fallen into a state of great anxiety and fear about a Parthian war, and remarks were heard from the soldiers that if they were being led against an enemy they would go, but that against a citizen and a consul they would not bear arms, he conducted his legions to Pergamum and the richest cities for winter quarters and bestowed on them very large bounties, and with the object of encouraging the men, allowed them to plunder the towns.

'Meanwhile sums of money, requisitioned with the utmost harshness, were being exacted throughout the province. Many kinds of extortion, moreover, were specially devised to glut their avarice. A tribute was imposed on every head of slaves and children; pillar-taxes, door-taxes, corn, soldiers, arms, rowers, freightage, were requisitioned; any mode of exaction, provided a name could be found for it, was deemed a sufficient excuse for compelling contributions. Men armed with military power were set not merely over cities but almost over every hamlet and stronghold. Among these he who had acted with the greatest harshness and cruelty was accounted the best of men and the best of citizens.'[16]

Whilst we must display caution with this source, given that that it is Caesar's own account of his enemy's activities, the point is made that the eastern provinces and kingdoms, freshly annexed to Rome, were now being forced to support a war, not in the East against Parthia, but in the West against other Romans. However, as well as extracting men and money from his allies, it seems that Pompeius turned his attentions to his enemies and dispatched an envoy to the Parthian court, to request aid in his war on Caesar. Details are scant and only recorded by two sources:

'Lucilius Hirrus, who had been sent by Pompeius to the Parthians.'[17]
    'That they [Parthians] had even imprisoned his [Pompeius'] envoy who came with a request for aid, though he was a Senator.'[18]

It is likely that this request was nothing more than a speculative effort on Pompeius' part, and the man dispatched, C. Lucilius Hirrus, seems to have been a low-ranking Senator and thus shows the low chance that Pompeius gave it.[19] Nevertheless, it clearly shows that Pompeius rated the civil war ahead of the war with Parthia. Nothing is known about what inducements were offered, if any, and the Parthians made their answer clear when they imprisoned Hirrus. Nevertheless, this blurring of the lines between the Roman Civil War and Romano-Parthian War became a continued theme in the years which followed.

Worse was to come for the kingdoms and provinces of the Roman east when it turned out that they had been forced into backing the losing side, when Caesar unexpectedly defeated Pompeius in a comprehensive victory at Pharsalus in Greece in 48 BC, after which Pompeius fled eastwards. Dio reports an interesting rumour which he must have found in earlier sources that Pompeius planned to flee to the Parthian court, but dismisses it:

> 'I have heard, indeed, that Pompeius even thought of fleeing to the Parthians, but I cannot credit the report. For that race so hated the Romans as a people ever since Crassus had made his expedition against them.
>
> 'And Pompeius would never have endured in his misfortune to become a suppliant of his bitterest foe for what he had failed to obtain while enjoying success.'[20]

In any event, Pompeius fled to Egypt and the court of Ptolemy XIII, son of the Ptolemy restored to the Egyptian throne by the Triumvirs. Yet Pompeius fatally underestimated the powers of realpolitik and the impact his defeat at Pharsalus had on his reputation. To the client kingdoms of the East, all that mattered was keeping on the right side of Rome, and Rome was now represented in the form of Caesar, not Pompeius. Pompeius was murdered when he set foot on an Egyptian beach, on the orders of Ptolemy XIII, in an abortive attempt to curry favour with Caesar. This act totally misunderstood the Roman character, which saw it as perfectly acceptable for a Roman to murder another Roman, but not for a 'foreigner' to do so. Caesar soon arrived in the Middle East and immediately got drawn into the latest round of the seemingly perpetual

Ptolemaic Civil Wars, as well as forging a 'close' alliance with one of its participants, Pharaoh Cleopatra VII.

Throughout this year of civil war we hear nothing of Parthia, with Orodes still presumably concentrating his efforts on securing his throne whilst waiting to see who would emerge victorious. For Rome's enemies, the calculation was clearly whether this collapse would lead to an opportunity or whether moving too soon would bring down the wrath of the victor. Far from a long drawn-out affair, as with Rome's First Civil War, Pharsalus and the subsequent death of Pompeius looked like it would settle the war quickly, which ironically was the opposite of what happened.

Orodes and the Parthian Empire did not immediately seek to exploit Rome's weakness, but took the more cautious route, a policy which seemed to fit with Orodes' personality and weak position. However, whilst the Parthians did not rush in to exploit Rome's collapse, another eastern power did, one with echoes of the First Civil War.

4. The Romano-Pharancean War (48–47 BC)

The Pontic King Pharances II, son of the legendary Pontic king and long-time opponent of Rome, Mithridates VI, was at this time ruler of the Bosphoran Kingdom (modern Crimea). Despite his lineage, he had actually rebelled against his father during the latter stages of the Eastern War (74–63 BC) and overthrew him, leading to his father's suicide. He then handed the body over to Pompeius as a token of his submission, earning him the kingship of the Bosphoran Kingdom, the only part of the Pontic Empire not conquered and annexed by Rome. Yet clearly Pharances had no love for the empire which had conquered his homeland, and thus in 48 BC, with the Romans distracted, he launched an attack on his neighbours, the kingdoms of Armenia and Cappadocia, both allies of Rome, in an attempt to reforge his father's empire.

We are fortunate that Caesar himself kept an accurate record of this war.[21] The Roman commander in the region was Cn. Domitius Calvinus (Cos. 53 BC), who had been appointed by Caesar to govern Asia Minor, and it was to him who the kings of Armenia and Cappadocia turned. Calvinus was in a weak position himself, having dispatched two of his three legions to Egypt to assist Caesar in the Ptolemaic Civil War, so had to face Pharnaces with just one legion, the Thirty-Sixth, supported by allied contingents from Armenia and Cappadocia:

'Taking with him one of the three, the Thirty-Sixth, he sent to Caesar in Egypt the other two which the latter had called for in his despatch. One of these two did not arrive in time for the Alexandrian war, as it was sent by the overland route through Syria. Cn. Domitius reinforced the Thirty-Sixth legion with two from Deiotarus, which the latter had had for several years, having built them up on our system of discipline and armament; he also adds to it 100 horsemen, and took a like number from Ariobarzanes. He sent P. Sestius to C. Plaetorius, the Quaestor, with instructions to bring the legion which had been formed from the hastily improvised forces in Pontus; and Quintus Patisius to Cilicia to muster auxiliary troops. All these forces speedily assembled at Comana according to the orders of Domitius.'[22]

Thus, Calvinus had some four legions at his disposal, two Roman (one newly created) and two Cappadocian. Calvinus had sent an order to Pharnaces to withdraw from both Cappadocia and Armenia, but received a reply stating that whilst he had withdrawn from Cappadocia he would not do so from Armenia, claiming it by hereditary right. Calvinus marched his army into Armenia to dislodge Pharances by force, making a base at the town of Nicopolis.

Pharances had drawn up his army in the vicinity, and was able to intercept messengers from Caesar, outlining his predicament in Alexandria and requesting further reinforcements from Calvinus. Pharnaces drew up his army in such a way that Calvinus had a route southward to withdraw from Armenia and march to Egypt. Calvinus, however, was more than aware that if he withdrew then Pharnaces would overrun the whole region, and thus gave battle.

Battle of Nicopolis (48 BC)

Caesar provides us with a highly detailed description of the dispositions of both sides, which can only have come from a first-hand report:

'Pharnaces drew up his line of battle according to his own established custom. This, in fact, was formed with its front as a single straight line, with each of the wings reinforced by three supporting lines; and on the same principle support lines were also posted in the centre, while in the two spaces, on the right hand and on the left, single ranks were drawn up.'[23]

'He [Calvinus] posted the Thirty-Sixth legion on the right wing and the Pontic one on the left, while the legions of Deiotarus he concentrated in the centre, leaving them, however, a very narrow frontage and posting his remaining cohorts behind them in support. The lines being thus arrayed on either side, they proceeded to battle.' [24]

'The signal to attack was given almost simultaneously on both sides: then came the charge, with hotly contested and fluctuating fighting. Thus, the Thirty-Sixth legion launched an attack on the king's cavalry outside the trench and fought so successful an action that it advanced up to the walls of the town, crossed the trench, and attacked the enemy in rear. The Pontic legion, however, on the other flank, drew back a little from the enemy, and attempted, moreover, to go around or cross the trench, so as to attack the enemy's exposed flank; but in the actual crossing of the trench it was pinned down and overwhelmed. The legions of Deiotarus, indeed, offered scarcely any resistance to the attack. Consequently, the king's forces, victorious on their own right wing and in the centre of the line, now turned upon the Thirty-Sixth legion. The latter, nevertheless, bore up bravely under the victors' attack and, though surrounded by large enemy forces, yet with consummate presence of mind formed a circle and so made a fighting withdrawal to the foothills, where Pharnaces was loth to pursue it owing to the hilly nature of the ground. And so, with the Pontic legion an almost total loss and a large proportion of the troops of Deiotarus killed, the Thirty-Sixth legion retired to higher ground with losses not exceeding 250 men. There fell in that battle not a few Roman knights, brilliant and distinguished men. After sustaining this defeat Domitius none the less collected the remnants of his scattered army and withdrew by safe routes through Cappadocia into Asia.'[25]

We can see that the Romans were defeated due to the inferior nature of their forces. The one veteran Roman legion, the Thirty-Sixth, was successful in routing Pharances' cavalry, but the newly formed Pontic legion fell into a trap, with ditches dug to narrow the field of battle, and was annihilated. It seems that the two Cappadocian legions were of little use and fled the field. The Thirty-Sixth legion found itself surrounded, but was able to stage a fighting withdrawal, retreating back into Cappadocia. Aside from the 250 dead of the Thirty-Sixth we do not know the total number of Roman fatalities, but it must have been at least 3,000–5,000 if we are to believe that the Pontic legion was destroyed.

The first engagement between Roman forces and those of the eastern kingdoms after the First Romano-Parthian War was thus yet another Roman defeat. Whilst it has to be recognized that the actual Roman content of the army was limited – only one veteran legion and one newly formed legion from Romano-Pontic citizens – this engagement shows the clear danger the Romans in the East faced in this civil war period, with its best forces fighting each other. It also again shows the questionable decision of Caesar to become embroiled in a Ptolemaic Civil War in Egypt, with riots and an attempted coup in Rome, the recovery of Pompeian forces in the West and now Rome's eastern empire coming under attack.

In the wider strategic sense, Nicopolis was another blow to Roman military prestige in the East. From the heights of the seemingly unstoppable conquests of the Great Eastern War, the Romans had been defeated first by the Parthians, who had overrun Syria, and then the Pontic forces of the Bosphorus, who proceeded to overrun not only Cappadocia but also the Roman provinces of Bithynia and Pontus. Pharnaces was able to overturn the result of the Great Eastern War, reoccupy his ancestral homeland of Pontus and recreate his father's Pontic Empire, which now spanned the length of Asia Minor (see Map 5).

We are not aware of any contact between Parthia and Pharnaces during this period, due to our only surviving sources being Roman. Nevertheless, these developments must have been looked on with some interest in Parthia, not only as a sign of Rome's ongoing military weakness, but also in terms of the isolated position of the Roman province of Syria. Although Caesar was still in Egypt with his legions, there would be no reinforcements coming overland now the route through Asia Minor had been cut off. We hear of no action from the Parthians to build on Pharnaces' success, but again Orodes must have been utilizing his natural caution as one battle against an understrength Roman army did not make a war. Clearly Caesar, if he survived the civil war in Egypt, would have to move against Pharnaces or lose the whole of the Roman East.

With the onset of winter, Pharnaces found himself in the same position as his father, Mithridates VI. He had defeated the Romans, ejected them from Asia Minor and recreated the Pontic Empire. It was from this high point that Pharances' fortunes began to turn. The first blow came from his Bosphoran heartland, when in a historical parallel, the man he left as governor of his Bosphoran kingdom, Asander, revolted, just as Pharnaces had done against his own father. This was followed by news that Caesar had emerged from the Ptolemaic Civil War victorious, albeit with the loss of the Great Library of Alexandria, and now had his 'ally' Pharaoh Cleopatra VII on the throne of Egypt, so had the whole resources of Egypt at his command.

Caesar was faced with a conundrum. He had originally travelled to the East in an attempt to capture Pompeius and bring an end to the Third Roman Civil War, but all he found was Pompeius' butchered corpse and another Ptolemaic Civil War. He now had with three competing priorities: securing Rome itself and political control of the Republic, which required his presence in Italy; stopping the remaining Pompeian/Senatorial forces from regrouping, requiring his presence in Africa; or recovering Rome's eastern empire, requiring his presence in Asia.

Pharnaces must have been hoping that Caesar would choose either Italy or Africa and come to some accommodation with him, much as Sulla had done with his father, Mithridates VI, in the First Roman Civil War. Indeed, Dio states the following:

'[Pharnaces] sent messengers to him [Caesar] before he drew near, making frequent proposals to see if he might on some terms or other escape the present danger. One of the principal pleas that he presented was that he had not cooperated with Pompeius, and he hoped to induce Caesar to grant a truce, particularly since the latter was anxious to hasten to Italy and Africa; and once Caesar was gone, he hoped to wage war again at his ease.'[26]

Yet for Caesar, the clearest threat came from Rome's enemies in the East, and here he may have had one eye on the Parthians. Had he moved to Africa to fight the regrouping Pompeian forces commanded by Metellus Scipio, Cato and the sons of Pompeius, or to Italy to regain control of the Senate and Assemblies, he would have been sending a clear message to the eastern powers that his priorities lay elsewhere and that he would not defend the eastern provinces. This would have been understood by Pharances, but also the Parthians and the inhabitants of the East. Furthermore, the richest prize in the East was Egypt, and he had just fought a close-run civil war to secure control of it. Caesar therefore put the ongoing Roman Civil War to one side, and in 47 BC marched on Pontus to face Pharnaces.

Caesar relates the whole campaign in some detail, including his attempts to reach a negotiated settlement with Pharnaces and have him withdraw from the territory he had conquered.[27] Pharnaces naturally stalled for time, hoping that necessity would force Caesar to abandon the East and march for Africa or Italy. In the end he chose to make his stand at the symbolic town of Zela, site of one of his father's most famous victories over the Romans.[28]

Battle of Zela (47 BC)

The two armies drew up opposing each other, but separated by a hill and ravine. Whilst Caesar's army was building its forward palisade, Pharances decided to launch a pre-emptive strike, catching Caesar off-guard:

'Having decided to engage, he [Pharnaces] began the descent down the steep ravine. For some little time Caesar laughed contemptuously at this empty bravado on the part of the king, and at his troops packed closely on ground which no enemy in his senses would be likely to set foot on; while in the meantime Pharnaces with his forces in battle array proceeded to climb the steep hill-side confronting him at the same steady pace at which he had descended the sheer ravine.'[29]

'This incredible foolhardiness or confidence on the part of the king disconcerted Caesar, who was not expecting it and was caught unprepared. Simultaneously he recalled the troops from their work of fortification, ordered them to stand to arms, deployed his legions to meet the attack, and formed line of battle; and the sudden excitement to which all this gave rise occasioned considerable panic among our troops. Disorganised as our men were, and as yet in no regular formation, the king's chariots armed with scythes threw them into confusion; but these chariots were speedily overwhelmed by a mass of missiles. In their wake came the enemy line: the battle cry was raised, and the conflict joined, our men being greatly helped by the nature of the ground.'[30]

'Heavy and bitter hand-to-hand fighting took place; and it was on the right wing, where the veteran Sixth legion was posted, that the first seeds of victory were sown. As the enemy were being thrust back down the slope on this wing, so too on the left wing and in the centre, much more slowly, but thanks nevertheless to the same divine assistance, the entire forces of the king were being crushed. The ease with which they had climbed the uneven ground was now matched by the speed with which, once dislodged from their footing, the unevenness of the ground enabled them to be driven back. Consequently, after sustaining many casualties, some killed, some knocked out by their comrades' falling on top of them, those whose nimbleness did enable them to escape none the less threw away their arms; and so, after crossing the valley, they could not make any effective stand from the higher ground, unarmed as they now were. Our men, on the contrary, elated by their victory, did not hesitate to climb the uneven ground and storm the entrenchments. Moreover, despite the resistance of those enemy cohorts which Pharnaces had left to guard his camp, they promptly won possession of it. With his entire forces either killed or captured Pharnaces took to flight with a few horsemen; and had not our storming of his camp afforded him a freer opportunity for flight, he would have been brought alive into Caesar's hands.'[31]

Having lost the element of surprise, Pharances' forces were defeated by the superior skill of the Roman forces in close order combat, combined with the advantage of the terrain, Pharances' forces fighting uphill. The success of the battle led Caesar to apparently issue his most famous quote, '*veni, vidi, vici*' – 'I came, I saw, I conquered.'[32] Having recovered Pontus, Caesar disposed of his forces and set about reorganizing the region and establishing firm Roman control:

'Having thus recovered Pontus and made a present to his troops of all the royal plunder, he himself set out on the following day with his cavalry in light order; instructing the Sixth legion to leave for Italy to receive its rewards and honours, sending home the auxiliary troops of Deiotarus, and leaving two legions in Pontus with Caelius Vinicianus.

'Thus, he marched through Gallograecia and Bithynia into Asia, holding investigations and giving his formal ruling on matters of dispute in all those provinces, and assigning due prerogatives to tetrarchs, kings and states.' [33]

Pharnaces himself survived and fled back to the Bosphorus, where he was killed fighting for control of the kingdom against his rebellious deputy, Asander:

'His enemy, Asander, attacked him again, and his men were defeated for want of horses, and because they were not accustomed to fighting on foot. Pharnaces alone fought valiantly until he died of his wounds, being then fifty years of age and having been king of Bosphorus fifteen years.'[34]

Asander himself did not have time to enjoy his victory, as Caesar appointed his close friend and ally, Mithridates, another son of Mithridates VI, as King of the Bosphorus and supplied him with the forces to conquer the kingdom and rule it as Rome's ally. Ironically, Mithridates' rule was short-lived, as Asander was later restored by Caesar's adopted son Octavianus.

With his overwhelming victory over Pharnaces, Caesar restored full Roman control of the East under the remaining Roman legions and Rome's client kings, allowing him to return west to pursue the civil war against the Pompeian forces. In Syria itself, Caesar left one legion under the command of his cousin Sex. Iulius Caesar.

The whole region, and Parthia especially, had been given a clear indication that despite the ongoing civil war, Rome's military might, when properly assembled and led, was as destructive as ever, as was their resolve to hold onto control of the region. Pharances had been a convenient, though accidental, stalking horse for Parthia to test Rome's control of the region. Rome, and ultimately Caesar, had not been found wanting, and though the shift of Rome's attention moved to the West – firstly in Africa and then Spain – the East lay very much in Caesar's mind.

5. The East and the Roman Civil War (46–44 BC)

No sooner had Caesar withdrawn westwards to fight the remaining Pompeian/Senatorial forces than civil war again broke out in Roman lands in the East. At the centre of this conflict was a Roman commander, Q. Caecilius Bassus. He had been a supporter of Pompeius, who had fled East after Pharsalus and taken up residence at Tyre. Though Bassus seemingly held no command, he waited until Caesar had left the region and instigated a pro-Pompeian rebellion against Caesar, apparently independent of the Pompeian forces in Africa. Both Plutarch and Dio preserve accounts of the civil war, but Dio's is by far the most comprehensive:

> 'So Bassus at first remained quiet, satisfied if only he might be allowed to live; but when some men in like case had associated themselves with him and he had attached to himself various soldiers of Sextus who came there at different times to garrison the city, and when, moreover, many alarming reports kept coming in from Africa about Caesar, he was no longer content with the existing state of affairs, but began to stir up a rebellion, his aim being either to help the followers of Scipio and Cato and the Pompeians or to win for himself some political power. But he was discovered by Sextus before he had finished his preparations and explained that he was collecting these troops for the use of Mithridates the Pergamenian in an expedition against Bosphorus; his story was believed, and he was released. So after this he forged a letter, which he pretended had been sent to him by Scipio, on the basis of which he announced that Caesar had been defeated and had perished in Africa and claimed that the governorship of Syria had been assigned to him.

He then seized Tyre with the aid of the forces he had got ready, and from there he advanced against the legions of Sextus but was defeated and wounded while attacking him. After this experience, he did not again make an attempt by force upon Sextus, but sent messages to his soldiers, and in some way or other won some of them to himself to such an extent that they murdered Sextus with their own hands.'[35]

Thus Bassus used the uncertainty about the ongoing civil war in Africa to claim that Caesar had been defeated and killed and that he had been appointed the new Governor of Syria. Thus he was able to gather enough men to his side to attack Sex. Iulius Caesar, but was defeated in battle. Yet Bassus turned defeat into victory by subverting Caesar's men – either through bribery, loyalty to Pompeius or news of Caesar's 'death' – who promptly rebelled and murdered Sex. Iulius Caesar, whose name was added to the list of Roman commanders murdered by their own troops.

This act of rebellion left Bassus in control of Roman Syria, but he soon had to contend with the fact that C. Iulius Caesar had not been defeated or killed in Africa but had emerged victorious and crushed the Pompeian and Senatorial forces at the Battle of Thapsus in North Africa (46 BC). Nevertheless, Bassus was able to retain control of Syria and fortified his position, as Dio relates:

'When Sextus was dead, Bassus gained possession of all his army except a few; for the soldiers who had been wintering in Apamea withdrew into Cilicia before his arrival, and although he pursued them, he did not win them over. Returning then to Syria, he took the title of praetor and fortified Apamea, so as to have it as a base for the war. And he proceeded to enlist the men of military age, not only freemen but slaves as well, to gather money, and to prepare arms. While he was thus engaged, one Caius Antistius besieged him. Later they had a fairly equal struggle, and when neither party was able to gain any great advantage, they parted, without any definite truce, to await the bringing up of allies. Antistius was joined by such persons of the vicinity as favoured Caesar and by soldiers who had been sent from Rome by Caesar, while Bassus was joined by

Alchaudonius the Arabian. He it was who had formerly made terms with Lucullus, as I have stated, and later joined with the Parthians against Crassus. On this occasion he was summoned by both sides but entered the space between the city and the camps and before making any answer called for bids for his services as an ally; and as Bassus outbid Antistius, he assisted him, and in the battle proved greatly superior in his archery. Even the Parthians, too, came at the invitation of Bassus, but on account of the winter failed to remain with him for any considerable time, and hence did not accomplish anything of importance. Bassus prevailed for a time, to be sure, but was later again held in check by Marcius Crispus and Lucius Staius Murcus.' [36]

Thus Bassus was able to mobilize the military resources of Syria and spent 45 BC resisting the Caesarian commander C. Antistius, who was by now receiving reinforcements from Rome, sent by Caesar. Naturally, as it was a Roman civil war, the bulk of the client kingdoms remained neutral, but Bassus reached out further afield and secured two allies: first Alchaudonius, an Arabian chieftain, and then the Parthians themselves. It is unfortunate that we have no further details of the Parthian involvement, which is confirmed briefly by Cicero:

'He has had a letter from Vetus, dated the last day of December, saying that when Caecilius was besieged and already within his grasp, the Parthian Pacorus came with a large force, and so Caecilius was snatched from his hands and he lost many men.'[37]

Given their brief appearance and lack of involvement in any fighting, we must question the scale of this Parthian contingent; it is more likely to have been a token presence, a measure of support for Bassus and nothing more. Nevertheless, their intervention, however brief, is an interesting one as it shows the Parthian court was taking an interest in the events in Syria when the civil war offered them an advantage, backing one side. The Parthians had failed to support Pompeius when he sent emissaries to them in 48 BC, but at that point, Pompeius was far way in Greece, and Syria was at peace. Now there was another Roman commander in charge of Syria, fighting against the faction in power at Rome, who thus would make for a more useful ally, especially given that he was not of the stature of Pompeius and so a more malleable tool. The year 45 BC therefore ended with Bassus in control of Syria and the Parthians indicating their willingness to involve themselves in the Roman Civil War, against Caesar.

6. Waiting for Caesar

Caesar, meanwhile, had not been idle in the West, and followed up his crushing victory over the Pompeian and Senatorial forces at Thapsus in 46 BC with another success, this time in Spain, over an army commanded by Pompeius' two sons at the Battle of Munda in 45 BC.

Caesar had clearly hoped that his comprehensive victory at Pharsalus would end the Third Roman Civil War. Yet Pompeius' murder on an Egyptian beach robbed him of any chance of reaching a settlement with his old colleague, and the remaining Pompeian and Senatorial forces chose to continue to oppose him rather than submit to a Caesarian-controlled Republic, a notable exception being Cicero. Caesar's eastern campaigns in 47 BC, first in Egypt and then in Pontus, were followed by an African campaign in 46 BC, which culminated in his victory at the Battle of Thapsus, and then a Spanish campaign in 45 BC, concluding with his triumph at Munda. It was not until late 45 BC that Caesar was able to return to Rome victorious, with the majority of the Republic and its empire under his control, Syria being the one obvious anomaly, with Bassus still fighting on.

Yet victory and the control of the Republic it brought seemed to always be a secondary concern. In truth, Caesar had not shone as a Roman politician, despite showing early promise. His Praetorship became tarred with questions around his possible involvement in the abortive coup that sparked the Second Civil War (63–62 BC), his Consulship had been as an agent of Pompeius and Crassus, and he had always been very much the junior partner of Rome's leading cabal, the Triumvirate. Yet Caesar's true talent lay on the battlefield, first with his unprecedented conquest of Gaul and then in the Third Civil War. It seems Caesar had no inclination to remain in Rome and deal with the harsh realities of trying to dominate an increasingly ungovernable Roman Republic. Naturally, his thoughts turned to another campaign, especially now that he was in his mid-50s and had the full resources of Rome's empire to back up his ambition. There was only one region he had in mind: the East.

Caesar, like most of Rome's ruling class, had an obsession with Alexander the Great and his conquest of the Persian Empire. This fixation had been fuelled by Rome's recent full-blown expansion into the East (74–63 BC) and his own experiences in Alexandria, including visiting Alexander's tomb. To many amongst the Roman oligarchy, both militarily and politically, Rome was now the inheritor of Alexander. Macedon had long fallen to Rome, as had the Seleucid Empire, and the Ptolemies of Egypt were effectively a Roman vassal state. Furthermore, the Parthians had inherited the mantle of the Persians and recreated much of their empire. Added to all this weight of history were the ghosts of Carrhae, the painfully stark defeat of a Roman army and the death of Caesar's old mentor and colleague M. Licinius Crassus. Caesar therefore set his mind and the whole resources of the Roman Republic to a great eastern campaign and the attempted conquest of the Parthian Empire.

Throughout the winter of 45/44 BC, Caesar prepared for a renewed war, targeting the Parthian Empire and beyond.[38] The surviving sources maintain a number of fragments of information about this great expedition, including its size and route:

'[Caesar] conceived the idea of a long campaign against the Getae and the Parthians. The Getae, a hardy, warlike, and neighbouring nation, were to be attacked first. The Parthians were to be punished for their perfidy toward Crassus. He sent across the Adriatic in advance sixteen legions of foot and 10,000 horse.' [39]

'But while Caesar was thus engaged, a longing came over all the Romans alike to avenge Crassus and those who had perished with him, and they felt some hope of subjugating the Parthians then, if ever. They [the People] unanimously voted the command of the war to Caesar and made ample provision for it.'[40]

'Then to make war on the Parthians by way of Lesser Armenia, but not to risk a battle with them until he had first tested their mettle.' [41]

We can see the scale of the campaign Caesar was planning. Where Crassus took seven legions, Caesar apparently sent an advance guard of sixteen legions, backed up by 10,000 cavalry, clearly aiming to avoid another Carrhae situation, where Rome's best hope had been the cavalry breakout spearheaded by Crassus eldest son Publius, himself on loan from Caesar's Gallic campaign. Caesar had several invaluable advantages over the first Roman invasion of Parthia, not only in resources but most importantly in experience. He must have quizzed as many of the survivors as he could, especially C. Cassius, whom he appointed as Praetor for 44 BC. The surviving note in Suetonius is especially valuable as it seems that Caesar chose to take a different route to Crassus, via Armenia, to the north, as opposed to the Euphrates route. He also appears to have intended to avoid an immediate set-piece battle to allow his troops to adjust to the different fighting style of the Parthians.

Caesar's Parthian campaign will always stand as one of ancient history's greatest 'what ifs'; whether Rome's leading general of the day, backed by unlimited military resources, could have indeed conquered and annexed the Parthian Empire and stretched Rome's empire to the borders of India. Given the relatively weak state of the Parthian Empire and the resources and brilliance of Caesar as a commander, we must assume that he would have indeed triumphed. Yet the Parthians were saved once again by the weakness and instability of the Republic, and the very campaign which Caesar planned hastened his downfall.

Despite having won three separate battles against his domestic opponents, the majority of the surviving Senatorial oligarchy were hardly enthusiastic Caesarian supporters, and Caesar's unsubtle political style made matters worse. In the preceding five years, Caesar had been Consul four times (48, 46, 45 and 44 BC) and Dictator another four times (49–46 BC). In 46 BC he became Dictator for a ten-year period, which became a *Dictator Perpetuus* in January 44 BC. Caesar's long-time ally, and later opponent, Pompeius had always avoided using the office of Dictator, which had become forever tainted with the sole rule of L. Cornelius Sulla (82–80 BC) and the bloody purges of his enemies. In choosing to so obviously flaunt his dominance in the Republic, Caesar clearly made himself enemies of even the moderate Senators, who believed in the founding principles of the Republic: not to suffer a king.

The intended Parthian campaign brought matters to a head. Firstly, his enemies set a story about that the Sibylline Oracle had stated that Parthia could only be conquered by a king, a rumour which Caesar reacted badly to, stripping two Tribunes of the People of their tribunician power for their actions in cracking down on those who were calling for Caesar to be king.[42] This heavy-handed show of power, backed by questionable legality, merely seemed to prove Caesar's opponents' point; that he was behaving in a tyrannical and thus un-Republican manner. Furthermore, this Parthian campaign would ensure that Caesar was out of Rome and surrounded by his army, far from his opponents, for a number of years, and if he was successful then he would return even more powerful and popular. Thus, before he had time to leave for Parthia, Caesar's opponents struck and enacted one of history's most famous assassinations in the Senate House on the Ides of March.

For the Parthians, the Ides of March was a gift from the gods. The Caesarian-led campaign for the conquest of the Parthian Empire died with Caesar, and Roman attention once more turned to domestic politics and the slow spiral into a renewed civil war.

Summary

We can see that the history of the Middle East and the Romano-Parthian conflict took a dramatic turn on the Ides of March 44 BC. The Second Romano-Parthian War should have started in that year with a massive Roman invasion of the Parthian Empire, commanded by Rome's leading general and with the full resources of Rome's empire at his command. As had been seen in Gaul in the 50s BC, Caesar had a taste for conquest, having overwhelmed the previously *terra incognito* of Gaul, and would have happily bought into the Alexandrian legend and taken his armies to the borders of India. Yet, as always in this period, events at Rome took precedence to those in the empire, and Caesar's enemies took their last chance to rid Rome of a tyrant. Once again, Parthia had been given a reprieve thanks to Roman domestic politics: it would not be the last time.

Part II

The Rise and Fall of Parthia (44–38 BC)

Chapter Three

Civil War and the Romano-Parthian Conquest of the East

1. Civil War and the Collapse of the Eastern Republic (44–42 BC)

Whilst Caesar had been able to extinguish the civil war in the western Republic, the same could not have be said for the eastern one, where the Pompeian general Q. Caecilius Bassus had seized control of the Roman legions of Syria and murdered Caesar's kinsman Sex. Iulius Caesar. Though Bassus had control of Syria, it seems that the other Caesarian commanders of the region – Bithynia, Pontus and Cilicia – went to war to recover Syria, though the details are obscure.[1] Nevertheless, by 44 BC Bassus still held Syria and remained a thorn in Caesar's side, not only in still fighting for the Pompeian cause but by blocking Caesar's proposed Parthian War and possibly allowing the Parthians a foothold in Syria.

Caesar appointed a new Roman commander for Syria, L. Staius Murcus. However, Murcus did not leave Italy until after the assassination of Caesar, in which he seems to have been implicated.[2] Following the murder, Murcus clearly judged it politic to leave for the East and take up his command, not only to safeguard his person but possibly to secure the province for the anti-Caesarian cause. By late 44 BC he entered Syria with three legions and met Bassus in battle:

'Caesar sent Staius Murcius against him with three legions. Bassus defeated him badly. Finally, Murcus appealed to Marcius Crispus, the governor of Bithynia, and the latter came to his aid with three legions.'[3]

'Caesar sent Staius Murcus against them with three legions, but they resisted bravely, Marcius Crispus was then sent from Bithynia to the aid of Murcus with three additional legions, and thus Bassus was besieged by six legions altogether.'[4]

Bassus still held Syria, facing six legions under the command of a supposedly Caesarian commander, though Murcus' loyalty must have been questionable. If this situation were not complicated enough, yet another commander in Syria had been appointed. This time it was Caesar's replacement as Consul, the young P. Cornelius Dolabella, who was appointed by popular legislation to replace Caesar as the commander for the proposed Parthian War:

> 'Antonius, knowing that this young Dolabella was himself ambitious, persuaded him to solicit the province of Syria and the army enlisted against the Parthians, to be used against the Parthians, in place of Cassius, and to ask it, not from the Senate, which had not the power to grant it, but from the People by a law. Dolabella was delighted, and immediately brought forward the law. The Senate accused him of nullifying the decrees of Caesar. He replied that Caesar had not assigned the war against the Parthians to anybody, and that Cassius, who had been assigned to the command of Syria, had himself been the first to alter the decrees of Caesar by authorising colonists to sell their allotments before the expiration of the legal period of twenty years. He said also it would be an indignity to himself if he, Dolabella, were not chosen for Syria instead of Cassius.' [5]
>
> 'Thus Dolabella became governor of Syria and general of the war against the Parthians and of the forces enlisted for that purpose by Caesar, together with those that had gone in advance to Macedonia.'[6]

The People appointed Dolabella as Caesar's successor and commander of the war against the Parthians, a command which Antonius chose not to pursue himself. Again this was a clear case of politics at Rome taking precedence over matters of war with Parthia. The murder of Caesar had created a power vacuum in Rome into which Antonius clearly intended to step, and appointing Dolabella to the eastern command accomplished two things. Firstly, it removed Dolabella, a rival, from Rome. Secondly, it stopped Cassius from securing the command, preventing one of the two leaders of the opposing faction from securing a major power base. As it was, Cassius only received the province of Cyrenaica, in North Africa, a backwater designed to nullify any future threat he might pose.

Whether Dolabella had thought of a war with Parthia we will never know. Clearly his main priority would have been to secure Syria from Bassus, and possibly Murcus. However, unfortunately for him, he took a leisurely overland route to Syria, possibly leaving in late 44 BC, but was overtaken by events in Rome. By early 43 BC Antonius, attempting to fill Caesar's shoes, overplayed his hand, with near fatal consequences. Having secured control of Rome and dispatched Dolabella, Brutus and Cassius from Italy, he deemed that the main threat to his control of Rome was one of the conspirators, D. Iunius Brutus, who held command of Cisalpine Gaul (Northern Italy) and thus had an army on Rome's doorstep. Antonius was able to persuade the Senate and People to go to war with Brutus. However, no sooner had he left Rome, than Caesar's recently adopted son, C. Iulius Caesar Octavianus, worked with factions in the Senate to undermine Antonius. Antonius and Dolabella were declared enemies of the state and Cassius was appointed Senatorial commander of Syria.

By early 43 BC Rome had four different commanders in Syria: Murcus, appointed by a Caesarian-controlled Senate (though a supporter of the Brutan-Cassian faction); Dolabella, appointed by the Antonine-controlled Assembly; Cassius, appointed by an anti-Antonine-controlled Senate; and Bassus, a Pompeian commander who had seized power. This goes to show the sheer chaos that had engulfed the Roman Republic. Even without the arrival of Cassius or Dolabella, there were eight legions in Syria, all fighting each other and ignoring the Parthians.

Critically, it was Cassius who moved the quickest. We must assume that he had already decided to pre-empt any aggressive move on Antonius' part and try to seize Syria himself. By the time he arrived he found that Antonius' domination of the Senate had been overthrown and that, far from seizing the province, he was now its latest officially appointed commander. Using both his new position and his experience and contacts in the province, Cassius reached the besieged Bassus and promptly took command of both the besieged and besieging armies, some eight legions in total:

'Affairs with them were in this state when Cassius came on the scene and at once conciliated all the cities because of the renown of his acts

while quaestor and of his fame in general and attached the legions of
Bassus and of the others without any further trouble. While he was
encamped in one place with all these forces, a great downpour from
the sky suddenly occurred, during which wild swine rushed into
the camp, through all the gates at once, overturning and throwing
into confusion everything there; hence some inferred from this his
immediate rise to power and his subsequent overthrow.'[7]

'Thereupon Cassius anticipated Dolabella by entering Syria,
where he raised the standards of a governor and won over twelve
legions of soldiers who had been enlisted and trained by Caius
Caesar long before.'[8]

'Cassius speedily intervened in this siege and took command at
once of the army of Bassus with its consent, and afterward of the
legions of Murcus and Marius, who surrendered them to him in a
friendly way and in pursuance of the decree of the Senate obeyed
him in all respects.'[9]

Thus the whole military resources of Syria, and the other eastern Roman
provinces, fell to C. Cassius Longinus, the man who had defended the
province nearly ten years earlier from the Parthians. Of the two main
commanders, Murcus, who was already involved in the plot to assassinate
Caesar, willingly served under Cassius, whilst Bassus, it seems, was
expelled from Cassius' force, unfortunately disappearing from history at
this point.[10]

The only remaining obstacle to his control was Dolabella, making
his way (incredibly slowly) through Asia Minor. Part of the reason for
Dolabella's tardiness was that he had become embroiled in another civil
war in Asia Minor, seemingly before he had even been outlawed by the
Senate. His path through Asia to Syria was hampered by the pro-Cassian
commander C. Trebonius, who attempted to slow him down, albeit
without violence. The same could not be said of Dolabella's reaction:

'Trebonius, governor of the province of Asia, was fortifying his
towns for them [Brutus and Cassius]. When Dolabella arrived,
Trebonius would not admit him to Pergamum or Smyrna, but
allowed him, as Consul, an opportunity of buying provisions

outside the walls. However, when he attacked the walls with fury, but accomplished nothing, Trebonius said that he would be admitted to Ephesus. Dolabella started for Ephesus forthwith, and Trebonius sent a force to follow him at a certain distance. While these were observing Dolabella's march, they were overtaken by night, and, having no further suspicions, returned to Smyrna, leaving a few of their number to follow him. Dolabella laid an ambush for this small number, captured and killed them, and went back the same night to Smyrna. Finding it unguarded, he took it by escalade.

'Trebonius, who was captured in bed, told his captors to lead the way to Dolabella, saying that he was willing to follow them. One of the centurions answered him facetiously, "Go where you please, but you must leave your head behind here, for we are ordered to bring your head, not yourself." With these words the centurion immediately cut off his head, and early in the morning Dolabella ordered it to be displayed on the Praetor's chair where Trebonius was accustomed to transact public business. Since Trebonius had participated in the murder of Caesar by detaining Antony in conversation at the door of the Senate-House while the others killed him, the soldiers and camp-followers fell upon the rest of his body with fury and treated it with every kind of indignity. They rolled his head from one to another in sport along the city pavements like a ball till it was completely crushed. This was the first of the murderers who received the weight of his crime, and thus vengeance overtook him.'[11]

Dolabella had taken Asia Minor, but was even more delayed in reaching Syria, allowing Cassius time to consolidate his position. Cassius even had the time to turn to the south and head off a Dolabellan force from Egypt:

'Just then Allienus, who had been sent to Egypt by Dolabella, brought from that quarter four legions of soldiers dispersed by the disasters of Pompeius and of Crassus, or left with Cleopatra by Caesar. Cassius surrounded him unawares in Palestine and compelled him to surrender, as he did not dare to fight with four legions against eight. Thus Cassius became the master, in a surprising way, of twelve legions, and laid siege to Dolabella, who was coming from Asia with two legions and had been received in Laodicea in a friendly manner.'[12]

Sensibly avoiding a set-piece battle, Dolabella took refuge in the city of Laodicea in Asia, which was put under siege.

'When Cassius had again made such preparations as he could with the forces in hand, he engaged Dolabella a second time. The first battle was doubtful, but in the next one Dolabella was beaten on the sea. Then Cassius completed his mound and battered Dolabella's walls till they trembled. He tried unsuccessfully to bribe Marsus, the captain of the night-watch, but he bribed the centurions of the day force, and while Marsus was taking his rest, effected an entrance by daylight through a number of small gates that were secretly opened to him one after another. When the city was taken Dolabella offered his head to his private sentry and told him to cut it off and carry it to Cassius in order to secure his own safety. The guard cut if off, but he killed himself also and Marsus took his own life. Cassius swore Dolabella's army into his own service. He plundered the temples and the treasury of Laodicea, punished the chief citizens, and exacted very heavy contributions from the rest, so that the city was reduced to the extremest misery.'[13]

2. The Roman Civil War, the Eastern Republic and the Parthians (42–41 BC)

Thus, ironically, it was Cassius who ended four years of civil war in the Roman East and brought the whole region under his control (see Map 6). Appian tells us that a proposed move on Egypt – ruled by Cleopatra, a Caesarian ally – was prevented by the need to link with Brutus in Macedonia.[14] Nevertheless, by capturing the four legions which A. Allienus had been dispatched with from Egypt, he had negated any threat from that region. Appian also contains an interesting passage concerning the presence of a Parthian force in Syria:

'He [Cassius] also sent back his Parthian mounted bowmen with
presents, and with them ambassadors to their king asking for a
larger force of auxiliaries. This force arrived after the decisive
battle, ravaged Syria and many of the neighbouring provinces as far
as Ionia, and then returned home.' [15]

It is difficult to know what to make of this passage, with on the one hand
Cassius having Parthian archers in his army and on the other them
attacking Syria and, incredibly, as far as Ionia (most likely meant to refer
to the Ionian coast of Asia). Having defended Syria from the Parthians in
the first war and successfully taken twelve legions without a blow struck,
it is unclear what the Parthians were doing here. We seem to have two
options. On the one hand, the Parthian King Orodes might have sent
them as a token of good will in their ongoing negotiations (see below),
whilst on the other, the Parthians may well have taken advantage of this
chaos in Syria to send raiding parties, which Cassius put a stop to.

In any event, it is clear that Cassius did open negotiations with Orodes
about coming to some accommodation, which would allow him to fight
his main enemy, the Caesarian faction in Italy. We know that he dispatched
a legate, Q. Labienus, to the Parthian court on some mission:

'He [Labienus] was an ally of Brutus and Cassius and having before
the battle been sent to Orodes to secure some reinforcements, was
detained by him a long time while the king was waiting the turn of
events and hesitating to join forces with him yet fearing to refuse.' [16]

Most ancient commentators assumed that Cassius was requesting military
reinforcements for his march into Macedonia, yet as we have seen he
already had at least fourteen legions at his command and no Parthian
forces had ever crossed the Bosphorus. It would be interesting to know
what exactly Cassius' offer to Orodes was; whether it was a reaffirmation
of friendship between the two empires or whether Cassius did indeed
want positive military assistance. Given his strong position in the East,
with fourteen legions under his control and his record of staunch
opposition to the Parthians, it seems unlikely that Cassius wanted help
from Parthian forces in the East, especially as it would be a propaganda

victory for his opponents, taking forces of Rome's greatest rival into Greece to fight other Romans.

Given this situation, it is more likely that he was hoping to secure an alliance with Orodes, to ensure his non-intervention in Syria whilst he left to fight the civil war in the West. This may well tie in with Appian's account of Parthian raiding parties in Syria. Had Cassius and his allies won the civil war, then they would have needed to go to Rome to secure their control of the Republic and its empire, ensuring his absence from the East for a number of years.

Naturally, Orodes was too cautious to throw his lot in with one of the factions of a Roman civil war and risk another Roman onslaught, but again preferred to bide his time and see if there were any weaknesses he could exploit. One consequence was that Q. Labienus was at the Parthian court for subsequent events. It also seems that Cassius sent M. Porcius Cato, son of the deceased Cato, to the Cappadocian court on a similar errand.[17] Thus, with time pressing, Cassius took the bulk of his Roman forces to Macedonia to link up with his ally M. Iunius Brutus, to await the arrival of the Triumviral forces which had retaken control of the Republic. Appian provides us with additional information:

> 'Cassius left his nephew in Syria with one legion and sent his cavalry in advance into Cappadocia, who presently killed Ariobarzanes for plotting against Cassius. Then they seized his large treasures and other military supplies and brought them to Cassius.'[18]

The death of King Ariobarzanes of Cappadocia, with his territory overrun, again highlighted the danger of a client king choosing the wrong side of a civil war. As with the earlier stages of the war between Caesar and Pompeius, the chosen battleground for this clash between the two leading factions of the Roman ruling elite was Greece, and the sides met at the two battles of Philippi.

The Philippi campaign falls outside the remit of this present work,[19] but the important aspect from the eastern perspective was the death of C. Cassius Longinus, who twice had brought peace to the region and ruled in Rome's name. Despite the First Battle of Philippi ending in a stalemate, Cassius believed that his cause was lost and took, what he believed, to be the 'honourable' way out and committed suicide rather than compromise with his enemies (and fellow Romans). He joined a growing list of notable Romans who committed suicide in the civil war, including, most notably, Cato and Metellus Scipio.

With the Triumvirs victorious in the second battle of Philippi, their immediate concern was to secure the East, which had staunchly supported Cassius, to secure both its loyalty and its resources. To that end, M. Antonius chose to take control of the Eastern Republic, whilst his colleague Octavianus returned to Rome, Lepidus having not left Italy. The war between the factions had been a costly one and the winners had inherited the headache of dismissing the bulk of the Roman forces – from both sides – back into civilian life, all of which took money; money which would have to be extracted from the Roman East, as though it were a conquered province. Appian provides details of a speech given by Antonius at Ephesus to an assembly of delegates from the eastern provinces and allies, where he made it clear that the burden of disbanding the legions would fall upon them, either voluntarily or by force.[20] Famously, even the Ptolemaic Pharaoh Cleopatra came from Egypt to Cilicia to meet Antonius, the new master of the Roman East.

The Near East had a new de-facto ruler, M. Antonius, one of Rome's ruling Triumvirs, armed with total authority to reorganize the region as he saw fit. The seat of power for this new regime naturally gravitated towards Alexandria, the largest and richest city of the East and the home of Cleopatra. The existing rulers and ruling elites in the patchwork of provinces and allied kingdoms of the East faced two choices: acquiesce with the new regime or oppose it. The majority chose the former and paid up. For those who refused to cooperate, for either practical or political reasons, the obvious problem was how to oppose the militarily dominant Rome. There would be little or no help from the Romans of the Brutan-Cassian faction. Those who survived Philippi had either changed allegiance to the new regime or fled to the West, having regrouped briefly at Rhodes,[21] to join the factions of Sex. Pompeius or Cn. Domitius Ahenobarbus who were still fighting the Triumvirs.

This left one obvious alternative, the Parthian Empire, which still held the Roman legate, Q. Labienus, now a political refugee at the court of Orodes and one who was determined not to accommodate with the

Triumviral regime in control of Rome. Yet despite all these factors, Orodes was hardly likely to rush into a fresh confrontation with Antonius for control of the East, especially given his power as one half (Lepidus being increasingly side-lined) of Rome's ruling oligarchy. Philippi, like Pharsalus before it, had been a crushing victory, but it had yet again failed to extinguish the civil war completely, with both Sex. Pompeius' and Cn. Domitius Ahenobarbus' factions still fighting. Nevertheless, whilst these began to pose a more serious threat to Italy, that fell into Octavianus' (and Lepidus') sphere of influence, not that of Antonius. Thus he had little to distract him from exercising his control of the Near East.

This was all to change during 41 BC, however, when a political dispute in Rome between one of Antonius' colleagues, Octavianus, and one of his brothers, the Consul L. Antonius, led to yet another collapse of the Republic into civil war, this time within the Triumviral regime. With civil war once again raging in Italy, and judging Antonius' grip and interest in the Near East to be vulnerable, the Parthians finally decided the time had come to exploit their rival's weakness.

3. The Romano-Parthian Invasion and the Second-Romano-Parthian War

In the spring of 40 BC a Parthian army crossed the Euphrates and invaded Roman Syria, sparking the Second Romano–Parthian War. As with the first war, the aggressor was intent on exploiting a civil war weakening their opponents, but on this occasion the roles were reversed, with Parthia the aggressor and Rome the weakened opponent. The Parthian army was led, not by Orodes, who seemed to have had little taste for actual command of an army, but by one of his sons, Pacorus, who had been part of the earlier Parthian invasion of Syria in 52/51 BC, and the Roman general Q. Labienus. The presence of Labienus in a leading role again blurred the lines between Roman civil war and Romano–Parthian War, much as they had been a generation earlier in the 70s BC during Rome's Great Eastern War when the forces of Mithridates VI of Pontus were 'commanded' by the Roman general M. Marius.[22]

Parthian Politics and the Origins of the War

Yet the clothing of this Parthian Army with the 'leadership' of Labienus was a convenient smokescreen, just as was Crassus' use of Mithradates IV, Orodes' deposed brother, in 53 BC (see Chapter One). As with the Roman invasion a decade earlier, this was an aggressive invasion with the intent of defeating their main regional rival and annexing territory. If Crassus and the Romans wished to emulate Alexander, then Orodes wished to emulate Cyrus the Great or Darius and recreate the Persian Empire. Both powers saw themselves as the inheritors of long-faded empires and their dreams of universal empire.[23]

Moving aside from matters of historical destiny, we need to question what motivated Orodes in this instance to launch an invasion of his rival? As stated before, we have no original surviving Parthian sources to build on and the only impressions we have of Orodes come from the pens of his rivals. Yet despite this, we get the impression that Orodes was a cautious character, driven perhaps by instinct, but certainly by circumstance. The Parthian throne was an unstable one in this period, and he had contrived to overthrow both his father and his brother to seize it. Furthermore, where his ancestors had forged an ever-expanding empire at the expense of decaying Hellenistic powers, in the West at least he had run into an empire whose expansionist tendencies and military prowess rivalled, if not exceeded, his own.

His lack of military activity in the west of the Parthian Empire and refusal to exploit the ongoing Roman Civil Wars in the 40s BC may have been guided by either his need to focus on securing his throne or to attend to matters in the east of his empire,[24] or a combination of both. The truth is, we simply do not have the surviving evidence, but we know that the Near East and Rome were never Parthia's sole focus.

Yet by 40 BC Orodes clearly saw that the time was right to exploit his rival's weakness. The presence of Labienus at court gave him an invaluable source for knowledge of the latest events in the Eastern Republic and the means to analyse and understand his rivals. The clear danger was that Labienus would hardly have been impartial in these matters and would naturally have played down the strength of the Caesarian faction. Yet the key question was the role of Pacorus, the Parthian prince. We do not know much of the Parthian court, or even Orodes' own family. Pacorus seems to have been the eldest son, certainly the leading one, yet in Parthian court politics this made him the most dangerous to Orodes. There were rumours that made their way into Romano–Greek sources that Pacorus had designs on the throne, or at least that it was believed that he had. He certainly fitted more into the mould of the traditional Parthian warrior monarchs that had forged their empire than his father. He also seems to have created a strong bond with Labienus, who apparently fed his desire for conquest in the West.

Therefore, the question we must ask ourselves is just who was the mastermind of this invasion and subsequent war: an increasingly strong Orodes, who had become secure enough in his role as Parthian king to attack his rival's empire, or a weakened Orodes, who was being dominated by the growing power of his eldest son and wished to remove him from court? Ultimately, with the sources we have, we will never know, but there certainly seems to be the hand of Orodes the master manipulator behind this. If Pacorus was successful, then it would enhance the glory of the Parthian Empire – under his rule, even if it did create a rival. If Pacorus failed, then his incompetence could be blamed and a dangerous rival humbled or even removed. Thus, for whatever reason, the Parthian court backed this invasion and the Second Romano–Parthian War began with Rome already on the back foot.

Eastern Politics and the Origins of the War
It is dangerous to think in terms of a clear dichotomy between the Roman and Parthian East in this period. Both powers were relatively new to the region, particularly Rome. Until just a century before there was no split in the region, and the territories on both banks of the Euphrates had been unified under the Seleucid Empire. The territories to the east of the Euphrates fell to the Parthians in the 140s BC, but those to the west remained Seleucid for several more generations.

For these western territories, centred on Syria, the fifty years prior to Pacorus' invasion had been tumultuous ones that had seen the province become the battleground of four empires (as detailed in Chapter One). First the Armenians had overthrown the Seleucids and they found themselves part of the newly emerged Armenian Empire. The Armenians were in turn overthrown by the Romans and, after a brief Seleucid restoration, they were part of the Rome's empire and being ruled from far overseas to the west for the first time (excluding a brief ten-year period of Macedonian rule under Alexander). Yet Roman rule seemingly brought no greater security. Firstly, the province found itself the front line of the Parthian retaliation to the failed Roman invasion, and then found it was a battleground for at least four different factions of squabbling Romans. For an eastern province used to rule from the East (first Seleucia and then Tigranocerta), we can see how attractive reintegration into an eastern empire would look, especially if it brought peace and security. Thus, in many ways the Parthians did not invade 'Roman' Syria but were merely the latest invader into a beleaguered Syria.

In 41 BC the eastern cities and provinces found themselves under the rule of the latest Roman commander, M. Antonius, a man with no background in the region – unlike Cassius – who proceeded to milk it dry. The surviving sources provide us with two examples of the heavy-handedness of the new regime and its impact:

'When Cleopatra returned home Antonius sent a cavalry force to Palmyra, situated not far from the Euphrates, to plunder it, bringing the trifling accusation against its inhabitants, that being on the frontier between the Romans and the Parthians, they had avoided taking sides between them; for, being merchants, they bring the products of India and Arabia from Persia and dispose of them in the Roman territory; but in fact, Antonius's intention was to enrich his horsemen. However, the Palmyreans were forewarned and they transported their property across the river, and, stationing themselves on the bank, prepared to shoot anybody who should attack them, for they are expert bowmen. The cavalry found nothing in the city. They turned around and came back, having met no foe, and empty-handed.'[25]

'It seems that this course on Antonius' part caused the outbreak of the Parthian war not long afterward, as many of the rulers expelled from Syria had taken refuge with the Parthians.

'At the time of Caesar's death and the internecine strife which followed, tyrants had possession of the cities one by one, and they were assisted by the Parthians, who made an irruption into Syria after the disaster to Crassus and co-operated with the tyrants. Antonius drove out the latter, who took refuge in Parthia.

'He then imposed very heavy tribute on the masses and committed the outrage already mentioned against the Palmyreans and did not wait for the disturbed country to become quiet but distributed his army in winter quarters in the provinces, and himself went to Egypt to join Cleopatra.'[26]

Unlike Appian, it is impossible to blame Antonius for the Parthian War, but it seems that his heavy-handedness did play into Parthian hands. In this respect his actions were no different to that of any other Roman commander entering an enemy territory, and he had the bigger picture to consider, namely Roman recovery from the recent civil war, and so had little time for the sensitivities of the locals. The aspect that he seemingly failed to understand was that, unlike the rest of Rome's empire, the inhabitants of this region did have an alternative to Roman rule or short-lived independence. There would have been many who would have welcomed the arrival of the Parthians and the incorporation into their empire. When news reached the East of the outbreak of yet another round of civil war – the third this decade – it seemed to galvanize Rome's opponents.

The Roman Reaction, or Lack of it

Actual details of the Parthian invasion are scant and only survive in outline. Dio preserves the best account.[27] We do not have an actual size for the invasion force only that it numbered more than twenty thousand.[28] Dio wrote:

'Now as soon as Labienus was aware of Antonius' demoralisation, of his passion, and of his departure for Egypt, he persuaded the Parthian king to make an attack upon the Romans. For he declared their armies were either destroyed utterly or impaired, while the remainder of the troops were in a state of mutiny and would again be at war; and he accordingly advised the king to subjugate Syria and the adjoining districts, while Caesar was busy in Italy with Sextus and Antonius was indulging his passion in Egypt. He promised to assume command in the war, and assured Orodes that if allowed to follow this course he would detach many of the provinces, inasmuch as they were already estranged from the Romans through the constant ill-treatment they had experienced.'[29]

Antonius was wintering in Egypt as a 'guest' at the court of the Pharaoh Cleopatra when news of the Parthian invasion broke. Unfortunately for him, this was soon followed by reports of the outbreak of civil war in Italy between his brother, Lucius, and his Triumviral colleague Octavianus. Antonius was faced with a conundrum, namely which of his two powerbases to defend, Rome or the East. Given that his role and power was based on control of Rome, he really had no option but to focus his efforts on regaining some measure of control of Rome or find himself ousted from the Triumvirate, much as his colleague Lepidus had been. Antonius would have to take the bulk of his forces westwards to confront Octavianus and invade Italy, in conjunction with Sex. Pompeius.

Whilst this was the wisest option for Antonius, it was not the best one for Rome's control of the East, showing the dangers to Rome's empire from the ongoing civil wars. When faced with the invasion of Syria by the rival Parthian Empire, the Roman reaction was to withdraw the bulk of their forces and return to Italy, leaving the provincial governors to deal with it as best they could. The province was left undefended and the locals yet again saw that the Romans would not protect them but instead concentrate upon internecine squabbles in the far west, a place which few had visited or understood. Defence of Rome's eastern empire therefore fell to one man: L. Decidius Saxa, governor of Syria.

Saxa appears to have been based in or near the city of Apamea, one of the largest in Syria, and Labienus and Pacorus drove their invasion force straight at the city. This is interesting and shows that Labienus and Pacorus, far from just raiding the province, were aiming for an immediate 'knockout' victory over the Roman garrison stationed in Syria. It was also the base of the Pompeian leader Caecilius Bassus. The city itself was commanded by Decidius Saxa's brother, a Proquaestor whose name is lost to us. Initially the city held firm, echoing the first Parthian invasion of Syria, when the Romans retreated behind city walls, which the Parthians were unable to breach as their army was not organised for siege warfare.

The initial Parthian assault was blunted, and it looked as though the pattern of the first war would be repeated, whereby the Romans held the cities and the Parthians controlled the countryside. Yet outside of Apamea, Labienus and Pacorus had far greater success, and it was here that the impact of the Roman Civil War became apparent:

'With them he [Labienus] invaded Phoenicia, and advancing against Apamea, he was repulsed from its walls but won the garrisons in the country to his side without resistance. For these garrisons consisted of troops that had served with Brutus and Cassius; Antonius had incorporated them in his own forces and at this time had assigned them to garrison Syria because they knew the country. So Labienus easily won over all these men, since they were well acquainted with him, with the exception of Saxa, their leader at the time, who was brother of the general Saxa as well as Quaestor and therefore refused to go over to the other side, being the only one who did [refuse].'[30]

It seems the rest of the cities of Syria were garrisoned and commanded by Roman forces which had formed part of Cassius' army of the East, who seemingly placed greater importance on the Roman Civil War than the defence of a Roman province. These other garrisons placed their loyalty with the defeated cause of Cassius and saw Labienus as the new leader of this faction, rather than as a front for a Parthian invasion. Loyalty to faction seemingly overrode loyalty to Republic. Cassius may have been defeated in battle – and taken the honourable way out – but the soldiers garrisoned in Syria chose to continue the fight against the Caesarian faction. Thus Syria, with the exception of Apamea and Tyre, fell to Labienus and the Brutan-Cassian faction or the Parthian Empire, depending on how one looked at it.

The two Saxa brothers continued to hold out at Apamea, with the Roman forces there still loyal to them and the Triumviral faction. Yet Labienus and Pacorus, with all the momentum and presumably the superior numbers, offered battle and the brothers accepted. We are not told why L. Decidius Saxa chose to give battle, but Dio alludes to questions over his army's loyalty and presumably he feared a similar desertion, especially with the loss of the other garrisons and Antonius' retreat westward.

The Battle of Apamea and the Fall of Syria

The result was the Battle of Apamea in early to mid-40 BC, for which we only have the scantest of details courtesy of Dio:

> 'Saxa the general he conquered in a pitched battle through the superior numbers and ability of his [Labienus'] own cavalry, and when the other later on made a dash by night from his entrenchments, he pursued them. The reason why Saxa fled was that he feared his associates would take up with the cause of Labienus, who was trying to lure them away by means of pamphlets which he kept shooting into Saxa's camp. Now when Labienus overtook the fugitives, he slew most of them, and then, when Saxa made his escape to Antioch, he captured Apamea, which no longer resisted, since the inhabitants believed that Saxa was dead; and subsequently he brought Antioch also to terms, now that Saxa had abandoned it.'[31]

Thus, the Roman forces were defeated by their Romano-Parthian adverseries. The surviving sources do not preserve any details as to number or tactics, but the Roman army of Saxa must have been comprehensibly outnumbered and can have been little more than a legion of Roman soldiers alongside native auxiliaries. The one crucial detail that is preserved by Dio is the role of the Parthian cavalry once more, as had been the case at the Battle of Carrhae. We are not told whether the Parthian cavalry were the heavily armoured cataphracts or the more manoeuvrable light cavalry armed with the deadly Parthian bow, that had done so much damage at the Battle of Carrhae. Saxa, in contrast, cannot have had much of a cavalry contingent in his army, and that, combined with being outnumbered, rendered the battle lost.

Defeat turned into rout when Saxa fled from Apamea rather than hold out against a siege, due to his justifiable worries over the loyalty of his men, many of whom must have been former Cassian supporters. Abandoned by Saxa, Apamea came to terms with the Romano-Parthians, as did Antioch after Saxa had passed through there. Saxa clearly abandoned his province – though we are not told about his brother – fleeing from Apamea to Antioch and then into Cilicia, with Labienus close on his heels.

4. The Dual Campaigns of Labienus and Pacorus

Following the Battle of Apamea, the Romano-Parthian forces seem to have split, with Labienus moving north, chasing Saxa into Cilicia, whilst Pacorus went south into Judea. This two-pronged approach would allow Labienus to ensure that there was no further Roman resistance from the north, whilst allowing Pacorus to consolidate the Parthian gains in the south, presumably with an eye to moving onto Ptolemaic Egypt, the richest prize in the East.

We are not told how the two commanders split their forces, but we must presume that Labienus had been reinforced by an unknown number of Roman legionaries from Syria. His goal must have been to press home the advantage and ensure that Saxa was not able to gain reinforcements and entrench Roman opposition. The remaining Roman provinces in the region were Cilicia – which traditionally never held a large garrison – Pontus-Bithynia – which usually did – and Asia Minor. We are not told how many other Roman forces remained in these provinces. The other source of opposition would have come from the client kingdoms of the region, which had supported Caesar earlier in the decade, notably Cappadocia, but they had already been attacked by Cassius two years earlier.

Yet it seems that no effective opposition was able to materialize, due to a combination of factors: the withdrawal of the bulk of the Roman forces, the antipathy in the region towards Rome, the lack of clarity whether this was merely another round of Roman civil war and the speed of Labienus' attack. It is notable that Pacorus and the bulk of the Parthian forces did not enter this region, which had been in Rome's orbit far longer. To all intents and purpose, it was not a Parthian invasion but yet another round of Roman civil war, which the locals were best steering clear of, for fear of ending up on the wrong side. This had been ably demonstrated by the chaos in Syria in the late 40s BC. L. Decidius Saxa was captured in Cilicia, although no details are provided,[32] and immediately executed – another on the long list of Romans murdered by Romans – and the whole region of Asia Minor fell to the control of Labienus.

We hear of no further opposition in either the Roman provinces or the client kingdoms. Labienus became a successor to Cassius and set up a pseudo-client kingdom in the Near East, the key difference being he was a client to the Parthian King Orodes, though it seems that he held the territory in the name of Rome:

> 'In the meantime Labienus had occupied Cilicia and had obtained the allegiance of the cities of the mainland except Stratonicea, since Plancus, in fear of him, had crossed over to the islands; most of the places he took without conflict, but for Mylasa and Alabanda he had to fight. For although these cities had accepted garrisons from him, they murdered them on the occasion of a festival and revolted; and because of this he punished the people of Alabanda when he had captured it and razed to the ground the town of Mylasa after it had been abandoned. As for Stratonicea, he besieged it for a long time, but was unable to capture it in any way.' [33]
>
> 'Now in consequence of these successes Labienus proceeded to levy money and to rob the temples; and he styled himself imperator and Parthicus, in the latter respect acting directly contrary to the Roman custom, in that he took his title from those whom he was leading against the Romans, as if it were the Parthians and not his fellow-citizens that he was defeating.'[34]

We have no surviving record of Labienus' long-term intentions here, or even if he had any.[35] Yet we can perhaps see the division of the Roman East that the two commanders had envisaged. Labienus would secure Asia Minor and perhaps push on into Greece, much as Mithridates VI had, ruling the region as a civil war fiefdom, albeit one backed by the Parthian Empire, whilst Syria and the rest of the Near East – Judea and presumably Egypt – would be annexed to the Parthian Empire. So whilst Labienus advanced north into Asia Minor, Pacorus moved south deeper into Syria and then into the Roman client kingdom of Judea. Again, Dio provides an excellent summary of his activities:

> 'After the death of Saxa, Pacorus made himself master of Syria and subjugated all of it except Tyre; but that city had already been occupied by the Romans who survived and by the natives who were in sympathy with them, and neither persuasion could prevail

against them nor force, since Pacorus had no fleet. They accordingly continued to be proof against capture, but Pacorus secured all the rest of Syria. He then invaded Palestine and deposed Hyrcanus, who was at the moment in charge of affairs there, having been appointed by the Romans, and in his stead set up his brother Aristobulus as a ruler because of the enmity existing between them.'[36]

We are fortunate that we have a non-Roman source whose narrative of these events survived: the works of the Jewish historian Josephus. He describes an ongoing civil war in Judea in which the Parthians intervened to install a pro-Parthian king:

'Now two years afterward, when Barzapharnes, a governor among the Parthians, and Pacorus, the king's son, had possessed themselves of Syria, and when Lysanias had already succeeded upon the death of his father Ptolemaeus, the son of Mennaeus, in the government, he prevailed with the governor, by a promise of a thousand talents, and five hundred women, to bring back Antigonus to his kingdom, and to turn Hyrcanus out of it. Pacorus was by these means induced so to do, and marched along the sea-coast, while he ordered Barzapharnes to fall upon the Jews as he went along the Mediterranean part of the country; but of the maritime people, the Tyrians would not receive Pacorus, although those of Ptolemais and Sidon had received him; so he committed a troop of his horse to a certain cup-bearer belonging to the royal family, of his own name [Pacorus], and gave him orders to march into Judaea, in order to learn the state of affairs among their enemies, and to help Antigonus when he should want his assistance.'[37]

The whole of Roman Syria fell to the Parthians, except the stronghold city of Tyre, which became the final bastion of Roman influence in the region. Aside from Tyre, Syria had been annexed to the Parthian Empire, while all Roman forces had fled with Saxa or withdrawn with Labienus. Judea remained a client kingdom, but now became a Parthian client, with a new (pro-Parthian) king on the Judean throne. Exactly how far Labienus extended his control is far from clear. It is generally accepted that Cilicia, Cappadocia, Pontus, Bithynia and Galatia all fell under his control, but it is not clear whether he successfully added the whole of the Roman province of Asia to his dominion. Appian provides the following:

> 'Antonius despatched Ventidius to Asia against the Parthians and against Labienus, the son of Labienus, who, with the Parthians, had made a hostile incursion into Syria and had advanced as far as Ionia during the late troubles.'[38]

If we are to believe Appian, Labienus had reached the Ionian shoreline of the eastern Aegean, meaning that at least a portion of the province of Asia had fallen, giving him virtually the whole of Asia Minor. Therefore, by the end of 40 BC, the Parthians had won a major victory. The Romans had been driven out of Syria, which had been annexed to their empire, Judea had been added as a client kingdom and the Parthian Empire now stretched to the borders of Ptolemaic Egypt. Furthermore, there were no hostile Roman forces east of the Aegean, with the Parthian Empire's northern flank now guarded by a pro-Parthian Roman fiefdom, ruled by Q. Labienus 'Parthicus' (see Map 7). Both commanders were well poised to continue their expansionist campaigns, with Greece and Egypt the next targets, both of which were lightly defended and ripe for conquest.

5. Antonius and the Roman Civil War in the West (40–39 BC)

As detailed earlier, despite the loss of their eastern empire, the focus of Rome's military effort lay in the civil war in the West. This war was no simple matter of Antonius fighting Octavianus, but involved at least six major Roman oligarchs in an ever-shifting pattern of alliances.[39] The year began with Octavianus at war with L. Antonius in northern Italy, but Antonius was defeated early in the year before his brother Marcus could intervene. Antonius himself was spared, but many of his supporters were butchered. This gave Octavianus control of Italy and the West. He was in alliance with the third member of the ruling Triumvirate, M. Aemilius Lepidus, a senior Caesarian leader. Lepidus had been undermined by Octavianus and Antonius after the Battles of Philippi in 42 BC, but staged something of a (short-lived) comeback. He secured command of Roman Africa as his own fiefdom, supported by a number of legions.

Clearly on the backfoot and having arrived in the West too late to aid his brother, M. Antonius made an alliance with the two other leading anti-Triumviral leaders. The first was Sex. Pompeius, who as well as leading the remaining Pompeian faction, had become a magnet for opponents of the Triumvirate and the surviving followers of L. Antonius.[40] He maintained a naval powerbase in the Mediterranean, centred around Sicily, and soon seized Sardinia and Corsica. The second figurehead was Cn. Domitius Ahenobarbus, the leader of a substantial faction of survivors of the Brutan-Cassian faction, who maintained a naval powerbase in the Adriatic.

M. Antonius' alliance with both men allowed him to surround Italy, with Pompeius to the south and west and Ahenobarbus to the east. This gave Antonius a springboard for an invasion of Italy from Greece. All-out war was averted when Octavianus and Antonius, along with Lepidus, reached a negotiated settlement – the Pact of Brundisium – and renewed the Triumvirate. Neither man wanted an all-out war, the results of which could be unpredictable, especially with Pompeius and Ahenobarbus in the mix. Antonius may have had the upper hand in Italy, but he needed a swift resolution to this matter if he were to turn and face Labienus and Pacorus, who were poised to attack his powerbases of Greece and Egypt respectively.

Antonius made several concessions, including waiving vengeance for the attack on his brother, who was packed off to Spain, and the loss of his command and forces in Transalpine Gaul. The Adriatic now became a dividing line between Octavianus and Antonius, with Antonius confirmed as de-facto ruler, in the name of the Republic, of the Eastern Republic and all the provinces and client kingdoms within its boundaries. Octavianus received control of the Western Republic, whilst Lepidus' reduced status was confirmed, leaving him in sole control of Roman Africa.

Of the other two figures, Ahenobarbus had accepted an offer by Antonius to join his forces and was offered a command in the overrun East, in Bithynia. Pompeius was originally left out of the renewal of the Triumvirate, but soon went on the offensive over the winter of 40/39 BC and used his naval power to cut off supplies to Italy and Rome, starving

Rome to the negotiating table. This was achieved in early 39 BC, the Triumvirate reached a formal agreement with the son of Caesar's old enemy and Pompeius was formally granted rule of the islands of Sicily, Sardinia and Corsica. Thus, the Roman Republic and its empire were cut into four separate fiefdoms (see Map 8). Octavianus ruled in Spain, Gaul and Italy; Pompeius in Sicily, Sardinia and Corsica; Lepidus in Africa; and Antonius in the East. This division into four fiefdoms was in reality five, as Labienus ruled Asia Minor, a fact not officially recognised in Rome. Nevertheless, Antonius was now in a position to face the twin challenges of Labienus and Pacorus in an attempt to recover his, and Rome's, possessions in the East.

Summary

The year 40 BC finally showed the Romans the dangers of their ongoing civil wars. Not only did their long-time rivals see them as weak and exploitable, but many of the client kingdoms within their sphere of influence did as well. Roman commanders from the various defeated factions continued to fight in opposition to the regime in control of Rome, first with Bassus, then Cassius and now Labienus. The Parthians chose the perfect time to invade, thanks to Roman intelligence, and Antonius' response was to evacuate what Roman forces were left to fight a war in Italy.

For at least the second time in the last fifty years, Asia Minor had been overrun and removed from the jurisdiction of Rome. Previously it had been by Mithridates and Pontus, now it was by Labienus. The Parthian Empire then achieved its greatest extent, finally reaching the Mediterranean and annexing the last of the old Seleucid Empire (Syria and Judea).

Chapter Four

From the Ashes; Ventidius and the Roman Recovery (39 BC)

1. The Position of Antonius

Whilst the Pact of Brundisium gave M. Antonius theoretical control of the whole of the Eastern Republic, its provinces and client kingdoms, his actual position at the beginning of 39 BC was far weaker. The only provinces he had actual control of were Macedonia and Greece, with Cilicia and Bithynia-Pontus having fallen to Labienus and Asia being contested by him. Syria and Judea were in the hands of Pacorus and the Parthian Empire, and Ptolemaic Egypt was under threat. Yet despite the loss of his eastern provinces, Antonius was in no position to return swiftly to the East and contest Labienus' and Pacorus' control of them. Whilst the civil war in Italy between himself and Octavianus had been settled, and Domitius Ahenobarbus and his faction had come to terms, there was still the matter of Sex. Pompeius.

Finding himself cut out of the reformed Triumvirate of Caesarian faction leaders, Pompeius had used his naval forces and control of Sicily, Sardinia and Corsica to blockade Italy and starve the Romans into submission. This policy proved to be so successful that the Triumvirs had no choice but to offer terms, resulting in the Peace of Puteoli, which resulted in Pompeius being given a quarter of the Republic to control (Sicily, Sardinia, Corsica and the Peloponnese), whilst not holding the office of Triumvir.

All this meant that Antonius could not leave Rome whilst the crisis was continuing, nor could he fully trust his partner Octavianus, the pair having fought two civil war campaigns in three years. Yet Antonius must have been painfully aware that the situation in the East was perilous, with Labienus poised to invade mainland Greece and Pacorus ready to strike at Egypt. Fortunately, the situation in Italy did not require Antonius' military forces, which he dispatched eastwards under the command of a triumvirate of promagistrates, whom he hoped would at least stem the advances of Labienus, Pacorus being too far east for Roman troops to reach from Greece.

It fell to these three men to spearhead Rome's response to the Romano-Parthian threat from the East and prosecute the war against Labienus and the Parthians. Antonius appointed each to command one of the three largest Roman provinces in the East (excluding Cilicia), despite them not being in Roman hands. Command in Asia fell to L. Munatius Plancus, command in Bithynia to Cn. Domitius Ahenobarbus, whilst command in Syria went to P. Ventidius. Antonius spent the majority of 39 BC in Rome, leaving for Greece towards the end of the year and wintering in Athens. Despite the losses of his eastern provinces, he left Italy in far stronger position than he had arrived the year before. Open warfare had been peacefully concluded and his position as a Triumvir reaffirmed, along with his official control of the Eastern Republic. Furthermore, whilst he had to reconquer his eastern provinces, he left his main opponent, Octavianus, the problem of dealing with Pompeius – no one believed the peace would hold for long – which would ensure that Octavianus would be too occupied to threaten his position, at least in the short term.

2. The Triumvirate of Antonine Commanders

The three men were an unusual mix: two staunch Antonine supporters and the leader of the largest group of the surviving Brutan-Cassian faction. Perhaps the most senior of the three was P. Ventidius (Bassus),[1] a loyal follower of M. Antonius and a commander in at least two civil war campaigns. Ventidius clearly represented the changing face of the Roman oligarchy and his rise to prominence encapsulated the history of the Republic in the First Century BC. Seaver presents an excellent article on Ventidius' background and career,[2] and Gellius provides the best short biography of his extraordinary rise to power:

'He was born in Picenum in a humble station, and with his mother was taken prisoner by Pompeius Strabo, father of Pompeius Magnus, in the Social [Civil] War, in the course of which Strabo subdued the Aesculani. Afterwards, when Pompeius Strabo triumphed, the boy also was carried in his mother's arms amid the rest of the captives before the general's chariot. Later, when he had grown up, he worked hard to gain a livelihood, resorting to the humble calling of a buyer of mules and carriages, which he had contracted with the State to furnish to the magistrates who had been allotted provinces. In that occupation he made the acquaintance of Caius Caesar and went with him to the Gallic provinces. Then, because he had shown commendable energy in that province, and later during the civil war had executed numerous commissions with promptness and vigour, he not only gained Caesar's friendship, but because of it rose even to the highest rank. Afterwards he was also made Tribune of the Plebeians, and then Praetor, and at that time he was declared a public enemy by the Senate along with M. Antonius. Afterwards, however, when the parties were united, he not only recovered his former rank, but gained first the Pontificate and then the Consulship.'3

Remarkably, Ventidius' first contact with the Roman military came in 89 BC as a baby when his home town of Asculum in Italy was besieged by the Roman army of Cn. Pompeius Strabo during the First Roman Civil War. His first visit to Rome was as part of Pompeius' Triumph, as one of the defeated. Yet he clearly rose through the ranks of the Roman military during the Gallic and the Civil Wars; a new man patronized by Caesar himself. By 45 BC Caesar had appointed him as a Plebeian Tribune, which granted him a seat in the Senate.

In 43 BC he was a serving Praetor, but sided with Antonius when he went to war with Octavianus and recruited three legions in his name in Picenum, an act which earned him condemnation as an enemy of the Republic. Following the establishment of the Triumvirate, however, not only was he pardoned, but he was elevated to a Suffect Consulship in 43 BC to see the rest of the year out, despite also being a Praetor that year. In an attempt to observe constitutional niceties, he resigned his Praetorship first, but still had the unique position of being holding a Praetorship and Consulship in the same year.

Yet Ventidius was also an accomplished military commander, perhaps the most accomplished of the three. He is likely to have served as a commander of one of the Gallic provinces in 42 BC, and the following year found himself once more serving the Antonine cause in the latest civil war in Italy, this time supporting L. Antonius (see Chapter Three). Along with another Gallic governor, he prevented the Octavian commander Q. Salvidienus Rufus Salvius from crossing the Alps and seizing Spain, and then made an attempt to relive L. Antonius, who was being besieged by Octavianus at Perusia. Having failed to lift the siege, he became commander of the Antonine forces in Italy and withdrew into southern Italy to await the return of M. Antonius. Following the Peace of Brundisium he was appointed Proconsul of Syria and seemingly de-facto overall commander of the Romano–Parthian War as Antonius' legate.

Following Ventidius was another staunch Antonine loyalist, L. Munatius Plancus, who had been one of the Consuls of 42 BC. During the latest civil war, he also had attempted to relieve Octavianus' siege of L. Antonius at Perusia and had defeated one of Octavianus' legions. Ultimately, however, he was unsuccessful and forced back.[4] When Perusia fell in early 40 BC, he fled Italy to Greece, along with M. Antonius' wife Fulvia, where they waited for Marcus' return from Egypt. After the Peace of Brundisium he was appointed Proconsul of Asia, but seems to have stayed with M. Antonius for longer than Ventidius and thus followed in his wake to his province.

The third commander was clearly the odd man out. Cn. Domitius Ahenobarbus had been an opponent of the Triumvirate and a supporter of the Brutan-Cassian faction. He had been a legate of M. Iunius Brutus and served in Macedonia, and thus fought against C. Antonius. In 42 BC he had been placed in charge of the Brutan-Cassian fleet in the Adriatic and was responsible for destroying the Triumviral relief fleet, which cut off Octavianus and M. Antonius in Greece prior to the Battles of Philippi. Following the battles, and the defeat of Brutus and Cassius, he remained in the Adriatic with his fleet and continued the war by attacking Roman coastal towns, including Brundisium, and disrupting traffic between Italy and Greece. By 41 BC M. Antonius had returned to Greece and needed to launch an invasion of Italy, which made Domitius, and his fleet, a key factor. This enabled him to come to terms with Antonius and join his faction, earning him the governorship of Bithynia and ultimately a Consulship in 32 BC.

3. The Campaigns of Ventidius – The Invasion of Asia Minor

With the most military experience of the three men and seniority in terms of former political office, Ventidius spearheaded the Roman counterattack against Labienus. We will never know what his orders from M. Antonius were, but at the very least he must have been expected to prevent Labienus from crossing into Greece and to secure a Roman foothold in Asia Minor, from which Antonius could lead his campaign against the Parthians the following year. As it turns out, Ventidius surpassed all of Antonius' expectations; indeed spectacularly so.

As is common in this period, Dio preserves the best surviving account of the campaigns. As stated earlier (Chapter Three), we are far from clear on how far Labienus penetrated into the Roman province of Asia, and there is no surviving record of any conflicts between Labienus and the local cities. Given that the region was now used to the ongoing Roman Civil War, we must assume that the cities there saw no reason to stand up to the latest Roman general to build a powerbase there and passively acquiesced to his 'rule'. Yet whilst this favoured Labienus in his conquest of the region, it would work against him in its defence and he would not be able to call on the local forces to defend his position. When Ventidius crossed the Aegean into Asia – we are not told where – Labienus had only his own Roman forces to defend the region. Again, Labienus' rapid conquest of the region had been aided by it being under the guise of the Roman Civil War rather than a Parthian invasion, and there seem to have been no Parthian forces present west of Syria.

Despite the fact that we have a number surviving sources which detail these campaigns, we have no numbers given for the size of either Ventidius' or Labienus' forces, so we are unable to judge the two sides' relative strength. Certainly Antonius must have raised a number of legions for his attack on Italy in 40 BC, but critically we don't know how many he sent with Ventidius. However, given that Antonius seems to have been planning on leading the great campaign against the Parthians himself the following year, we must assume that he kept the bulk of his forces with him, mustering in Greece, and only sent Ventidius with a few legions to secure Asia Minor as an advance guard. Nevertheless, it seems that Ventidius' forces were the larger in number, as Dio alludes to:

'This officer [Ventidius] came upon Labienus before his coming and terrified him by the suddenness of his approach and by his legions; for Labienus was without his Parthians and had with him only the soldiers from the neighbourhood. Ventidius found he would not even risk a conflict with him and so thrust him forthwith out of that country and pursued him into Syria, taking the lightest part of his army with him.'[5]

Ventidius was able to recapture the Roman province of Asia without a fight, Labienus' control of the region proving to be fragile. Labienus retreated eastwards towards the Roman province of Cilicia and closer to the Parthian forces occupying Syria. Again we do not know what Ventidius' orders from Antonius were, but rather than secure Asia and await the arrival of Antonius, he chose to press on and give chase to Labienus, splitting his forces into two. The lighter and faster forces he took with him, while the heavier troops followed some days behind. This was certainly a bold strategy, as Ventidius could not have been clear about the location of the Parthian forces. He clearly wanted to prevent Labienus from meeting up with them, but it seems that he was taking a calculated risk that he could catch Labienus before he met up with the Parthians, otherwise he would be facing a far superior army, having only a portion of his own with him.

For Labienus, this was a tactical retreat. He clearly did not feel that he could defend Asia with the forces available to him, and we must assume therefore that he sent word to his Parthian allies in Syria for reinforcements, moving eastwards to meet up with them. His strategy was to avoid a confrontation with Ventidius until he could be reinforced, draw Ventidius out of Asia, defeat him in Cilicia or Syria and then reoccupy Asia Minor before Antonius could invade with his army. Thus both sides set off on a chase through Asia Minor.

4. The Campaigns of Ventidius – The Battle of the Cilician Gates

However, it was Ventidius who seems to have had the faster army and was able to catch up with Labienus and his forces near the Taurus Mountains, preventing him from retreating further:

'He overtook him near the Taurus range and allowed him to proceed
no farther, but they encamped there for several days and made no
move, for Labienus was awaiting the Parthians and Ventidius his
heavy-armed troops.'[6]

It seems that neither side wanted to commit to battle, with both awaiting
reinforcements. For Labienus, he would naturally want to wait for his
Parthian allies, but for Ventidius, this was another gamble. If the Parthians
arrived before the other part of his army, he would have been forced to
retreat. We can only assume that he did not gamble on attacking Labienus
before this happened due to the reduced strength of his army, which
must have made the sides fairly evenly matched in terms of numbers.
The matter became a waiting game, broken by the timely arrival of both
sets of reinforcements, the rest of Ventidius' army from the west and a
large contingent – the number unknown – of Parthians from the south-
east, including mounted archers, which had done so much damage at the
Battle of Carrhae. With both sides suitably reinforced, battle commenced:

'These reinforcements, however, arrived during the same days on
both sides, and though Ventidius through fear of the barbarian
cavalry remained on the high ground, where he was encamped,
the Parthians, because of their numbers and because they had been
victorious once before, despised their opponents and rode up to the
hill at dawn, without even waiting to join forces with Labienus; and
when nobody came out to meet them, they actually charged straight
up the incline. When they were at length on the slope, the Romans
rushed down upon them and easily hurled them down-hill. Many
of the Parthians were killed in hand-to hand conflict, but still more
caused disaster to one another in the retreat, as some had already
turned to flight and others were still coming up; and the survivors
fled, not to Labienus, but into Cilicia.'[7]

'Ventidius, keeping his own men in camp on pretence of
fear, caused the Parthians and Labienus, who were elated with
victorious successes, to come out for battle. Having lured them
into an unfavourable situation, he attacked them by surprise and so
overwhelmed them that the Parthians refused to follow Labienus
and evacuated the province.'[8]

Ventidius emerged victorious and the Parthian forces were defeated, though we have no surviving details as to Parthian casualties. Key to the whole battle were two factors: the Roman occupation of the high ground, negating the Parthian cavalry, and the lack of coordination between the Parthian forces and those of Labienus. We are not told who was commanding the Parthians, but whoever it was, he was clearly at fault for the rash decision to attack uphill and without coordination with Labienus' forces. On the other hand, Ventidius' skill shone through, from his decision to occupy the high ground, negating the danger of the Parthian cavalry, to his ruse of not immediately coming to meet the Parthian advance, leading to the folly of the Parthians rushing uphill in an uncoordinated manner.

The Parthian forces made matters worse by their uncoordinated flight from the battlefield. Rather than retreat to Labienus' forces and regroup, they seem to have fled the battlefield altogether. We are not told whether the Parthian commander was still alive, but their discipline seems to have deserted them, ensuring Ventidius' victory. Surviving accounts do not record Labienus' thoughts or actions during this rout. Having waited weeks to meet up with his Parthian reinforcements, he must have watched aghast as they immediately attacked the Romans without waiting for a coordinated attack, which quickly turned into a full-blown rout. He then had to endure the sight of them fleeing the battlefield. With the Parthian element of the opposition dealt with, Ventidius was free to move against the army of Labienus:

> 'Ventidius pursued them as far as the camp but stopped when he saw Labienus there. The latter marshalled his forces as if to offer him battle but perceiving that his soldiers were dejected by reason of the flight of the barbarians, he ventured no opposition at the time, although when night came, he attempted to escape somewhere.'[9]

Strangely, there was to be no battle between the two Roman contingents. Labienus' forces were clearly dejected by the defeat of the Parthian allies, which had been the linchpin of Labienus' whole strategy. Furthermore, we must assume that again they were numerically inferior. We are left wondering why Ventidius did not press home his advantage; the second time he had refused to attack Labienus, despite this time having the vastly superior position. He clearly had experience of fighting fellow Romans during the civil wars in Italy, yet chose not to on this occasion.

The clear danger was that so long as Labienus was alive, there would be the possibility of him rallying forces to the anti-Triumviral banner once more, in a region that had been a powerbase for anti-Triumviral forces. Ventidius must have calculated that Labienus' forces would desert a losing position, which clearly they did, but he played a high-risk game by not destroying the threat of Labienus once and for all. We must assume that there were communications between the two men during the standoff, so perhaps Ventidius was hoping that Labienus would come to terms and surrender without the need for further Roman bloodshed. If this did indeed take place, then Labienus used them to his advantage as he stalled Ventidius' attack until nightfall, when he attempted to slip from the battlefield and escape:

> 'Nevertheless, Ventidius learned his plan beforehand from deserters and by setting ambushes killed many in the retreat and gained over all the rest, after they had been abandoned by Labienus.'[10]

Ventidius had wasted an advantage and had to attack Labienus' retreating army at night, and although he was successful in killing a number of them, the main prize eluded him and Labienus escaped, somewhat tainting Ventidius' victory. Although he had secured victory over the Romano-Parthian alliance and recovered the provinces of Asia and Cilicia, driving the Parthians out and defeating Labienus' Romans, Labienus himself remained alive and free, potentially to reignite the civil war element of the conflict. Fortunately for Ventidius, Labienus was not able to do so, and after hiding in Cilicia for a while seems to have been captured by an agent of Antonius on the island of Cyprus:

> 'The latter [Labienus] by changing his dress gained safety at the time and escaped detection for a while in Cilicia, but was afterwards captured by Demetrius, a freedman of the former Caesar, who had at this time been assigned to Cyprus by Antonius; for Demetrius, learning that Labienus was in hiding, made a search for him and arrested him.'[11]

No source is explicit in recording Labienus' fate upon capture, but both the *Periochae* of Livy and Plutarch record that Labienus was killed, with Plutarch assuming it was in battle.[12] Labienus' death removed the civil war element from this war between the two empires, though Ventidius had effectively done this by the destruction of Labienus' army.

His next step was the reconquest of the Roman province of Cilicia – we are not told of the fate of Bithynia-Pontus – which was where the surviving Parthian forces had retreated. There are no surviving accounts of any further clashes, but we must assume that the Parthians retreated to the mountain passes that divided Cilicia from Syria (see below). Dio refers to Ventidius reorganizing the provinces, most likely to purge it of its pro-Labienan element: 'After this Ventidius recovered Cilicia and attended to the administration of this district himself.'[13]

5. The Campaigns of Ventidius – The Battle of Mount Amanus (Cilicia)

Whilst the Parthians may have been defeated and removed from Asia Minor, the bulk of their forces, under the command of Pacorus, still occupied Syria and Judea. In order to protect Cilicia from further incursion, it would be necessary for Ventidius to secure the mountain passes which separated the two provinces. To those ends, he moved his force towards the mountains to occupy the main route between the provinces and prevent a Parthian counterstrike. Again, he seems to have separated his forces into two, sending the faster troops ahead of the main body of the army. On this occasion Ventidius stayed with the main army, whilst command of the advance guard was given to a legate, Q. Pompaedius Silo.

The key pass at Mount Amanus had already been occupied by a deputy of Pacorus, a Parthian general named Pharnapates. We do not know when Pharnapates secured this pass, either before or after the defeat at the Battle of the Cilician Gates, nor whether he had been present at the battle itself. It may have been the case that having received news of the defeat at the Taurus mountains, and the fall of Labienus, Pacorus sent him to guard the pass and prevent Ventidius from moving on Syria. It is also possible that Ventidius was made aware of the advance of Pharnapates and assumed that this was the advance guard of the main Parthian army, intent on invading Asia Minor.

Whatever the cause, Pompaedius found that Pharnapates had secured the pass and its fortifications, and seems to have launched an immediate attack on them, without waiting for the main army. Dio provides us with the most detailed account for this battle, but it seems Pompaedius was on the verge of being defeated when Ventidius and his corps showed up and swung the battle in Rome's favour:

'But (Ventidius) sent ahead Pompaedius Silo with cavalry to the Amanus. This mountain is on the border between Cilicia and Syria and has a pass so narrow that a wall and gates were once built across it and the place received its name from that fact. Silo, however, was unable to occupy it and actually came near perishing at the hands of Pharnapates, a lieutenant of Pacorus in charge of the garrison at the pass. This would certainly have been his fate, had not Ventidius by chance come upon him when he was fighting and reinforced him. For Ventidius fell upon the barbarians when they were not expecting him and were at the same time in smaller force and slew Pharnapates and many others.'[14]

Frontinus writes of this clash:

'The same Ventidius, having himself only a small force available for use against the Parthians under Pharnastanes, but observing that the confidence of the enemy was growing in consequence of their numbers, posted eighteen cohorts at the side of the camp in a hidden valley, with cavalry stationed behind the infantry. Then he sent a very small detachment against the enemy. When these by feigning flight had drawn the enemy in hot pursuit beyond the place of ambush, the force at the side rose up, whereupon Ventidius drove the Parthians in precipitate flight and slaughtered them, Pharnastanes among them.'[15]

It seems that the Parthians once more fell into a trap set by Ventidius, who drew them in with a feigned retreat and ambushed them. Frontinus makes a point of referring to all three Roman victories over the Parthians in succession – one for Cassius and two for Ventidius – with all coming from Roman feints and ambushes. He is clearly drawing his readers' attention to the Parthians falling for the same tactic on multiple occasions. It is worth speculating whether Ventidius, before he left Rome, had consulted veterans of the First Romano-Parthian War, and especially of Cassius' victory over the Parthian general Osaces. Putting aside any notion that Frontinus manipulated the accounts so that they all fitted the same pattern – an outside possibility – we are left with the notion that the Parthians did seem susceptible to falling for an ambush and rashly attacking a retreating enemy. It also seems that once their cavalry were committed then their speed proved to be an Achilles heel, as it was difficult to pull them from a rash attack and back into formation.

Despite the accounts of both Dio and Frontinus, we are not given any numbers for the size of the armies, nor their causalities. However, Ventidius won his second battle in a row with the Parthians, though we must note that both had been little more than skirmishes and Ventidius had yet to face the full Parthian army. Nevertheless, each battle had brought tangible results and Ventidius had accomplished everything that Antonius had ordered him to do. Labienus had been defeated, the Parthians driven out of Asia Minor and the route from Syria secured against further Parthian incursion.

6. The Campaigns of Ventidius – The Absence of Pacorus

With two quick victories to his name and much of the campaigning year still available, Ventidius went on the offensive, in doing so most likely exceeding the orders he had received from Antonius. He gathered his forces and crossed the mountains into Syria unopposed. It is here that our lack of surviving sources proves problematic, as we have to contend with the complete absence of Pacorus or the Parthian army for the rest of the year.

All Dio has to say is the following: 'In this way he took over Syria without a battle, now that it was deserted by the Parthians.'[16] The clear assumption here is that the Battle at Mount Amanus dealt the Parthians a serious blow and destroyed their forces in Syria. Yet this battle seems to have been no more than a glorified skirmish for a mountain pass, certainly not a major clash between armies, and nor did Pacorus take part. It does seem clear that, although Ventidius encountered some opposition in reoccupying Syria, it was certainly not from Pacorus and the main Parthian army.

We are left with two critical questions: firstly, did Pacorus withdraw from Syria, and if so, why; and secondly, was this done before Ventidius invaded or afterwards? The traditional school of thought states that the two battles – Cilician Gates and Mount Amanus – destroyed the majority of the Parthian army, forcing Pacorus to evacuate the province and regroup in Parthia. Yet none of the surviving sources for these two battles seem to depict a major confrontation for the Parthians. No troop numbers are given and the question of command, and more particularly the absence of Pacorus, is perhaps the most interesting aspect. At the Cilician Gates, we are not told who the Parthian commander was, but by their tactics they were clearly not one of the finest Parthian generals. At Mount Amanus we are told that it was a deputy of Pacorus. The question we are faced with, if we are to believe that Ventidius defeated the bulk of the Parthian army, is where was Pacorus?

It is interesting that Pacorus is not named as being present in Syria between 40 BC, when he intervened in Judea, and 38 BC, when he invaded Syria in force once more. The only time his name occurs is in connection with Pharnapates, the commander at Mount Amanus, who is named a deputy of Pacorus, but that did not mean that Pacorus sent him. There is a section of Justin which draws attention to the absence of Pacorus: 'Ventidius, who, like Cassius before him, had routed the Parthian army in the absence of Pacorus.'[17] Given this absence and the seemingly uncoordinated nature of the Parthian forces this year, it is tempting to consider whether Pacorus was present in Syria at any time in 39 BC or whether he had already returned home to the Parthian court in the winter of 40 BC?

This would also account for the seemingly stalled nature of the Parthian advance. In 40 BC the Parthians had swept aside all the defending Roman forces, except in Tyre, and annexed Syria and installed a puppet ruler in Judea. With Labienus securing control of Asia Minor, the next logical target was the Ptolemaic Kingdom of Egypt, whose own forces had never been tested against Parthian opposition and were generally considered to be insufficient to defend the richest kingdom in the Middle East. For any commander or empire wanting to secure control of the East, Egypt was surely the prize, and had fallen to the Persians, Alexander the Great and then his general Ptolemy, and was now a Roman client. With no Roman forces to defend it, other than some garrison troops, we would have expected Pacorus to follow in the footsteps of those other Persian and Hellenistic leaders and attack Egypt, before Rome could reinforce it.

Yet this attack never came, and we must question whether that was because Pacorus considered it too well defended (unlikely), was distracted by Ventidius' invasion of Asia (possible) or was not present at all (also possible). If Pacorus was not present in Syria, then we must further question why he had withdrawn to Parthia? Here we seem to have three main options, the first of which is whether he withdrew to raise a far larger army to face the inevitable Roman counterattack, headed, or so everyone believed, by M. Antonius.

This would have made strategic sense, as we do not have any numbers for the Parthian invasion force of 40 BC, and it may well be that it was sufficient to overwhelm the garrisons of the East but not to confront a great Roman army. This may have been bolstered by the fact that the Parthians must have thought that they would have more time. The Parthians were probably kept well informed of events in Rome and would have assumed that an Antonine invasion of Italy would lead to several years of civil war, giving them plenty of time to raise fresh forces and consolidate control of the East. The Pact of Brundisium brought a swifter end to the war than anyone in Rome or the East imagined, so the Parthians may well have been caught out.

The second factor is of course the great unknown, namely events in Parthia. We must never allow ourselves to see the Parthians as a one-dimensional foe, solely through the lens of simply being an opponent of the Romans. For the Romans, the Middle East was but the fringes of a large Mediterranean-based empire and, as we have seen, it had spent the last twenty years being an afterthought in Roman strategic thinking. The same also held true for the Parthians, for whom the Middle East was but the most western fringes of a large Eurasian-based empire that stretched from the Caspian in the north to the Indus in the east. The key difference between the two empires was that we are well informed as to what was distracting the Romans in the West, but not of any potential distractions for the Parthians in the rest of their empire. It may well have been the case that they too had other priorities and enemies to fight.

The third factor is Parthian court politics. As we have seen, King Orodes II was an insecure monarch, both in terms of position and temperament. We have seen that the Parthian noble Surenas had fallen from grace, and been executed, due to his victory against the Romans at Carrhae bringing him more glory than the king. The surviving sources had already reported rumours of a rift between Orodes and Pacorus, who was probably his eldest son and heir, but certainly the highest-profile of his heirs and it seems the most militarily successful. This was in comparison to Orodes, who came to the throne by overthrowing his father and then his elder brother in palace coups.

There is also the possibility that Orodes allowed Pacorus to invade Syria in a bid to get rid of a troublesome rival at court, hoping that he would be defeated and possibly killed. If this was the case, then the plan backfired spectacularly, as events in 40 BC showed. The Romans had been driven from the East, Syria had been annexed to the Parthian Empire, Judea added as a client kingdom and a new client kingdom of Roman Asia Minor had been created. In less than a year Pacorus had extended the Parthian Empire nearly to the Nile and the Aegean, and advanced far further eastwards than any Parthian monarch, or any eastern leader since the fall of the Persian Empire, three centuries before. Thus, with Pacorus poised to attack Egypt, it would not have been difficult to imagine Orodes recalling him to court in order to trim his wings on some pretext, whether it be civil or military.

In any of the three scenarios, it is not just hindsight to say that Pacorus withdrawing from Syria and not pressing an attack on Egypt was a tactical mistake. In wars of this nature, momentum was everything. In 40 BC Pacorus had gambled on the Romans being too distracted by their civil war to properly defend the East and he had been proved right, and the result had been the greatest Parthian westward advance in their history. Recent history had shown that Rome was vulnerable when they collapsed into civil war, but that they recovered and then advanced anew. Just a generation earlier, in 88 BC, Mithridates VI of Pontus had rolled over all of Asia and invaded and even annexed Greece and Macedonia, before Rome recovered and not only retook its lost territory but pushed further into the Middle East than ever before.[18]

Thus, as events did indeed show, the Romans recovered quickly once more and Pacorus would have been better off continuing the assault and denying Rome the use of Egypt as an ally. Looking at his career, Pacorus strikes us as a bold general, a throwback to the previous century of expansionist Parthian rulers, who had turned a small rebel kingdom into the one of the greatest empires in Eurasia. It seems out of character for him to ignore the prize of Egypt and withdraw to Parthia, especially given how quickly and easily the rest of the Roman East fell. For those reasons, this author is of a mind that Pacorus was recalled to Parthia rather than went of his own volition. As subsequent events showed, it was to be a major strategic error on the part of the Parthians.

7. The Campaigns of Ventidius – The Recovery of Syria and Judea

As we have stated, we do not know what Ventidius' orders were from Antonius, but surely the remit must have been no more than to gain a bridgehead in Asia Minor – recovering the lost Roman provinces and defeating Labienus – which Antonius could use as a springboard for a full war against the Parthians the following year. In this respect Ventidius' campaign had been a total success: the Parthian client kingdom of Labienus had been overthrown, with Labienus (eventually) being captured and killed, and the route into Syria had been secured against the Parthians, providing the Romans with the perfect base for an invasion of Syria.

Unfortunately for Antonius, it was Ventidius who used this position to launch an invasion of Syria and the recovery of the Roman East, not him. We don't know at what point Ventidius chose to exceed his orders – whether implicit or explicit – but we must assume that having defeated the Parthians to secure the route through the Taurus Mountains, he found out about the weak position of the Parthians in Syria (i.e., only garrisons and no Pacorus). We do not know whether it was Parthian prisoners who revealed this information or pro-Roman elements in Syria, yet at some point soon after the Battle of the Taurus Mountains, Ventidius discovered how weak the Parthian position in Syria really was.

In many ways, Ventidius had a similar military style to Pacorus: he liked to strike quickly and decisively, and knew the importance of momentum, as both of his previous battles this year had shown. Thus, despite the fact that his campaign was merely the vanguard for a full-blown campaign by Antonius the following year, he took the opportunity that presented itself and decided to attack Parthian Syria before the Parthians had a chance to send reinforcements, putting the needs of Rome – and himself – ahead of those of his patron.

The surviving sources preserve few details of Ventidius' campaigns in Syria, other than to confirm that 'Parthian' Syria fell as quickly as 'Roman' Syria had the year before, and for the same reasons; namely that the cities of the region were neither Roman nor Parthian, but acquiesced to whichever outside power marched through the region. All Dio has to say on the matter is: 'In this way he took over Syria without a battle, now that it was deserted by the Parthians, with the exception of the Aradii.'[19]

It seems that 'Parthian' Syria fell to Ventidius without a fight, and presumably the remaining Roman garrison at the city of Tyre was relieved. The only fighting that took place was between Ventidius and the Arabian tribe of the Aradii, of whom Dio provides some further explanation:

'As for the Aradii, they were afraid they would have to pay the penalty for their boldness against Antonius, and so would not come to terms with him, though they were captured by others after much difficulty.'[20]

The fighting here seems to have dragged on into the next year, but was nothing more than a distraction for the Romans. Ventidius was therefore able to recover the cities of the province of Syria without a major battle. Dio does not preserve details about any Parthian garrisons which may have remained, but we must assume that they retreated. So we are still left with the mystery of the Parthian collapse in Syria and again face questions about how many Parthian forces were actually left in the province? We hear of no Parthian withdrawal from Syria, so must assume that the two Parthian forces that Ventidius fought at the Cilician

Gates and Mount Amanus did indeed comprise the bulk of the forces that remained stationed in Syria. A further note in Plutarch makes it seem that the commander of the remaining Parthian forces in Syria was indeed Pharnapates, who is referred to as 'the most capable general of King Hyrodes [Orodes]'.[21]

Once Ventidius had defeated these, then there were insufficient forces to defend the province. Ventidius' boldness had exposed the Parthian decision to withdraw from Syria, for whatever reason. Their policy had clearly been to rely on the Romano-Parthian client kingdom of Labienus to defend their northern flank, with the bulk of their remaining forces stationed to the north to lend support to Labienus and the final garrison to defend the approach to Syria. With all three of these elements defeated, Syria fell to the Romans, undoing all of Pacorus' work in 40 BC. Having recovered Syria, Ventidius spent the remainder of the year ensuring that the native client kingdoms of the region renounced their allegiance to Parthia and returned to the Roman fold. Principally this centred on the Judean and Arabian Nabatean kingdoms, as related by Dio:

> '[Ventidius] left occupied Palestine without trouble, after he had frightened the king, Antigonus, out of the country. Besides accomplishing all this he exacted large sums of money from the rest individually, and large sums also from Antigonus and Antiochus and Malchus the Nabataean, because they had given help to Pacorus.'[22]

In the case of the Judean kingdom, this meant intervening once more in the power struggles between the rival claimants to the throne, Antigonus and Herodes (Herod). Antigonus II was the rightful king, born of the native Hasmonaean dynasty, but had declared for the Parthians. By contrast, Herodes was the pro-Roman usurper, son of Antipater, a pro-Roman official in Judea who had been elevated by Caesar for his support. Having been evicted from Judea by Antigonus and the Parthians, Herodes had fled to Rome and Antonius, and, at his instigation, had been declared the rightful King of Judea by the Senate, thus toppling, in theory, the native Hasmonaean dynasty.

However an order from the Senate and Antonius meant little in practice in Judea, especially as Ventidius had already been campaigning in Judea to ensure that Antigonus abandoned his pro-Parthian stance and came back into line as a Roman client and paid for the privilege. Josephus wrote of these events:

'In the meantime Ventidius, the Roman general, was sent out of Syria, to restrain the incursions of the Parthians; and after he had done that, he came into Judaea, in pretence indeed to assist Joseph and his party, but in reality to get money from Antigonus; and when he had pitched his camp very near to Jerusalem, as soon as he had got money enough, he went away with the greatest part of his forces; yet still did he leave Silo with some part of them, lest if he had taken them all away, his taking of bribes might have been too openly discovered. Now Antigonus hoped that the Parthians would come again to his assistance, and therefore cultivated a good understanding with Silo in the meantime, lest any interruption should be given to his hopes.

'Now by this time Herodes had sailed out of Italy, and was come to Ptolemais; and as soon as he had got together no small army of foreigners, and of his own countrymen, he marched through Galilee against Antigonus, wherein he was assisted by Ventidius and Silo, both whom Dellius, a person sent by Antonius, persuaded to bring Herodes. Now Ventidius was at this time among the cities, and composing the disturbances which had happened by means of the Parthians, as was Silo in Judaea corrupted by the bribes that Antigonus had given him; yet was not Herodes himself destitute of power, but the number of his forces increased every day as he went along, and all Galilee, with few exceptions, joined themselves to him.'[23]

The Romans under Ventidius marched on Jerusalem once more but stopped short of the city and, once an appropriate donation had been made to the Roman cause, withdrew into Syria, but left Pompaedius Silo behind with a garrison to ensure their loyalty. Judea erupted into civil war between Herodes and Antigonus, with Ventidius not willing to commit his forces fully to placing Herodes on the throne, having come to an accommodation with Antigonus.

By the end of 39 BC Roman rule had been restored to the province of Syria and the two greatest local kingdoms, Judea and Nabataea, had formally restored their ties to Rome. Yet as we can see, the loyalty of both the province of Syria and these kingdoms was paper thin and would change at a moment's notice; that moment being the perceived Parthian military superiority.

8. The Shadows of Pacorus and Antonius

With winter approaching, Ventidius dispersed the Roman army, staying in Syria with part of it but dismissing the rest to Cappadocia, which presumably had greater resources to sustain an army over winter, especially given the disruption to Syria caused by the fighting in the last five years. This allowed Ventidius time to plan for the coming year and the potential war which was to accompany it.

On the one hand Ventidius had plenty of reason to be well pleased with his year of campaigning: the civil war in the East had been ended, two Parthian forces defeated and all of the territory lost the previous year recovered. Yet he must have realized that despite all these accomplishments, the war was far from over. Although he had defeated two Parthian forces, neither seems to have been the main Parthian army, which still lay undefeated across the Euphrates, as did the Parthian prince Pacorus. Ventidius had clearly benefited from being bold and pushing on into an undefended Syria, yet he must have expected a Parthian backlash the following year. We do not know why Pacorus left Syria and returned to Parthia, nor do we know whether Ventidius knew. The assumption must have been that Pacorus would return the following year to reply to this Parthian reversal, which meant that Ventidius would have to face a full Parthian army commanded by its skilled leader.

As we have seen in the campaigns of 40 and 39 BC, conquering Syria seemed to be easy, as the cities and client kingdoms acquiesced to whichever army was the stronger. Holding onto it was another matter. We cannot go so far as describing this year as a 'phoney war', due to two battles having been fought, yet all sides must have assumed that this was but a prelude to the main war still to come. Neither the Romans nor the Parthians had committed anywhere near their full forces; if anything, this year saw a Roman advance guard, commanded by a legate, defeat a Parthian rearguard, led by a deputy. The bulk of the Roman forces lay in Greece with M. Antonius, whilst the main Parthian army was in Parthia with Pacorus.

Ventidius had to wait to see which army reached Syria first: the Roman reinforcements or a renewed Parthian invasion. There must have been great uncertainty for him which would arrive first, as he could be certain of neither. M. Antonius was showing no great hurry to cross into Asia, wintering in Athens and enjoying the hospitality of the city:

> 'It was while he [Antonius] was spending the winter at Athens that word was brought to him of the first successes of Ventidius, who had conquered the Parthians in battle and slain Labienus, as well as Pharnapates, the most capable general of King Hyrodes [Orodes]. To celebrate this victory Antonius feasted the Greeks and acted as gymnasiarch for the Athenians. He left at home the insignia of his command, and went forth carrying the wands of a gymnasiarch, in a Greek robe and white shoes, and he would take the young combatants by the neck and part them.'[24]

Even more uncertainty surrounded whether the Parthians would launch a renewed invasion. Under normal circumstances they would attack again, but no one, including Ventidius himself, can have been certain why Pacorus withdrew in the first place or if he would even be allowed to invade once more by his father, the king? In many ways this situation resembled that in 51 BC where the Romans managed to defeat a Parthian force commanded by a deputy of Pacorus and expected the full Parthian invasion the following year, an invasion which never came. So much depended upon the Parthian king, Orodes, and whether the situation within the Parthian Empire was stable enough for a renewed war in the West, especially given that the civil war element had been removed.

Would Orodes sanction his son – and rival – to launch another war against Rome? All these questions must have been going through Ventidius' mind during the winter of 39/38 BC, along with the question of what the reaction would be of his own commander. Antonius would not have expected Ventidius to reconquer the whole of the eastern provinces and drive the Parthians beyond the Euphrates. Clearly, he intended that this honour would be his, and now Ventidius had stolen his glory. Ventidius cannot have even been sure that he would be in command the following year, or whether word would come from Antonius that he had been replaced. Dio summed up Ventidius' position thus:

> 'Ventidius himself received no reward for these achievements from the Senate, since he was not acting with independent authority but as lieutenant to another; but Antonius was honoured with eulogies and thanksgivings.'[25]

Summary

The second year of the Second Romano-Parthian War was as eventful as the first. Just as Pacorus and Labienus had swept the Romans from the East the year before, they too were swept away, with the year ending with the pre-war status quo restored. Yet as we have discussed, in essence the warfare of this year was a prelude, between an advance guard and a rearguard, with neither side committing their full might. Furthermore, although Ventidius had military control of Syria and the Near East, this control was tenuous and could crumble at the first Roman defeat. We can see at this point that the Near East was neither Roman nor Parthian, but a buffer zone between the two empires, a region to be fought over, with armies advancing and retreating and the local cities and kings pledging dubious allegiance to whichever side was in the ascendancy.

As the year drew to an end, attention was focussed on Parthia and whether there would a renewed response to the temporary restoration of Roman ascendancy, or whether the inherent weakness of the Parthian court would postpone a clear military conflict for control of the Near East.

Chapter Five

The Battle of Gindarus and the Collapse of Parthia (38 BC)

1. The Race for Syria

U nder normal circumstances the Romans should have been racing to reinforce Syria, as the province had only just been freshly reoccupied, but only due to the absence of any significant Parthian forces. The Romans were faced with a province that still had not been fully subdued and were surrounded by allies of dubious loyalty. More importantly they were expecting a full-scale Parthian invasion led by Pacorus. Facing them would be Ventidius, a proven military leader, albeit one who would be outnumbered by a full Parthian army. However, as we have seen, these were not normal circumstances and once again the Romans seemed to prioritise the Civil War over the Romano–Parthian War.

Not only did Antonius not hasten to Syria with his legions, in order to strengthen the province and face Pacorus, but he remained in Greece and eventually turned in the opposite direction and made his way back to Italy. Once again Antonius had prioritised the Civil War when the inevitable breakdown between the Triumvirate – or more accurately Octavianus – and Sex.Pompeius occurred. In truth a peace treaty between the son of Caesar and the son of Pompeius was never going to hold, especially with one in charge of Italy and the other in charge of Sicily. This breach plunged the Western Republic back into three years of civil warfare fought off the very shores of Italy.

Yet rather than leave his Triumviral partner to deal with this fresh bout of civil war, Antonius left Greece and journeyed to Italy to meet Octavianus at the latter's invitation. He landed at Brundisium to find that Octavianus was not there, so promptly left and returned to Greece. The upshot was that Antonius did not hasten to Syria with the large Roman army he had assembled until the middle of the year, so Ventidius was left on his own to face an expected Parthian invasion. This shows the value of the Parthian tactical thinking, launching an attack on Rome when it was in the middle of a civil war, gambling – successfully as it seemed – that the Romans would be too preoccupied to defend their eastern territories with any vigour.

For Pacorus, though, the previous year had definitely been a setback. As we have seen, it is not recorded why he was not in Syria to defend it against Ventidius' attack, why there seemed to have been so few troops left in Syria to defend it, nor why he did not move against Egypt. In his absence, however, the Romano–Parthian client state in Asia Minor had crumbled and Labienus had been defeated and killed. He had seen a Parthian detachment destroyed at the Battle of the Cilician Gates and another under his deputy, Pharnastanes, defeated at the Battle of Mount Amanus. The Romans had then poured into Syria and started to re-secure the province, and the Parthian allies of Judea and Nabataea had deserted back to Rome. Furthermore, all this had been achieved by Antonius' deputy with an advance army, with the main army, commanded by the Triumvir Antonius, expected to arrive shortly. Pacorus' absence had seen all the gains he had made in 40 BC overturned.

However, unlike Antonius, Pacorus saw the importance of a swift counter-strike. If the main Parthian army could invade Syria again and overcome the Roman advance guard, then he could secure the province and either move into Asia to face Antonius or prevent him from crossing into Syria. If Pacorus had indeed been recalled in 39 BC, then clearly he had been able to impress upon his father the need to reinvade, and in force, or else lose Syria – and access to the Mediterranean – to the Romans for at least a generation. The king, it seems, agreed, or was overruled, and Pacorus was able to assemble the Parthian army once more and make plans to invade Syria at the earliest opportunity.

2. The Parthian Invasion & Ventidius' Double Bluff

Ventidius must have been expecting the Parthians to reinvade, unless he had intelligence stating that Pacorus had indeed fallen foul of Orodes once more, but the swiftness of the Parthian invasion seems to have caught him by surprise. Again it is Dio who preserves the most detailed account of the war:

'Publius Ventidius heard that Pacorus was gathering an army and invading Syria, and became afraid, since the cities had not yet become quiet and the legions were still scattered in their winter-quarters.'[1]

Ventidius, who had built his recent success upon his own boldness, faced being undone by the boldness of Pacorus. The bulk of his army was wintering in Cappadocia and would not be ready to repulse the Parthian invasion. Ventidius faced two choices: either evacuate Syria without striking a blow or try to buy time to summon and assemble his army. Added to this was the fact that even if he did assemble his army in time, he would still be outnumbered. We do not know the size of Ventidius' forces, but they were only ever meant to be the advance guard of a larger invasion force. Neither do we know the size of the Parthian army for certain, but we are told that it numbered more than 20,000. Ventidius once again gambled and attempted to delay Pacorus' invasion by means of a double bluff, feeding Pacorus false information via a known Parthian sympathizer to alter his route:

'Knowing that a certain prince Channaeus, with whom he, too, was acquainted, favoured the Parthian cause, he honoured him in all respects as if he had his entire confidence and took him as an adviser in some matters wherein he could not be injured himself and yet would cause Channaeus to think he possessed his most hidden secrets. Having reached this point, he affected to be afraid that the barbarians might abandon the place where they customarily crossed the Euphrates near the city of Zeugma and use some other road farther down the river; for this other place, he said, was a plain and convenient for the enemy, whereas the former was hilly and best suited to his own forces. He persuaded the prince to believe this and through him deceived Pacorus also; for the Parthian leader took the route through the flat district, which Ventidius kept on pretending to hope he would not take, and as this was longer than the other, it gave the Roman time to assemble his forces.'[2]

Frontinus adds further detail:

'When Ventidius was waging war against the Parthian king [*sic*: prince] Pacorus, knowing that a certain Pharnaeus from the province of Cyrrhestica, one of those pretending to be allies, was revealing to the Parthians all the preparations of his own army, he turned the treachery of the barbarian to his own advantage; for he pretended to be afraid that those things would happen which he was particularly desirous should happen, and pretended to desire those things to happen which he really dreaded. And so, fearful that the Parthians would cross the Euphrates before he could be reinforced by the legions which were stationed beyond the Taurus Mountains in Cappadocia, he earnestly endeavoured to make this traitor, according to his usual perfidy, advise the Parthians to lead their army across through Zeugma, where the route is shortest, and where the Euphrates flows in a deep channel; for he declared that, if the Parthians came by that road, he could avail himself of the protection of the hills for eluding their archers; but that he feared disaster if they should advance by the lower road through the open plains. Influenced by this information, the barbarians led their army by a circuitous route over the lower road and spent above forty days in preparing materials and in constructing a bridge across the river at a point where the banks were quite widely separated and where the building of the bridge, therefore, involved more work. Ventidius utilized this interval for reuniting his forces.'[3]

To the Romans, this ruse must have become quite famous, certainly for its inclusion in Frontinus, even if the two versions above have two different men named as the mole – Channaeus in Dio and Pharnaeus in Frontinus. It may well have been that Ventidius told all of his allies the same story, namely that he preferred the Parthians to come via Zeugma rather than downstream. On the one hand, this stratagem certainly reveals that Rome had few allies in the region it could really count on, and that there were many in Syria who favoured the Parthians over the Romans, showing how little actual control of the province Rome had after twenty-five years. On the other hand, we have a duty to question this story, as to take it at face value merely devalues the Parthians into unthinking stooges, a danger made all the easier by only having one side's account of the war. The question we have to ask is whether Pacorus allowed himself to be swayed by this pseudo-intelligence. From what we know of Pacorus' character and record, he does not strike us as a man who would change his invasion strategy on the word of a source. We also have to ask ourselves if he really cared what Ventidius thought or wanted. He had the larger army and the impetus, and as events showed he did not see that fighting in hilly terrain was going to put him at a disadvantage. Furthermore, it is not as if the Parthians had never fought in hills, given the wide-ranging and mountainous terrain of many parts of the Parthian Empire itself, including Media and Armenia.

As Frontinus later records, the Parthians crossed into Syria just three days after Ventidius had finished assembling his army. We have to consider that Pacorus may have wanted Ventidius to assemble his army, in order to deliver a hammer blow to the Romans in the East. Ventidius' army represented the only substantial Roman force between Greece and the Parthian Empire. If Pacorus could destroy it in battle, then he could again show that the Romans were not able to defeat the main Parthian army and thus the whole East would fall to the Parthians without any further resistance. If, however, Ventidius was not able to assemble his force in time, then he would evacuate Syria, but even though that would give the Parthians the province, Ventidius would still be in Asia Minor, meaning that the native cities and rulers would continue to 'hedge their bets' and thus reduce Parthian control of the region.

We may question whether Pacorus did indeed change his invasion route on the word of an informer, one whose loyalty could easily be questioned. It may have been a case of both generals having the same strategy, namely ensuring that there was a decisive battle between the two armies and empires for control of Syria and the East.

3. The Battle of Gindarus (38 BC)

In northern Syria, early in 38 BC, the second great battle between the Roman and Parthian armies took place. On this occasion, the Parthians were the aggressors and the Romans outnumbered. The battle was in the northern Syrian region of Cyrrhestica, near the city of Gindarus and that of Heracleium (though only Strabo provides the latter detail).[4] No surviving ancient source formally names the battle, but Gindarus is the most commonly used today. There are scattered references to the battle throughout a number of surviving sources, and enough detail survives to recreate its key elements:

'In this way he [Ventidius] met Pacorus in Syria Cyrrhestica and conquered him. For when he had not prevented them from crossing the river and had not attacked them at once after they had got across, they imputed sloth and weakness to the Romans and therefore marched against their camp, although it was on high ground, expecting to take it without resistance. But when a sally was suddenly made, the assailants, being cavalry, were driven back down the slope without difficulty; and although at the foot they defended themselves valiantly, the majority of them being in armour, yet they were confused by the unexpectedness of the onslaught and by stumbling over one another and were defeated by the heavy-armed men and especially by the slingers; for these struck them from a distance with their powerful missiles and so were exceedingly difficult for them to withstand. The fall of Pacorus in this struggle was a very great loss to them; for as soon as they perceived that their leader had perished, although a few men zealously fought for his body, yet when these also were slain, all the rest gave way. Some of them desired to escape homeward across the bridge and were unable to do so, being cut off and killed before they could reach it, and others fled for refuge to Antiochus in Commagene.'[5]

'Had not Ventidius, another lieutenant of Antonius, with marvellous good luck severely defeated the forces of Labienus and Pacorus himself and all the Parthian cavalry over the whole area between the Euphrates and the Orontes. The defeated force numbered more than 20,000. The defeat was not inflicted without a stratagem on the part of the general, who, under a pretence of panic, allowed the enemy to approach so close to the camp that he prevented them from making use of their arrows by depriving them of room to shoot. The king [*sic*: prince] died fighting with great gallantry. After his head had been carried round the cities which had revolted, Syria was recovered without further fighting.

Thus we obtained compensation for the disaster of Crassus by the slaughter of Pacorus.'[6]

'Ventidius, pretending to be afraid, kept himself a long time in his camp, and suffered the Parthians to insult him. At last, however, when they were full of security and exultation, he sent out part of his legions upon them, and the Parthians, put to flight by their onset, went off in several directions; when Pacorus, supposing that his fugitive troops had drawn off all the Roman forces in pursuit of them, attacked Ventidius' camp, as if it had been left without defenders. Upon this, Ventidius, pouring forth the rest of his troops, put the whole force of the Parthians, with their king [*sic*: prince] Pacorus, to the sword; nor did the Parthians, in any war, ever suffer a greater slaughter.'[7]

'Ventidius utilized this interval for reuniting his forces, and having assembled these, three days before the Parthians arrived, he opened battle, conquered Pacorus, and killed him.'[8]

'Ventidius, when fighting against the Parthians, would not lead out his soldiers until the Parthians were within five hundred paces. Thus by a rapid advance he came so near them that, meeting them at close quarters, he escaped their arrows, which they shot from a distance. By this scheme, since he exhibited a certain show of confidence, he quickly subdued the barbarians.'[9]

'In the meantime Pacorus, the king's son, advanced again with a large army of Parthians against Syria; but Ventidius engaged and routed him in Cyrrhestica and slew great numbers of his men. Pacorus fell among the first.'[10]

'Here is Gindarus, a city, which is the acropolis of Cyrrhestica and a natural stronghold for robbers; and near it is a place called Heracleium. It was in the neighbourhood of these places that Pacorus, the eldest of the sons of the Parthian king, was killed by Ventidius, when he made an expedition against Syria.'[11]

'Also Lucius [*sic*: Publius] Ventidius Bassus defeated the Persians [Parthians], who were making incursions into Syria, in three engagements. He killed Pacorus, the son of king Orodes, on that very day on which Orodes, the king [*sic*: prince] of the Persians [Parthians], had before put Crassus to death by the hands of his general Surena. He was the first who celebrated a most legitimate Triumph at Rome over the Parthians.'[12]

'In this engagement, he killed Pacorus, the king's son, on the same day on which Crassus had been defeated, lest the death of a Roman commander ever be left unavenged.'[13]

In terms of the sources, it is interesting that by the time the later of our surviving sources came to be written, the story of the battle had changed in two minor but revealing aspects. Firstly, Pacorus was elevated from being a Parthian prince and heir to the throne to being the king, increasing the Roman accomplishment in slaying him. Secondly, the date of the battle had changed, from early in the year to being on the anniversary of the Battle of Carrhae, thus tying the two battles together and stating that no Roman defeat goes unavenged.

Ventidius did become the first Roman general to defeat a full Parthian army[14] and chalked up his third victory in a row against the Parthians, a feat not matched by many subsequent Romans. This was done despite having numerical inferiority. There were three key elements, all of which confirm Ventidius' place in the pantheon of great Roman commanders: he had to neutralize the key elements of the Parthian army; he was facing superior numbers; and he overcame their heavy cavalry (*cataphractii*) and archers, the latter of which had proved so decisive at Carrhae.[15]

Critical to Ventidius' success was his choice of battleground. Rather than meet the Parthians in open territory and give their cavalry and numbers the advantage – as Crassus had done – he chose to hold the high ground, as he had the previous year in the Battle of the Cilician Gates. As he had shown the year before, he also chose to utilize the element of surprise and draw the Parthians onto him by feigning inaction. Here we have to be careful whether the surviving sources are confused over the three battles, as some clearly seem to be, and thus project backward elements of this battle onto the ones the year before. That aside, it does seem that Ventidius had a clear battle plan in mind whenever he fought the Parthians, namely to only fight on high ground and draw the Parthians into attacking him by feigning inaction.

That the tactic worked two years in a row does point to Ventidius understanding a clear weakness in the Parthian tactics, the desire to swiftly engage the enemy and hit them quickly with their *cataphractii*. We do not know whether any survivors of the Parthian force destroyed at the Cilician Gates made it back to Parthia to let their kin know of Ventidius' ambush tactics, but it seems unlikely. Thus Pacorus fell into the same trap that his deputy had a year earlier, launching a full-scale cavalry charge uphill and not allowing his forces to pepper the Romans with their arrows, a tactic which had proved decisive at Carrhae, or utilize superior numbers to surround the Romans, which again was done at Carrhae.

Both Dio and Florus point out that Ventidius held back his forces when the Parthian cavalry attacked, to give the impression that the Romans were either not ready to give battle or would flee – a very un-Roman tactic – thereby encouraging Pacorus and the Parthian cavalry to be more reckless than they might naturally have been. Having only attacked the Romans with their cavalry, with their infantry moving up behind them, a sudden Roman surprise attack, along with a hail of slingshots, meant that any collapse of the attack and reversal would ensure total chaos. The cavalry charge was blunted and turned back, collapsing back into retreat and running straight into the advancing infantry, totally destroying the cohesion of the Parthian army.

Interestingly, it is Justin who seems to provide the most detailed information on this tactic used by Ventidius, presumably taken from his source, Pompeius Trogus (see Appendix Two). It is worth analysing the Justin extract above in detail, as it reveals a two-stage process:

'Ventidius, pretending to be afraid, kept himself a long time in his camp, and suffered the Parthians to insult him. At last, however, when they were full of security and exultation, he sent out part of his legions upon them, and the Parthians, put to flight by their onset, went off in several directions.'[16]

'When Pacorus, supposing that his fugitive troops had drawn off all the Roman forces in pursuit of them, attacked Ventidius' camp, as if it had been left without defenders. Upon this, Ventidius, pouring forth the rest of his troops, put the whole force of the Parthians, with their king [*sic*: prince] Pacorus, to the sword; nor did the Parthians, in any war, ever suffer a greater slaughter.'[17]

Justin here highlights two clear stages to this ambush. Firstly, Ventidius does not reply to the Parthian advance on his camps, nor their verbal taunts, but then ambushes them with part of his force and scatters the Parthian advance cavalry guard. Unlike in Dio, they do not seem to head straight down the hill into the oncoming infantry, but are scattered 'in several directions'. The second phase has Pacorus, assuming that the Romans have all fled from his cavalry, then moving to attack what he believes to be an empty camp, being ambushed by Ventidius' main force and slaughtered.

This account seems to me to be an odd one. Why did Pacorus assume that the Roman army had fled from his fleeing cavalry and choose to attack an empty camp rather than pursue the Romans and perhaps surround them? This assumes that Pacorus was not in the first wave and was unsighted on the numbers of Romans who faced the cavalry. Dio's account does not state whether Pacorus was in the first wave of cavalry that was beaten back, but he was clearly in a position to try to restore order at the bottom of the hill. Justin's account also seems to take no notice of the terrain. If the Parthian cavalry were routed and fled, some must have come down the hill where the rest of the Parthian army was advancing, even if others did not, allowing him to see any pursuing Romans. Using Justin's account, we may assume that the others fled to the far side of the Roman camp, putting the camp between them, and any pursing Romans, and Pacorus.

Having ambushed and turned the Parthian cavalry, the final part of Ventidius' tactics paid dividends, the use of slingers, another very un-Roman tactic. One of the key elements of the Roman defeat at Carrhae had been the endless barrage of armour-piercing arrows, which the Parthians had used and to which the Romans had no response. This allowed the Roman army to be pinned down, unable to strike back at their assailants, who slowly killed them off at their leisure. Roman armies certainly utilised a barrage of pilum as an opening tactic, but then moved to the short sword (*gladius*) and won their victories at close range.

The defeat at Carrhae and the totally alien manner of the Parthian fighting there must have been discussed and analysed at the highest levels of the Roman oligarchy. There would have been enough survivors – C. Cassius being the most senior – to provide detail on the Parthian tactics. Here we see the military genius of Ventidius, utilizing what must have been native slingers, a common enough form of warfare in the East, and integrating them into his army. We don't know when Ventidius recruited his slingers, but it does seem unlikely that he brought them from Greece or that he used them in the two battles of 39 BC, where there is no mention of them. We must assume that he determined on the idea over the winter of 39/38 BC, when he knew that he may well face the full Parthian army and must develop a solution to the long-range attack of the Parthian archers. He may well have drawn from the earlier experience of Lucullus who used slingers in his army when he faced the Armenians in the 60s BC.

The Romans having repulsed the Parthian cavalry into the oncoming infantry, it seems that Pacorus was able to rally his forces at the foot of the hill and prepare to withstand the Roman advance. It was here that the slingers were able to do the most damage, utilizing their higher position to rain down a barrage of slingshots on the Parthians below, a detail only preserved by Dio. Despite Ventidius having seized the initiative, the Parthians still had a numerical superiority; had they regrouped or been allowed to withdraw from the hill then the Parthian invasion could still be salvaged.

However, the key final element of the battle then occurred, the death of Pacorus, which swung it decisively in Ventidius' favour. The sources seem to differ on when he was killed, with Plutarch stating that he was one of the first to fall and Dio placing it after the Parthians had rallied at the foot of the hill. Given the greater detail of Dio, we must prefer his account. There is also no clear indication how he was killed, whether by sword or slingshot. All we have is Florus' note that he 'died fighting with great gallantry'.[18]

Having focused so heavily on Ventidius' tactical genius, what can we say about his fallen opponent, the Parthian prince Pacorus? In many ways his fate does seem to have mirrored that of Crassus some fifteen years earlier. He went into the battle with the larger army and confident that his forces were superior to those of his opponents. As with Crassus, under normal circumstances Pacorus' army should have defeated a smaller Roman force; one without archers or *cataphractii*. Yet as with Crassus, he faced an opponent who was a cut above the standard commanders of his day.

In 53 BC Surenas fashioned an army designed to play to his strengths and Roman weaknesses – in cavalry and archers – fighting a mobile war rather than a toe-to-toe infantry one. As Surenas had fashioned a Parthian army for the occasion and ensured they fought on his choice of ground, so did Ventidius, with slingers and hilly territory.

Pacorus was equally guilty of the mistakes which Crassus made a decade and a half earlier, namely overconfidence and a battleplan which assumed his opponents would fight in the 'traditional' way and not have a customised force. He also found that his opponent had turned one of his greatest assets against him: his boldness. Pacorus seems to have been a daring general, who led from the front and always preferred taking the battle to his enemies. Ventidius counted on this in drawing up his plan of attack, relying on the boldness of his opponent and desire to attack the Romans fast and hard. Pacorus' decision to attack uphill removes any doubt about him being reticent about fighting the Romans on hilly ground, as the story about the informer seems to imply.

Having fallen into Ventidius' trap, it seems he attempted to regroup his forces, which would have benefitted from re-forming away from the hill and being able to bring their greater number, and distance weapons, to bear. Unfortunately for him, and the Parthian cause, it was not to be and he fell in battle, the last of a long line of aggressive and expansionist Parthian war leaders.

It seems that the death of Pacorus, the charismatic prince and leader of the Parthian army, proved to be the final straw for the Parthians at Gindarus. The army fragmented and fled, giving Ventidius and the Romans a decisive victory in the war. The fragmentation of the Parthian army, as recorded by Dio, is an interesting aspect:

> 'Some of them desired to escape homeward across the bridge and were unable to do so, being cut off and killed before they could reach it, and others fled for refuge to Antiochus in Commagene.'[19]

So part of the army fled eastwards for the bridge over the Euphrates and back into the Parthian Empire, whilst others retreated north-east towards the independent client kingdom of Commagene (see Map 4), which like the others sandwiched between Rome and Parthia had scant allegiance to either. We must assume that some of the senior Parthian officers survived and can wonder whether the move to Commagene was to allow the army to regroup and fight on, rather than retreat back into the empire proper.

The other interesting aspect is the destruction of that section of the army which fled for the Euphrates bridge. All Dio tells us is that they were 'cut off and killed before they could reach it'. Did this mean that they were caught by the pursuing Romans, or that Ventidius had hidden a reserve force to cut off access to the bridge and who thus were ahead of the retreating Parthians, who became trapped between the two Roman forces? It is also tempting to speculate that the emergence of such a force led to the other parts of the Parthian army choosing to retreat to Commagene, with the Euphrates bridge in Roman hands. If this is the case, then it again illustrates the strategic brilliance of Ventidius, who, planning for victory, wanted to ensure that the Parthian army was not only defeated but destroyed, ending the invasion in one decisive battle.

The bulk of the Parthian army of 20,000 or more was destroyed, with their leader, the Parthian prince, dead and the survivors – an unknown number – fleeing to Commagene. The body of Pacorus was located and, partly for practical reasons but also to avenge the treatment of Crassus' body, was beheaded, with the head sent around the cities of Syria in a clear demonstration of Roman power, as recorded by Dio and Florus:

> 'Ventidius easily brought into subjection all the rest out of Syria, which had been hesitating while awaiting the outcome of the war, by sending the prince's head about through the different cities; for the Syrians felt unusual affection for Pacorus on account of his justice and mildness, an affection as great as they had felt for the best kings that had ever ruled them.'[20]
>
> 'After his head had been carried round the cities which had revolted, Syria was recovered without further fighting. Thus we obtained compensation for the disaster of Crassus by the slaughter of Pacorus.'[21]

Thus Ventidius sent messengers to all of the Syrian cities and the client kingdoms declaring his victory, the destruction of Parthian army and the death of Pacorus, and – more importantly – giving a clear statement that Syria, and the Near East, was Roman.

4. The Romano-Commagene War – Ventidius

Ventidius did not rest on his laurels, setting off after the retreating remains of Pacorus' army and invading the client kingdom of Commagene. Commagene was a Hellenistic kingdom formed from a breakaway province of the Seleucid Empire, which gained its independence in the mid-second century BC (c.163 BC). However, it soon found itself surrounded by three expanding empires: the Armenians to the north, the Romans to the west and the Parthians to the east. By 63 BC the Seleucid and Armenian Empires were no more, and Commagene became a buffer state between the expanding Roman and Parthian Empires.

The ruler of Commagene at this time was Antiochus I Theos (70–38 BC), who had allied himself to Pompeius in Rome's Great Eastern War. His reward was official recognition by the Senate and People of Rome as an ally. During the first Romano-Parthian War he kept the Romans, including Cicero, quietly informed of Parthian movements, but, as with the other client kingdoms, would have tried to balance his loyalties between the two empires. During the Roman Civil War, Antiochus seems to have provided troops to Pompeius, as did much of the East, and to have kept a low profile during the Pharnacean War. However, according to Dio, at some point Antiochus had married his daughter off to the Parthian King Orodes, technically making him Orodes' father-in-law and Pacorus' grandfather-in-law. We do not know when this took place, but the marriage did produce young sons, giving him Parthian princes as grandchildren.

It is not perhaps surprising that a number of Parthian survivors chose to flee to the kingdom ruled by Pacorus' kinsman by marriage. We do not know whether they assumed they would get a friendly welcome from a pro-Parthian monarch, or simply chose it as a convenient crossing point into Parthia, now that the Euphrates bridge had been captured. Whatever their reason, it placed Antiochus in a perilous position as it gave the Romans an excuse to invade and possibly annex his kingdom, already on the suspect list for supporting both Pompeius and probably the Parthians in 39 BC. Ventidius, it seems, sent Antiochus an ultimatum to hand over the Parthians who had fled there, but whether Antiochus was in a position to do so is not known. It may have simply been the case that the Parthians had fled into Commagene and then crossed into

Parthia. Regardless, Ventidius now had his excuse and launched an attack on Commagene.

Dio adds that Commagene's wealth, it being on the east–west trading route – later to be known as the Silk Road – attracted Ventidius' interest:

'And Ventidius himself made an expedition against Antiochus, on the plea that the latter had not delivered up to him the refugees, but really because of the vast wealth which he possessed.'[22]

It may well have been that Ventidius, like most Roman elites, was able to tie together the interests of the Republic and his own and secure a payoff to restore Antiochus into Rome's good books. He must have assumed that eventually Antonius would arrive in the East to take command, and therefore wanted to finish on a personal and profitable high note. We hear of no battles taking place in Commagene, which is hardly surprising given the military disparity between the two sides. It seems that Antiochus shut himself in his capital city of Samosata, prepared for a siege and opened negotiations with the approaching Ventidius. Plutarch is the only surviving source to provide any detail for Ventidius' campaign:

'But he [Ventidius] attacked and subdued the peoples which had revolted from Rome, and besieged Antiochus of Commagene in the city of Samosata. When Antiochus proposed to pay a thousand talents and obey the behests of Antonius, Ventidius ordered him to send his proposal to Antonius, who had now advanced into the neighbourhood, and would not permit Ventidius to make peace with Antiochus.'[23]

Ventidius laid siege to Samosata, but was unable to take the city before the long-delayed arrival of Antonius.

4. The Romano-Commagene War – Antonius

M. Antonius finally arrived in Syria to find the Parthian army crushed, Pacorus slain and the Parthian War all but over, which probably made him the one Roman who was not celebrating the military exploits of

Ventidius. It is clear from the start that Antonius wanted himself to be the hero of the Parthian War and be the first general to defeat the Parthians, yet instead he found his deputy had stolen all the glory. For this Antonius only had himself to blame, having wintered in Athens and then returned to Italy, rather than rushing to Syria to defend Rome's eastern possessions from the invading Parthians.

Antonius was lucky that Ventidius was such an able general, as if the Battle of Gindarus had gone the way that many expected – with a Parthian victory – Antonius would have found himself facing a victorious Pacorus at the head of a battle-hardened Parthian army. Rome's relations with the Parthians throw up a number of highly intriguing 'what-if' scenarios, and this surely must be one of them: Pacorus vs Antonius for control of the East. Had Antonius fallen, then the Parthian Empire would have annexed Syria, whilst the Western Republic fought a civil war between the sons of Caesar and Pompeius. Egypt too may have fallen, leaving Octavianus, who would have found himself with sole control of the Republic several years earlier than actually happened, with a decision on whether to wrest control of the East from the Parthians.

Antonius found himself effectively at a loose end, with nothing more than mopping-up operations in the East. Almost inevitably he took out his frustrations on the hero of the hour, Ventidius, who ironically, like Surenas after his victory at Carrhae, found himself in trouble for overshadowing his master, the titular power, be it King or Triumvir. Dio tells us:

> 'When he had got to this point, Antonius suddenly came upon him,
> and so far from being pleased, was actually jealous of him because
> he had gained the reputation of having carried out a brave exploit
> independently. Accordingly, he not only removed him from his
> command but employed him on no other business either then or
> later, although he himself obtained the honour of thanksgivings for
> both achievements and a triumph for his assistant's work.'[24]

Ventidius found himself summarily dismissed from the eastern armies and sent home to Rome, to a hero's welcome, becoming the first man to celebrate a Triumph over the Parthians, not to mention being the first

Roman to both celebrate a Triumph as a victorious general and take part in one as a captive, as a child in Pompeius Strabo's triumph of 89 BC. Ventidius disappears from history after this point, the assumption being he died soon after returning, though whether of natural or unnatural causes will never be known.[25] Gellius records that he received a public funeral when he died, but not how or when.[26]

Antonius found he now had little to do, but took over command of the siege of Samosata:

'He insisted that this one exploit at least should bear his own name, and that not all the successes should be due to Ventidius. But the siege was protracted, and the besieged, since they despaired of coming to terms, betook themselves to a vigorous defence. Antonius could therefore accomplish nothing, and feeling ashamed and repentant, was glad to make peace with Antiochus on his payment of three hundred talents.'[27]

'This, to be sure, took place at a later period; at the time under consideration Antonius attacked Antiochus, shut him up in Samosata and proceeded to besiege him. But when he found he was accomplishing nothing and was spending his time in vain, and when he also suspected that the soldiers were alienated from him on account of the disgrace of Ventidius, he secretly opened negotiations with the foe and made a pretended compact with him so that he might have a plausible reason for withdrawing. At any rate, Antonius got neither hostages (except two and these of little importance) nor the money which he had demanded, but he granted Antiochus the death of a certain Alexander, who had earlier deserted from him to the Roman side.'[28]

Not only was Antonius not able to capture the city of Samosata, but he seems to have negotiated a worse deal with Antiochus than that which was offered to Ventidius. According to Dio, Antiochus offered Ventidius 1,000 talents to end the siege, yet Antonius only secured 300. It seems that Antonius grew bored of the whole affair and settled it as quickly as possible. Antiochus duly paid up and was once again confirmed as an ally of the Senate and People of Rome, though he did not live long to enjoy it.

For Antonius, the whole campaign had been a personal failure: the Parthians had already been defeated and he became bogged down in the siege of an insignificant city. It is safe to say that his much-anticipated eastern campaign had been a total shambles thus far, with him paying the price for his lack of focus. This soon came to the fore once again, as, rather than push on and press home Rome's advantage over a weakened Parthia, he turned around and left Syria, returning to Greece once more:

'After doing this he set out for Italy, and Caius Sosius received from him the governorship of Syria and Cilicia.'[29] 'After settling some trivial matters in Syria, he [Antonius] returned to Athens.'[30]

It seems that Antonius, having been denied the chance of military glory, soon tired of Syria and the East and returned to the comforts of Greece, leaving Roman military affairs once again in the hands of a subordinate. However, Appian adds an interesting note, that Antonius received an emissary from his Triumviral colleague Octavianus, a certain C. Maecenas. Octavianus' war against Pompeius had suffered a disastrous start when his fleet was hit by a storm and badly damaged, and he needed his colleague's assistance:

'Less than half of Octavianus' ships were saved, and these badly damaged. He left certain officers in charge of them and proceeded to Campania much cast down, for he had no other ships and he needed many; nor did he have time to build them, pressed as he was by famine and by the people, who were again harassing him about a new treaty and mocking at the war as being in violation of the old one.

'He [Octavianus] sent Maecenas to Antonius to change the mind of the latter respecting the things about which they had lately had some bickering, and to bring him to an alliance.'[31]

Antonius' focus once again shifted to the West and matters in the ongoing Roman Civil War, rather than on Rome's interests in the East, which on a personal note is understandable. Antonius' whole position rested on his, and Octavianus', control of Rome, the Senate and People.

Whilst he no doubt would have taken pleasure at Octavianus' military setbacks, Pompeius seizing Rome would undo his whole powerbase and see Antonius declared an enemy of Rome. So, with the situation in the East stabilised, he returned westward once more. C. Sosius was placed in charge of Syria and Cilicia, and given command of the civil war in Judea (see Chapter Six). Of the two other men sent with Ventidius, it seems that L. Munatius Plancus remained as governor in Asia and Cn. Domitius Ahenobarbus in Bithynia and Pontus, both seemingly having contributed little to the war effort. The war against Parthia was effectively put on hold until Antonius returned to take up command, when he found time to prioritise it over events at Rome.

6. The Collapse of Parthia

Whilst the effects on Rome of the victory over Parthia did not spread beyond Syria, there were profound effects in the Parthian Empire, and in particular at its court. As has been noted throughout this work, we are far from clear what standing Pacorus had at the Parthian court, especially in relation to his father, the king. We know that Pacorus had a number of half-brothers from his father's various wives, the latest of which seems to have been the daughter of Antiochus, King of Commagene. We also believe that Pacorus had been designated as Orodes' successor. Yet the Parthian rules of succession were far from fixed, and like many oriental monarchies was a matter for the incumbent ruler. Orodes definitely had reason to be jealous of Pacorus, his military prowess and popularity, and was therefore wary of him.

Pacorus seemed to hark back to the Parthian monarchs of old, warrior kings carving out an ever-expanding empire. Yet this line of kings had petered out with Mithradates II, after which the Parthian Empire had collapsed into a protracted civil war. The monarchs who emerged seemed to be more court-based and less militarily adventurous, and thus seemed smaller than their more illustrious forebears (see Appendix One). All of this was exemplified in the person of the current king, Orodes II, who had seized power following two palace coups, the first against his father Phraates III and the second against his brother Mithradates IV (see Chapter One). Pacorus had been the natural choice for successor, but one whom Orodes clearly worried may overthrow him. There are two surviving sources, Justin and Dio, who detail the impact of the Parthian defeat at Gindarus on the Parthian Empire, and in particular its court:

'When the news of this disaster reached Parthia, Orodes, the father of Pacorus, who had just before heard that Syria had been ravaged, and Asia occupied by his Parthians, and was boasting of his son Pacorus as the conqueror of the Romans, was affected, on hearing of the death of his son and the destruction of his army, at first with grief, and afterwards with disorder of the intellect. For several days he neither spoke to any one, nor took food, nor uttered a sound, so that he seemed to have become dumb. Sometime after, when his sorrow found vent in words, he did nothing but call upon Pacorus; Pacorus seemed to be seen and heard by him; Pacorus appeared to talk with him and stand by him; though at other times he mourned and wept for him as lost. After long indulgence in grief, another cause of concern troubled the unhappy old man, as he had to determine which of his thirty sons he should choose for his successor in the place of Pacorus. His numerous concubines, from whom so large a progeny had sprung, were perpetually working on the old man's feelings, each anxious for her own offspring. But the fate of Parthia, in which it is now, as it were, customary that the princes should be assassins of their kindred, ordained that the cruellest of them all, Phraates by name, should be fixed upon for their king.

'Phraates immediately proceeded to kill his father, as if he would not die, and put to death, also, all his thirty brothers. But his murders did not end with his father's sons; for finding that the nobility began to detest him for his constant barbarities, he caused his own son, who was grown up, to be killed, that there might be no one to be nominated king.'[32]

'The Parthian state, in fact, with no outside interference underwent a severe revolution from the following cause. Orodes, the Parthian king, had succumbed to age and to grief for Pacorus as well, but before he died had delivered the government to Phraates, the eldest of his remaining sons. Phraates after receiving the kingdom proved himself the most impious of men. He treacherously murdered his brothers, sons of the daughter of Antiochus, because they were his superiors in virtue, and, on their mother's side, in family; and when Antiochus chafed under this outrage, he killed him also, and after that destroyed the noblest men in the state generally and kept committing many other crimes. Consequently, a large number of the most prominent persons abandoned him and betook themselves to various places, some, including Monaeses, going to Antonius.'[33]

Though Orodes may have distrusted his son, it seems that his defeat and death brought about a complete mental collapse in the king. Not only was the Parthian monarch, the absolute ruler of the empire, debilitated, but his nominated successor had been killed, plunging the empire into another succession crisis. It seems that full-scale civil war was only averted by Orodes naming Phraates, his eldest remaining son, as his successor. It is more than a little ironic that Orodes had spent his whole reign worried that his son Pacorus would overthrow him, only to be immediately overthrown by the son he nominated in Pacorus' place. Orodes himself seems to have been the final casualty of the Battle of Gindarus, murdered by his successor, paying the price for his son's failure on the battlefield.

Phraates became Phraates IV of Parthia, the third king in a row to seize the throne by overthrowing his predecessor. Rather than having a monarch cut from the old warrior king mould, the Parthian Empire got a new style 'oriental despot' who seems to have lived up to the stereotype by murdering all thirty of his brothers, as well as his own son and heir, and then engaging in a wholesale purge of the aristocracy, including the King of Commagene, Antiochus. We can see that Ventidius did far more lasting damage to the Parthian Empire at Gindarus than simply defeating one of its armies. Just as the Parthians changed the course of Roman history by killing Crassus in 53 BC, now the Romans returned the favour. The Parthian Empire fragmented once more, with a number of nobles fleeing Parthia and Phraates' rule, again presenting the Romans with not only a weakened enemy, but just as in 55–54 BC an excuse to intervene in Parthia itself. The only question was whether Antonius would have the focus to exploit this opportunity or be dragged into the ongoing Roman Civil War in the Western Republic.

Summary – Stalemate in the East

The year 38 BC saw the second of the great battles between the Romans and Parthians, which ended as decisively as the first, this time with the destruction of the Parthian army and the death – and decapitation – of its leader Pacorus. Just as Carrhae ended the Roman invasion of the Parthian Empire, so Gindarus ended the Parthian invasion of Rome's empire.

Not only did this bring to an end the first phase of the war, with Parthia as the aggressor, but it plunged the Parthian Empire into a near state of collapse, reversing each sides' fortunes and putting Parthia on the back foot as the weaker of the two empires. However, it is important to remember that although Ventidius had destroyed a Parthian army and chalked up three victories in a row, none of them had come from standard open warfare. All three had come in mountainous terrain, which neutralized the Parthian cavalry, and had seemingly involved a ruse that encouraged the Parthians to attack with a headlong cavalry charge. None of these victories had come in a battle on level ground, as seen at Carrhae, and in open battle with the two armies standing toe-to-toe. We must realise that these victories did not mean that the Romans could defeat the Parthians at will, nor that other commanders would marshal their resources as efficiently as had Ventidius.

Part III

The Rise and Fall of Rome (38–36 BC)

Chapter Six

Roman Consolidation in the East;
Judea and Armenia (38–37 BC)

1. The Absence of Antonius

As we have seen, Antonius' contribution to the war had so far amounted to a leisurely progression from Greece to Syria at the head of an army, the replacement of the talented and victorious Roman commander in the region and then a half-hearted siege in Commagene which ended with a financial settlement. Having accomplished little of note, Antonius appointed new commanders for Syria and Cilicia (C. Sosius) and Armenia (P. Canidius Crassus), and promptly headed for Italy, concerned about the conflict between Octavianus and Sex. Pompeius, and more importantly about his own Triumviral powerbase.

The Triumviral pact made in 43 BC between the three leading Caesarian faction leaders had benefitted Antonius handsomely and given him more formal power than any Roman leader outside of the first-century dictators, Sulla and Caesar. Under the various consecutive Triumviral agreements, Antonius had been granted formal command of the whole of the Eastern Republic, the richest area of the ancient world. Yet the whole basis of this power rested on a grant of Triumviral power by the Senate and People of Rome. Whoever physically controlled Rome itself controlled the Senate and People, and thus for all Antonius' power, it was on a shaky foundation. Should the Triumvirate's enemies take Rome, then his power would be rescinded and he would be declared an enemy of the People, as he had been in 43 BC.

It was not just his enemies he needed to be wary of, but also his allies. In the previous five years he had twice been to war with his erstwhile ally Caesar Octavianus, and even if the Triumvirate held Rome, there was still the possibility that his position could be pulled from beneath him, much as it had for his other Triumviral colleague, M. Aemilius Lepidus. We can see what lay behind Antonius' frequent loss of concentration in the East: until he could be sure that his position was secure, he could not commit to a lengthy eastern campaign.

In 37 BC Octavianus and Antonius met once more and renewed their alliance for another five years; the last such time this was done. This renewal, sometimes known as the Treaty of Tarentum, reaffirmed the division of the Roman Republic between the two men and their now junior colleague, Lepidus, on much the same terms as before. Octavianus held onto the Western Republic, excluding Africa, whilst Antonius was re-reconfirmed as Triumvir for the Eastern Republic, with Lepidus still holding Africa. Antonius had once more absented himself from the war in the East to shore up his shaky relationship with Octavianus.

In Antonius' absence, his commanders were left with instructions to bring the region firmly back into Roman control and prepare for a possible renewed attack on the Parthian Empire itself. The men in question were the new Proconsul of Syria and Cilicia, C. Sosius, and P. Canidius Crassus (Cos. 40 BC), a legate of Antonius. It is interesting to speculate that neither man boasted the pedigree of Ventidius. We can perhaps see two elements at play here: firstly, the reduced risk factor in the East, now that the Parthian army had been defeated; and secondly, Antonius' experience with Ventidius, a more than capable commander who pursued his own campaign and effectively trumped Antonius to the glory of defeating the Parthians. Seemingly Antonius did not wish for a repeat, so chose men who could be relied on not to pursue their own agenda.

2. Pacifying Syria (38 BC)

With the Parthians defeated and having fled from the province, there remained the matter of its final pacification. Whilst the majority of the region had quickly transferred its loyalty back to Rome, one region held out: the island city of Aradus (Arwad). We only have scant details and nothing to explain why the Aradii had taken such an anti-Roman line, but the Roman attack on the island city had been started in 39 BC by Ventidius, yet it seems the Aradii had been able to hold out over the winter into

38 BC. We do not know whether the Roman campaign had been broken off by Ventidius in early 38 BC when he recalled much of his army to face Pacorus' invasion. Any respite they may have received was short-lived as the new Proconsul of the Syria – and Ventidius' replacement – C. Sosius picked up the campaign and took it to a successful conclusion:

> 'Caius Sosius received from him the governorship of Syria and Cilicia. This officer subdued the Aradii, who had been besieged up to this time and had been reduced to hard straits by famine and disease.'[1]

The last major openly anti-Roman elements of Syria were thus defeated, and the province fully secured, at least in the short term, for Rome. Having secured Syria, the next obvious challenge lay further south with the Kingdom of Judea, currently being ruled by a king placed on the throne by Parthia.

3. The Romano-Judean War (39–37 BC)

At first glance, this war was one waged by Rome against a Parthian client kingdom, much as had happened in Commagene earlier in the year. However, the reality of the situation was far from clear cut and mirrored the wider situation in the Middle East at the time, when internal civil war and the external Romano-Parthian War became intertwined. In many ways this war was a microcosm for the conflict wracking the whole region.

i) Judea and Rome – A Study in Roman Intervention
The Kingdom of Judea had suffered a turbulent history, and the recent period was no exception. The fate of Judea found itself increasingly tied to that of Rome, for both good and ill. At the start of the second century BC, Judea was a province of the Seleucid Empire and on the front line of the wars between the Seleucid and Ptolemaic Empires. These wars reached their zenith in 168 BC when the Seleucid King Antiochus IV invaded a weakened Ptolemaic Empire, but was promptly ejected by the Romans, whose intervention was neatly encapsulated by the Roman

Commissioner C. Popillius Leanas infamously drawing a line around the Seleucid King with a stick in the sand and demanding an answer to the Senate's ultimatum before he left the circle. Thus, the Romans faced down the Seleucid king and his army armed with nothing more than a stick – and the threat of overwhelming Roman military force, which had that very year defeated and then dismembered Macedon.

Having been faced down in Egypt, Antiochus retreated northwards, taking his umbrage out on Judea, sacking Jerusalem and attempting to outlaw the key tenets of Judaism. This naturally led to a Jewish (Maccabean) revolt and a renewed push for independence.[2] By the 140s BC Judea had taken advantage of the Parthian-induced militarily weakened Seleucid Empire, which had collapsed into another round of civil war. By 141 BC Judea had gained autonomy within the Seleucid Empire under the rule of a new native Hasmonean dynasty of kings. In c.141–139 BC this autonomy received a major boost when a Hasmonean embassy was received at Rome and granted the status of friends of the Roman People (*amicitia*).[3] The Judean Kingdom became one of Rome's first de-facto client states in the region, a useful buffer against the Seleucids.[4]

As the Seleucid Empire weakened, Hasmonean Judea grew in strength, until the Romans themselves turned their attention to the region in earnest. Having been drawn into the region in wars against the rising Pontic and Armenian Empires (see Chapter One), the Romans under Pompeius determined to establish a permanent presence and annexed Syria, the last remnant of the Seleucid Empire. This brought the Roman Empire right to Judea's borders, and an ongoing Hasmonean Civil War – between Aristobulus II and Hyrcanus II – gave the Romans the excuse to intervene and annex Judea, taking their empire to the borders of Egypt. This short Romano-Judean War culminated in 63 BC, when Jerusalem itself was laid siege to and captured by Pompeius, who promptly desecrated the Jewish Holy of Holies, the most sacred inner sanctuary of the Temple on the Mount, to add insult to significant injury. Judea had come full circle and exchanged one master for another.

Of the two warring Hasmonean brothers, Aristobulus, the stronger, was taken as a prisoner to Rome, whilst Hyrcanus II was restored to power, albeit as High Priest and Ethnarch. Rome had ensured that there would be a weak ruler on the throne, someone who was less likely to challenge their rule. Hyrcanus came more and more to rely upon one of his officials, Antipater, who became second only to him in status within the kingdom. Given that their fortunes were tied up with those of Rome, when the Third Civil War broke out in 49 BC the effects were felt in Judea. As Pompeius had been their 'patron', Hyrcanus – and Antipater – had no choice but to support him. Caesar therefore turned to the other rival ruler, Aristobulus, perhaps intending to install him as puppet ruler of Judea. However, this plan was cut short when Aristobulus was poisoned by pro-Pompeian sympathizers whilst en-route to Judea and his eldest son, Alexander, was executed by Metellus Scipio in Antioch.

The murder of Pompeius changed everything and placed Hyrcanus and Antipater in a precarious situation, which was resolved by Antipater leading a force of Judean soldiers to relieve Caesar when he was besieged at Alexandria in 47 BC. As a reward, Hyrcanus was confirmed as Ethnarch of Judea, while Antipater received Roman citizenship and was appointed the official Roman Procurator of Judea, making him a clear rival to Hyrcanus' throne. The potential for chaos in Judea was increased by the presence in the region of the younger son of the murdered Aristobulus, named Antigonus, who petitioned Caesar to restore his branch of the family to the throne. However, Caesar refused the proposition.

When the civil war between the Caesarian and Brutan-Cassian factions broke out in 44/43 BC, Hyrcanus and Antipater again found themselves having to make a difficult and potentially life-threatening choice. As detailed earlier (Chapter Two), the Eastern Republic fell to C. Cassius in 42 BC and Judea had little option but to comply with his demands. Antipater, however, was soon murdered by another rival (Malichus); a rivalry in part stoked by Cassius' demands for monies from the various regions to support his civil war campaign. His place was taken by his eldest son, Herodes, better known as Herod the Great.

If being torn apart by the various internecine struggles of the Romans was not enough, then came the intervention of the Parthians. Having been refused by the Romans, Antigonus, son of the deposed Aristobulus II, turned to the Parthians, who were all too willing to have their puppet ruler on the Judean throne. Thus, as detailed earlier (Chapter Three), Pacorus used his invading forces to place Antigonus on the Judean throne, as Antigonus II, and depose the ruling Hyrcanus, who was mutilated, his ears being severed, and transported into captivity in Babylon amongst the exiled Jewish community. Judea now became a Parthian client kingdom, the third empire that the Hasmonaean dynasty had served under. Internal, pro-Roman opposition naturally centred on the figure of Herodes, who fled Judea to Rome and appealed to the Senate. Seemingly at Antonius' instigation, the Senate and People of Rome ordered the deposition of the Hasmonaean dynasty and the elevation to the Judean throne of Herodes, whose family had proven their loyalty to the Caesarian cause.

ii) The Romano-Judean War (39–37 BC)

Herodes may have been declared King of Judea by the Romans, but installing him in Jerusalem was another matter. Campaigning against Antigonus had to come second to the Parthian War itself. Ventidius, the first Roman commander tasked with installing Herodes on the throne, campaigned in Judea and Palestine in late 39 BC, having recovered Syria. Yet, as we have seen (Chapter Four), Ventidius chose not to fully engage in the civil war in Judea, preferring to leave Antigonus on the throne in return for a payment to himself. In all fairness, Ventidius did have the wider Parthian War to think of and could not afford to become bogged down in a war of attrition in Judea. Antigonus, wisely for him, showed no signs of offering the Romans a set-piece battle and the campaign dragged out into a series of sieges, including that of Jerusalem. Ventidius took Antigonus' money and dubious offerings of loyalty to Rome, then moved back north to prepare for the winter and the anticipated Parthian offensive the following year.

Given the Senate's instruction, which would have been reaffirmed by Antonius, and the need to keep a Roman presence in the region to remind Antigonus of his loyalty, Ventidius left behind a Roman force – again we are not told how large – under the command of Q. Pompaedius Silo. Silo is accused by Josephus of taking bribes from Antigonus,[5] but nominally assisted Herodes, who returned from Italy in 39 BC and was able to raise Antigonus' own siege of the fortress of Masada, held by his brother Joseph, and march on Jerusalem.

As Josephus relates, the Roman contribution to the siege was half-hearted at best, and the Roman contingent soon found itself winter quarters and the occasional opportunity for plunder:

'And here it was that Silo discovered he had taken bribes; for he set many of the soldiers to clamour about their want of necessaries, and to require their pay, in order to buy themselves food, and to demand that he would lead them into places convenient for their winter quarters.'[6]

'After the making of which entreaty, he went hastily into the country, and brought thither so great an abundance of necessaries, that he cut off all Silo's pretences.'[7]

'Yet was Herodes not idle, but took with him ten cohorts, five of them were Romans, and five were Jewish cohorts, together with some mercenary troops intermixed among them, and besides those a few horsemen, and came to Jericho; while the Romans fell upon the rest of the city, and plundered it, having found the houses full of all sorts of good things. So, the king left a garrison at Jericho, and came back, and sent the Roman army into those cities which were come over to him, to take their winter quarters there.'[8]

Thus, 39 BC ended with Antigonus still on the throne of Judea and in control of Jerusalem itself whilst Herodes attempted to subdue the rest of Judea, with the Roman contingent seemingly unwilling to assist him to any great extent in pressing his claim. With the renewal of the war against the Parthians, both Silo and Herodes were recalled by Ventidius to face the invasion of Pacorus:

'In the meantime, Antonius remained at Athens, while Ventidius called for Silo and Herodes to come to the war against the Parthians but ordered them first to settle the affairs of Judaea; so Herodes willingly dismissed Silo to go to Ventidius, but he made an expedition himself against those that lay in the caves.'[9]

So Silo returned to the main Roman army, but Herodes it seems stayed in Judea to campaign against those who would not recognize his elevation to the throne. As we have seen, Ventidius did not miss Herodes' assistance and went on to crush the Parthian army at Gindarus, a victory which ultimately ensured that the Judean Civil War would be won by Herodes, with Antigonus' patron dead and all hopes of Parthian assistance ended. Nevertheless, as the last monarch of the ruling Hasmonean dynasty, he chose to fight on. With the Parthian threat removed, and seemingly annoyed at Ventidius' half-hearted efforts on Herodes' behalf, Antonius, then making his way from Greece, issued Ventidius with a clear instruction: 'Ventidius, by Antonius's command, sent a thousand horsemen, and two legions, as auxiliaries to Herodes, against Antigonus.'[10]

Ventidius himself chose to pursue the retreating Parthian survivors of Gindarus, and invaded the Kingdom of Commagene in the north, leaving command of the legions in Judea to an individual known only as Machaeras.[11] We must question how many men Machaeras actually took with him, as the detailed narrative of the campaign provided by Josephus seems to indicate that he had nowhere near that size of force. It wasn't until Sosius took command that two legions were actually sent into Palestine and Judea. Given how condensed Dio's account of the campaign is, and the fact we seem to have a duplicate account of two legions being sent at different times, it does seem that the Roman force sent by Ventidius was not as large as Dio assumes. It is always possible that Antonius ordered two legions to be sent south, but that Ventidius, tied up with the siege of Samosata in Commagene, and knowing that his time in Syria was coming to an end, did not comply.

Regardless of the size of force he commanded, Machaeras seemed to have been no more enthusiastic in his pursuit of this war than Silo had been before him. Antigonus fell back on his tried and tested method of financial inducement, an offer which was countered by Herodes himself, meaning that Machaeras was being paid by both protagonists in the Judean Civil War. Machaeras withdrew from Jerusalem without attacking it, making clear his displeasure at the whole venture:

> '[Machaeras] retired to Emmaus to Herodes; and as he was in a rage at his disappointment, he slew all the Jews whom he met with, without sparing those that were for Herodes, but using them all as if they were for Antigonus.'[12]

The Roman-Herodian alliance was in such a poor state that Herodes had to break off his campaigns in Judea and head north to find Antonius himself, who had taken over the siege of Samosata in Commagene, and plead his case in person. This break proved to be costly, at least in the short term, as command of his forces fell to his brother Joseph, who also had command of the five Roman cohorts. Unfortunately, Joseph fell into a trap marching towards Jericho and was killed, along with his forces, including the Roman cohorts:

> 'But when his [Joseph's] enemies attacked him in the mountains, and in places which were difficult to pass, he was both killed himself, as he was very bravely fighting in the battle, and the entire Roman cohorts were destroyed; for these cohorts were new-raised men, gathered out of Syria, and there was no mixture of those called veteran soldiers among them, who might have supported those that were unskilful in war.'[13]

Though in the short term this was a victory for Antigonus, in the longer term it sealed his fate: Roman soldiers, no matter how inexperienced, had been killed by a foreign king. Antonius, it seems, left the new Proconsul of Syria, Ventidius' replacement C. Sosius, in no doubt as to his wishes. With the Commagene War concluded, Sosius marched south with the whole Roman army, sending two legions in advance:

> 'But Sosius sent two legions before him into Judaea to assist Herodes and followed himself soon after with the rest of his army.'[14]
>
> 'Sosius also joined him with a large army, both of horsemen and infantry, which he sent before him through the midland parts, while he marched himself along Phoenicia; and when the whole army was got together, which were eleven regiments of footmen, and six thousand horsemen, besides the Syrian auxiliaries, which were no small part of the army, they pitched their camp near to the north wall. Herodes' dependence was upon the decree of the Senate, by which he was made king; and Sosius relied upon Antonius, who sent the army that was under him to Herodes' assistance.'[15]

For the second time in twenty-five years a Roman army laid siege to Jerusalem. When the city fell is a matter for debate. Josephus' detailed narrative indicates that the siege did not start until the following year, with the march of Herodes and Sosius southwards and a subsequent battle between Herodes and Antigonus' general, Pappus, taking them up to the winter of 38/37 BC. Thus the siege of Jerusalem, which was to last five months, took place in early to mid-37 BC. The only argument against this is Dio's account, which condenses the whole campaign into a few lines, after which he states:

> 'This was the course of events in the Consulship of Claudius and Norbanus [38 BC]; during the following year the Romans accomplished nothing worthy of note in Syria.'[16]

Given the far greater detail of the accounts of Josephus, we must prefer his timeline and place the siege and fall of Jerusalem, and the overthrow of the Hasmonaean dynasty, in 37 BC. Jerusalem was able to hold out for five months until the city was stormed and sacked by the Roman forces:

> 'Indeed, though they had so great an army lying round about them, they bore a siege of five months, till some of Herodes' chosen men ventured to get upon the wall, and fell into the city, as did Sosius' centurions after them; and now they first of all seized upon what was about the temple; and upon the pouring in of the army, there was slaughter of vast multitudes everywhere, by reason of the rage the Romans were in at the length of this siege, and by reason that the Jews who were about Herodes earnestly endeavoured that none of their adversaries might remain; so they were cut to pieces by great multitudes, as they were crowded together in narrow streets, and in houses, or were running away to the temple; nor was there any mercy showed either to infants, or to the aged, or to the weaker sex; insomuch that although the king sent about and desired them to spare the people, nobody could be persuaded to withhold their right hand from slaughter, but they slew people of all ages, like madmen.'[17]

The sacking only ended when Herodes promised to pay Sosius' men a bounty equivalent to the plunder they would receive. Sosius and the

Romans then withdrew, taking with them Antigonus, the last of the Hasmonean monarchs of Judea,[18] a dynasty Rome helped to gain their independence before taking it away a century later. Antigonus himself was taken before Antonius and executed, an act which the sources remark on as being a first; a native monarch being flogged and beheaded by the Romans:

'But Antigonus he [Antonius] bound to a cross and flogged, a punishment no other king had suffered at the hands of the Romans, and afterwards slew him.'[19]

'Antigonus the Jew, whom he [Antonius] brought forth and beheaded, though no other king before him had been so punished.'[20]

Thus, finally, after an eighteen-month campaign, the pro-Parthian ruler of Judea was overthrown and a pro-Roman one installed. This campaign marked the end of yet another native dynasty caught up in Rome's civil wars, to join those of Numidia and ultimately Egypt. Judea, however, maintained its nominal independence and received a new dynasty – the Herodian – which would have significant religious and political consequences. In strategic terms, the Romans had replaced a Parthian client king with one of their own who could be trusted to ensure Roman influence in the south of the Middle East, act as a buffer against the Nabatean Arabs to the south-east and provide support to the Roman province of Syria to the north.

Yet throughout this campaign we see all too clearly the reticence of the Roman commanders to engage in anything more than a half-hearted manner. Ventidius, Silo and Machaeras all preferred not to involve themselves in the Judean Civil War and leave the fighting to Herodes, despite the Senatorial and Antonine decrees ordering his installation as king. They also found it easier to take Antigonus' money and his protestations of loyalty to Rome. In some way they may have been right. As we have seen, throughout the region all the native rulers paid lip service to Roman rule, but quickly changed sides when the Parthians were in the ascendancy. With the Parthians crushed at Gindarus, Antigonus had little choice but to follow Roman rule. Yet Herodes had convinced Antonius that a change of dynasty would be better for Rome, and Antonius, who didn't have to do any of the fighting himself, agreed. Judea, or what was left of it, was once more in the Roman fold.

In the Judean campaign we can detect the Romans' changing view of their empire in the East. Pompeius was happy to defeat Judea and leave the native Hasmonean dynasty in nominal control. Yet the Hasmonean dynasty had risen to the fore fighting for independence from an imperial overlord, and such rule would always chafe at them. Even without the dynastic civil war between the rival Hasmonean candidates, the ruler's loyalty would always be suspect. Thus the Senate and Antonius put in place a new dynasty, which would owe their elevation and survival to Rome, and we can see Rome beginning to shape its newly acquired eastern empire.

4. The Armenian and Caucasus Campaigns (37 BC)

Whilst Sosius was securing the south of the region, the other major campaign of this period was taking place to the north, in the Armenian and Caucasus region. The Armenian Empire had been defeated and dismantled by Lucullus and Pompeius some thirty years earlier in Rome's Great Eastern War (74–63 BC), the Kingdom of Armenia becoming a Roman client.[21] Pompeius had further campaigned against the tribes of the Caucasus regions, but no permanent settlement had been made, meaning that these tribes had been left alone by Rome for the intervening twenty-five-year period.

Antonius, clearly thinking ahead for any forthcoming invasion of Parthia, had seemingly determined that rather than follow the route Crassus had taken – crossing the Euphrates and marching down through Mesopotamia – he would take a northern course and invade via Armenia (see Chapter Seven). To that end he appointed a legate, P. Canidius Crassus, with a remit to subdue the tribes of the region and ensure a smooth passage of any invading Roman army. We only have three references to Crassus' campaign, pursued throughout 37 BC, and no additional details as to the size of the Roman force nor how many battles were fought. What is clear is that Crassus fought a series of successful campaigns and widened Roman control of the region:

'Publius Canidius Crassus made a campaign against the Iberians in Asia, conquered in battle their King Pharnabazus and brought them to make an alliance; with this king he invaded Albania, the adjoining country, and, after overcoming the inhabitants and their King Zober, conciliated them likewise.'[22]

'Canidius, who was left by Antonius in Armenia, conquered that people, as well as the kings of the Iberians and Albanians, and advanced as far as the Caucasus. Consequently the name and fame of Antonius' power waxed great among the barbarians.'[23]

'The passes from Armenia into Iberia are the defiles on the Cyrus and those on the Aragus ... These passes were used first by Pompeius when he set out from the country of the Armenians, and afterwards by Canidius.'[24]

The sources give us three separate campaigns. Firstly, there came the resubmission of Armenia, mentioned only in Plutarch. This is interesting as we have no surviving evidence for Armenia's involvement in the Parthian War to date. We must assume that the king, Artavasdes II, offered his support to Pacorus when he invaded in 40 BC, if only to avoid outright annexation to the Parthian Empire. However, given a Roman punitive expedition led by Crassus, we can assume that – at least in Roman eyes – the Armenians offered Pacorus more than token support. The Armenians were reminded that their loyalty was to Rome and not Parthia. It is always possible that elements of the retreating Parthian forces from Gindarus passed into Armenia. Nevertheless, Crassus seemingly brought Armenia back into the fold as a Roman client state.

Having re-subdued Armenia, Crassus then moved against the two strongest tribes in the region, the Iberians (modern Georgia) and Albanians (modern Azerbaijan), both located in the Caucasus region, and not to be confused with their present usage and position (see Map 4). Again we have scant details for these campaigns but they both ended in Roman victories, with the two tribes becoming 'allies' of Rome. Crassus' campaigns extended Rome's influence and control of the East, right up to the Caspian Sea, ensuring that they did not fall into Parthia's orbit once more and securing a safe passageway for any invasion of the Parthian Empire via a northern route. By the end of 37 BC, despite what Dio states,

Rome was in a far stronger position in the East and these two Antonine commanders, Sosius and Crassus, had restored and widened Rome's control of the region, building on the work done by Ventidius. Antonius, when he returned, would have an excellent platform from which to launch the next stage of the Second Romano-Parthian War: the Roman invasion and potential annexation of the Parthian Empire.

5. Parthian Divisions and Defections

Whilst Rome was consolidating and strengthening its position in the East during these years, Parthia's strength, by contrast, was being weakened by the continued internal divisions caused by the loss of Pacorus and accession of Phraates IV. Whilst Parthia, ironically, unlike Rome, seemingly avoided a full-scale civil war, the surviving sources lay bare the divisions and bloodletting going on in the Parthian court and amongst its nobility:

> 'And after that destroyed the noblest men in the state generally and kept committing many other crimes. Consequently a large number of the most prominent persons abandoned him and betook themselves to various places, some, including Monaeses, going to Antonius.'[25]
>
> 'And now Phraates put Hyrodes [Orodes] his father to death and took possession of his kingdom, other Parthians ran away in great numbers, and particularly Monaeses, a man of distinction and power, who came in flight to Antonius.'[26]

On the one hand, Phraates had successfully consolidated his grip on the throne through the execution of all thirty of his half-brothers and a number of their supporters. Clearly this purge extended to the Parthian aristocracy, which would have seen a number either executed or fled. By the end of 37 BC, Phraates had purged the Parthian court of any dissent or rivalry and seemingly had a firm grip on the levers of power within the Parthian Empire.

On the other hand, Phraates had made enemies amongst much of the aristocracy and created an exile community of powerful nobles who would work for his downfall, including those who fled to the Roman East. Chief of these exiles was Monaeses, of whom we know little other than he was a powerful exiled Parthian noble, determined to see Phraates overthrown, possibly with himself as a replacement. The Romans had already overthrown one native dynasty – the Hasmoneans in Judea – and the thought of doing the same in Parthia and replacing the Arsacids, having them rule over a reduced Parthian Empire, must have appealed. Monaeses, it seems, found a warm welcome with Antonius, who by late 37 BC had returned to Syria:

'Now Antonius was elated by all this and furthermore based great hopes upon Monaeses, who had promised him to lead his army and bring most of Parthia over to him without trouble, and so he took in hand the war against the Parthians and gave Monaeses, in addition to other presents, three Roman cities to occupy until he should finish the war, and promised him the Parthian kingdom besides.'[27]

'Antonius likened the fortunes of the fugitive to those of Themistocles, compared his own abundant resources and magnanimity to those of the Persian kings, and gave him three cities, Larissa, Arethusa, and Hierapolis, which used to be called Bambyce.'[28]

Antonius now finally felt secure enough in his Triumviral position and with the state of the ongoing Roman Civil War – by late 37 BC Octavianus clearly had the upper hand militarily against Pompeius – to consider an attack on, and conquest of, the Parthian Empire. The aims of the war seemed clear: defeat the Parthian army, oust Phraates and the Arsacid Dynasty and replace them with a new Parthian dynasty and a client king in the form of Monaeses, a copy of the policy that had occurred in Judea and a variation of Crassus' original plan in 54 BC. Parthia would become a client state of Rome, and in particular of Antonius, further increasing his powerbase, especially with regard to his erstwhile ally and rival Octavianus. In this scenario it was more than likely that Rome would annex the border territories of the Parthian Empire, though we will never know for sure.

Summary

The end of 37 BC saw Antonius finally making preparations to renew the war with Parthia and launch a fresh invasion of their empire, building on the successes of Ventidius in 39/38 BC and taking advantage of the divisions within the Parthian nobility and the weak position of the new king. As we have seen, although Antonius had spent the majority of the last eighteen months in Greece and Italy, his commanders had consolidated and expanded Roman control of the East, re-securing Syria, Judea and Armenia and expanding Rome's rule to the tribes of the Caucasus (the Iberians and Albanians). Rome and Antonius were now in a strong position to take the war to Parthia.

Chapter Seven

The Roman Invasion of the Parthian Empire I (The Invasion)

T he year 36 BC saw the culmination of the two wars affecting both the Western and Eastern Republics. In the West, Octavianus, Lepidus and Agrippa launched an attack on the Sicilian stronghold of Sex. Pompeius in an attempt to bring to an end the latest round of the Third Roman Civil War. In the East, meanwhile, Antonius was poised to invade the Parthian Empire to bring a victorious end to the Second Romano-Parthian War.

1. A Clash of Diplomacy

However, before the invasion actually took place, Phraates, clearly understanding the danger he was facing, made overtures to the Parthian dissidents, and Monaeses in particular, hoping to lure him way from the Romans and reconcile him to his rule:

'While they were thus occupied Phraates became terrified, especially because the Parthians took the flight of Monaeses very much to heart, and he opened negotiations with him, offering him everything conceivable, and so persuaded him to return. When Antonius found this out, he was angry, quite naturally, but did not kill Monaeses, though he was still in his power; for he could not hope to win to his side any other barbarians, in case he should do such a thing. Accordingly, he not only released Monaeses, just as if Monaeses were going to bring the Parthians under his control, but even sent envoys with him to Phraates. Nominally he was negotiating peace, on the condition of getting back the standards and the prisoners captured in the disaster of Crassus and with the purpose of taking the king off his guard because of his hope of reaching a settlement;

but, as a matter of fact, he was getting everything in readiness for war.'[1]

'But when the Parthian king made an offer of friendship to Monaeses, Antonius gladly sent Monaeses back to him, determined to receive Phraates with a prospect of peace, and demanding back the standards captured in the campaign of Crassus, together with such of his men as still survived.'[2]

So Monaeses was sent to the Parthian court along with Roman ambassadors, to demand the return of the Roman standards lost at Carrhae and any Roman prisoners taken either at Carrhae or the retreat, mostly living in the city of Merv on Parthia's eastern border.[3] We cannot believe that Antonius would have been happy with such a meagre return and clearly he had a glorious military campaign in mind, bringing about the submission of the Parthian Empire. Yet the cover of a diplomatic mission did allow Monaeses to return to the Parthian court to stir up further dissensions, if he could be trusted. On the other hand, it did allow for Phraates to bring Monaeses back to his side and remove a pro-Roman pretender to the crown. There is also the time factor to consider, as Antonius did not launch his invasion of the Parthian Empire early in the year. It may be that this diplomatic mission was cover for Antonius' assembly of what was to be a very large army indeed.

We are not told what the formal response was to the Roman offer of peace in return for the standards and prisoners, nor explicitly whether Monaeses returned to the Roman fold. Yet judging by later events, it seems he was fighting for the Parthians. Diplomacy had therefore gained Antonius little and he had lost his preferred candidate to put on the Parthian throne, a powerful domestic opponent of Phraates and the Arsacid dynasty. Whilst it is true that there would have been a number of other candidates whom Antonius could have put on the throne as puppet rulers, Phraates had in the short term scored an early victory over Antonius without firing a shot.

2. Roman Preparations for the Invasion – Route and Army

With the cover of diplomacy cast aside, Antonius began his long-planned invasion of the Parthian Empire, the second such Roman incursion.

Rome's first invasion had seen Crassus cross from Syria into Parthia over the Euphrates, then following the Euphrates southwards towards the key Mesopotamian cities of Seleucia and Ctesiphon, a Parthian capital.[4] There were advantages and disadvantages of this direct approach. On the one hand, it made for a direct attack on the administrative and commercial heart of the Parthian Empire, enabling any attacker to potentially deliver a 'knock-out' blow. On the other hand, much of the terrain that had to be crossed was arid, wide open and made for perfect conditions for Parthian cavalry, as Crassus found to his cost. Taking into account the disastrous defeat at Carrhae at the hands of the Parthian horse archers, Antonius planned a different and more cautious route, which seems to have fitted with his mentality. He selected to invade the Parthian Empire not from the west, but the north-west, and move through Armenia into the Parthian client kingdom of Media-Atropatené (modern Azerbaijan, see Map 9), a more mountainous terrain.

Again, this route had both its advantages and disadvantages. The obvious advantage was that it negated the chance of the Parthians deploying thousands of horse archers and surrounding a Roman army, as had happened at Carrhae. It also built on the three most recent Roman victories against the Parthians – all commanded by Ventidius – where the Romans had used hilly terrain to negate the Parthian cavalry and deploy their greater infantry strength. Antonius would also, in theory, be able to establish a strong supply chain through the allied Kingdom of Armenia, which could be used as an effective base from which to launch an attack into neighbouring Media-Atropatené. The obvious downsides were that this route would not deliver a speedy 'knock-out' blow to the Parthians and he would have to fight his way through Media to eventually reach the Parthian capital. In other words, this route was the slow and steady one. The other problem was that it would take longer for the Roman forces to march through Syria to Armenia, and then through Armenia into Media-Atropatené.

Nevertheless, we can see that Antonius had this route in mind for some time, by the preparations undertaken by his general P. Canidius Crassus in the preceding year, who re-subdued Armenia and the neighbouring kingdoms of Iberia and Albania. We can disregard Dio's notion that Antonius attempted to attack Parthia via Syria, but had his mind changed:

'And he [Antonius] went as far as the Euphrates, thinking it was destitute of a garrison; when, however, he found that whole region carefully guarded, he turned aside from it, but undertook to make a campaign against Artavasdes, the King of the Medes, being persuaded thereto by the King of Greater Armenia, who had the same name and was an enemy of the other.'[5]

Whatever his actual military ability, many of the surviving ancient sources follow an Augustan tradition and portray Antonius as a man easily persuaded by others, especially non-Roman 'foreigners', most infamously Cleopatra, who in Roman eyes suffered from being both foreign and a woman. Antonius' ultimate fate – waging, and losing, a war on Rome itself, just as both Caesar and Octavianus themselves had done – could be put down to him being led astray, just as any other Roman military failures could be. Yet there was clear military logic behind Antonius' chosen route: a more cautious approach than had been taken by Crassus, and a clear desire to fight Parthian forces on ground more conducive to the Roman method of fighting than the Parthian one. Thus, Antonius made Armenia the gathering point for his army and assembled a formidable invasion force. Unlike the armies of Ventidius, we have multiple sources providing a variety of differing estimates for the size of this force:

'Antonius himself, however, after sending Cleopatra back to Egypt, proceeded through Arabia and Armenia to the place where his forces were assembled, together with those of the allied kings. These kings were very many in number, but the greatest of them all was Artavasdes, King of Armenia, who furnished six thousand horse and seven thousand foot. Here Antonius reviewed his army. There were, of the Romans themselves, sixty thousand foot-soldiers, together with the cavalry classed as Roman, namely, ten thousand Iberians and Celts; of the other nations there were thirty thousand, counting alike horsemen and light-armed troops.'[6]

'M. Antonius invaded Media rather late, and brought war to Parthia with eighteen legions and 16,000 horsemen.'[7]

'For Antonius with thirteen legions after passing through Armenia and then through Media.'[8]

'On this prince Antonius made war, with sixteen effective legions.'[9]

Here we have estimates ranging from thirteen to eighteen legions. What we need to bear in mind is that this was at least twice as large as Crassus' invasion army in 53 BC, which was only seven legions. This was a clear signal of Antonius' intent: a full-blown Roman effort to, once and for all, knock out their eastern rival and add the resources of the Parthian Empire to those of Antonius' Eastern Republic. We should also note the large number of cavalry which Antonius took with him. This countered one of the main criticisms of the first Roman invasion of Parthia, namely that they took too few cavalry and were overwhelmed by the Parthian cataphracts and horse archers at Carrhae. There were also great numbers of allied forces which accompanied Antonius, the largest of which were with the King of Armenia, but also included that of the rump client Kingdom of Pontus.

3. Parthian Preparations for the Invasion – Army and Tactics

It is often said that generals prepare to fight the previous war, and we can see elements of this here. Antonius' army and invasion plans were clearly influenced by the ghosts of Carrhae and Crassus. In response, the Parthians would have needed to amend their tactics too. We have no estimates for the size of the Parthian army, which relied on the Parthian noble houses levying their vassals. In theory, the Parthians could have shrugged off the losses sustained at Gindarus and easily put an army in the field that matched Antonius'. However, key to the mustering of the Parthian army was the loyalty of the Parthian nobles to the throne, and in particular its incumbent, the widely disliked Phraates IV. However, as we have seen, Phraates, realising that his throne was in danger, seems to have gone on a charm offensive with the disaffected Parthian nobility, curbed his murderous streak and reached out to them.

Typically, the surviving sources do not clearly state how large an army the Parthians were able to put into the field, nor even who its overall commander was. The closest we come to a figure for the size of the Parthian army is a passage from Justin commenting about the nature of the Parthian society and army:

'They have an army, not like other nations, of free men, but chiefly consisting of slaves, the numbers of whom daily increase, the power of manumission being allowed to none, and all their offspring, in consequence, being born slaves. These bondmen they bring up as carefully as their own children, and teach them, with great pains, the arts of riding and shooting with the bow. As any one is eminent in wealth, so he furnishes the king with a proportionate number of horsemen for war. Indeed, when fifty thousand cavalry encountered Antonius, as he was making war upon Parthia, only four hundred of them were free men.'[10]

So it seems that Phraates was able to raise at least 50,000 cavalry to resist the Roman invasion. It is not clear exactly who was in charge of the Parthian army which faced Antonius, but there are three candidates, all of whom may have played a role. The most prominent in our surviving sources is the Parthian king, Phraates IV himself, who unlike his father seems to have left the Parthian court and taken command of the army in Media, either directly or through a subordinate. All the sources name him as commanding the army in Media.

There are two other figures who may have taken some role in commanding the Parthian forces. One is the King of Media, Artavasdes I, who would have commanded the Median contingent of the forces present. The other is the former Parthian defector, Monaeses. Though he is absent from any of the major surviving narratives, he does figure in an odd passage of Horace, the Augustan poet:[11] 'Twice have the troops of Monaeses and Pacorus crushed ill-omened offences.'[12]

Thus, in near contemporary Augustan literature, Monaeses is placed on a par with Pacorus, leading many to suggest, or even blithely assume, that he was the Parthian general responsible for fighting Antonius.

Moving onto tactics, the first Roman invasion had been met with a set-piece battle, which had brought victory to the Parthians. Since then, however, the Romans had won three major clashes against the Parthians, and both the size and composition (cavalry-heavy) of the Roman army and its strategy (invading via Media) did not present a similar opportunity for the Parthians to replicate Carrhae and meet them in open battle. Phraates may well have wanted to avoid another set-piece battle due to the fragile nature of his hold on the throne. A clear Roman victory in the field would demonstrate the weakness of his position and open up opportunities for him to be replaced. Momentum was clearly with Antonius, and a victory would enhance his position and cause many waverers to change sides.

The Parthians did hold two clear advantages, however: the terrain and the time of year. The fighting would be on territory they knew well – unlike the battles in Syria and Asia Minor – and Antonius had seemingly invaded quite late in the campaigning year, having had to mass his troops in Armenia. A viable tactic was to hold Antonius off until winter set in and his supply lines became stretched.

4. The Invasion of Media-Atropatené

A number of ancient sources blame Antonius for the delay in invading Media, which many unfairly lay at the feet of his infatuation with Cleopatra. Nevertheless, Plutarch provides the following summary:

> In the first place, then, though he ought to have spent the winter in Armenia and to have given his army rest, worn out as it was by a march of eight thousand furlongs, and to have occupied Media at the opening of spring, before the Parthians had left their winter quarters, he could not hold out that length of time, but led his army on, taking Armenia on his left, and skirting Atropatené, which country he ravaged.'[13]

Other sources state that Antonius was duped by the Armenian king and taken on a circuitous route, as best exemplified by Strabo:

> 'It was not the nature of the country that made the expedition difficult for Antonius, but his guide Artavasdes, the King of the Armenians, whom, though plotting against him, Antonius rashly made his counsellor and master of decisions respecting the war.

Antonius indeed punished him, but too late, when the latter had
been proved guilty of numerous wrongs against the Romans, not
only he himself, but also that other guide, who made the journey
from the Zeugma on the Euphrates to the borders of Atropatené
eight thousand stadia long, more than twice the direct journey,
guiding the army over mountains and roadless regions and
circuitous routes.'[14]

In all cases the sources – all post-Augustan – seem to take great pleasure
in marking out Antonius as a dupe, someone who is easily manipulated
by others, whether it be Cleopatra or the King of Armenia. In the field
of politics this was a man who had risen to command half of the Roman
Republic and amassed power which had only been eclipsed by the
dictators Sulla and Caesar. On the other hand, his military record does
have a number of black marks against it. In the civil wars which followed
the death of Caesar, he found himself defeated by the Consuls Hirtius
and Pansa and forced from Italy.

These military defeats were only salvaged through political acumen
in forging an alliance, first with his old colleague Lepidus and then his
enemy Caesar Octavianus. In the subsequent war between the Triumvirate
and the Brutan-Cassian faction, which culminated in the two Battles of
Philippi, Antonius was victorious in both engagements, but both had
been close-run events. Furthermore, as we have seen, Antonius' various
delays in the early stage of this Second Romano–Parthian War, though
understandable from a political point of view, could have been costly for
the Romans, had not Ventidius intervened. We can say that Antonius'
military record was patchy at best, with him being a competent but not
brilliant Roman military commander.

Bearing that in mind, aside from the sources' desire to downplay
Antonius' ability and re-emphasize that he was easily led, there were
sound military reasons for the timing of his attack. Firstly, he had to
move all the Roman forces into Armenia from Asia Minor and Syria and
then coordinate them with the arriving allied contingents, all of which
would have taken time. Secondly, having gathered such a large force, he
deemed it better to strike quickly, rather than have them sit idle over a
winter in Armenia, giving the Parthians even more time to gather their

forces and prepare for his arrival. As Ventidius had shown in the early stages of the war, it was better to seize the initiative against the Parthians and press them, rather than sit back.

Although there was nothing fundamentally wrong with Antonius choosing to attack Media later in the year, there were two downsides. Firstly, this strategy relied on achieving some quick wins, most notably securing winter quarters within Media; and secondly, he would need to secure his supply lines back into Armenia. At this point we must raise a note of caution, as Antonius' record to date does seem to portray him as being an impatient commander, especially when it came to the arduous work of warfare, such as sieges. We need only think back to the siege of the Commagene capital city of Samosata, where he took over from Ventidius, made no progress and soon gave up and left.

Nevertheless, Antonius seemed to have had a clear strategy in mind for the early stages of his invasion (see Map 9). He thrust quickly into Media-Atropatené and set his sights on the city of Praaspa, the site of the royal court. If the city could be subdued, then Antonius would have his winter quarters and Media-Atropatené could be occupied and held by the Roman army, to use as a springboard for a deeper incursion into the Parthian Empire the following year. However, it was shortly after his invasion that his intelligence told him that the Median king, Artavasdes I, had fled his capital, seemingly leaving his family behind, to link up with the King of Parthia.

5. The Division of the Army

It was here that Antonius took a fateful decision and divided his army. He took the faster elements of his army, including the cavalry, in a lightning assault on the city, leaving behind the slower elements, including all his siege engines, and two legions under the command of Oppius Statianus, who would catch up later. In many ways this decision echoes that made by Ventidius in 39 BC when he split his army into faster and slower elements to chase after the Parthians. However, there were two key differences between Ventidius' position and that of Antonius. Ventidius was not setting out to attack a city, for which he would need siege engines, and he roughly knew where the opposing army was; Antonius, it seems, did not. The key to Antonius' decision was his apparent belief that the city of Praaspa would fall without a siege:

> '[Antonius] left behind the beasts of burden and a portion of the army with Oppius Statianus, giving orders for them to follow, while he himself, taking the cavalry and the strongest of the infantry, hurried on, confident that he would capture all the enemies' strongholds without a blow.'[15]

In this assumption, however, he was to be proved wrong, as the city was well prepared for a siege. Antonius, with only his cavalry and infantry, was in no position to conduct an effective investment until Statianus arrived with his siege train. As Plutarch points out:

> 'Secondly, his engines necessary for siege operations were carried along on three hundred waggons, and among them was a battering ram eighty feet long. Not one of these, if destroyed, could be replaced in time to be of use, because the upper country produced only wood of insufficient length and hardness.'[16]

Antonius' gamble had failed, and he had to lay siege to the city as best he could:

> 'He assailed Praaspa, the royal residence, and proceeded to heap up mounds and to make assaults.'[17]
>   'But the exigencies of the case at once proved what a mistake he had made in leaving behind him his engines and coming to close quarters he began to build a mound against the city, which rose slowly and with much labour.'[18]

On the face of it, Antonius' gambit, to strike quickly and catch the enemy unawares and thus secure the royal residence without having to undertake a long siege, was a balanced one. It is here again, however, that we can perhaps detect a streak of impatience in Antonius. At first glance it seemed that there was no danger involved in this manoeuvre; even if he didn't capture the city quickly, his siege train would catch up and the siege could begin in earnest. However, Antonius made one fatal error as he seemingly did not take into account the existence, or location, of the Parthian army. His whole strategy here was based on the assumption, presumably backed up by intelligence on the ground, that the Parthian army had either not mustered or was ahead of him in Parthia proper. Unfortunately for him this was not the case, and once again the Romans grossly underestimated their opponents.

6. The First Battle (Unnamed)

Again, we can only judge this first battle of the invasion from the Roman perspective, due to the lack of surviving Parthian sources. Nevertheless, it seems that Phraates had been able to outmanoeuvre the Romans. The Parthians would have roughly known the route that the Roman invasion force would take from Armenia and into Media-Atropatené, and had as much time as the Romans to muster and prepare their army. Rather than immediately face the Romans, as they had in 53 BC, Phraates held back, understandably worried about losing a major battle.

However, it appears that the Parthian army, with him in command, was held in the vicinity of Media-Atropatené, seemingly without the Romans noticing. We are not told how this was achieved. It seems that the Romans took the absence of opposition and the retreat of the Median king to mean that the Parthian army was ahead of them. Critically, however, it appeared to be on their flank. When the Roman army split into two and Antonius took the bulk of the legions and cavalry with him, he unwittingly exposed the remaining Roman force to the full might of the Parthian army. The Partians quickly seized the opportunity, although we are not told exactly where the battle took place:

> 'When the Parthian and the Mede ascertained this, they left him [Antonius] to continue his idle toil, for the walls were strong and were well-manned by defenders, but assailed Statianus while off his guard and wearied from the march and slew his whole detachment, with the exception of Polemon, King of Pontus, who was then accompanying Statianus; him alone they took alive and released for a ransom.'[19]

> 'In the meantime, however, Phraates came down with a great army, and when he heard that the waggons carrying the engines had

been left behind, he sent a large number of his horsemen against them. By these Statianus was surrounded and slain himself, and ten thousand of his men were slain with him. Moreover, the barbarians captured the engines and destroyed them. They also took a great number of prisoners, among whom was Polemon the king.'[20]

A large Parthian army of cavalry – whose number is unknown, but may have been anything up to 50,000 – fell upon Rome's siege train, defended by only two legions. The result was the destruction of the legions, the only doubt raised by the sources being whether the Romans were all slaughtered (Dio) or a number were taken prisoner (Plutarch). Amongst the dead was the Roman commander Statianus, whilst the client King of Pontus was taken alive.

By any measure this defeat was a disaster for the Romans and ensured that Antonius' gamble had backfired spectacularly. On the face of it, the loss of two legions, from an invasion force of thirteen to eighteen legions, was far from a decisive blow to Antonius, but the wider ramifications were far more serious. Firstly came the destruction of Antonius' siege train, severely limiting his plans to conquer cities which resisted and thus slowing down the whole campaign. Perhaps more important was the psychological blow and dent to Roman military prestige.

Antonius had invaded Parthia with a huge army on the back of the Roman victory at Gindarus, hoping to capitalize on the weak domestic position of Phraates IV. Yet the first victory had gone to Phraates, which would have significantly boosted his position and gone a long way to ensuring that any Parthian nobles with wavering loyalty would commit themselves to the throne. The manner of the victory also seemed to throw the two leaders' military abilities in sharp focus and compare them in an unfavourable light for Antonius. Antonius had been the one to make the first mistake and split his army, leading to the destruction of the lesser element, whilst Phraates was able to pounce on the Roman army undetected. The psychological blow of this defeat soon reaped further rewards for the Parthians as it led to the retreat of the Armenian forces commanded by their king:

'Because the Armenian King, on the one hand, was not present at the battle, but, when he might have helped the Romans, as some say, neither did so nor joined Antonius, but retired to his own country.'[21]

'This calamity naturally distressed all the followers of Antonius, for they had received an unexpected blow at the outset; besides, Artavasdes, the King of Armenia, despairing of the Roman cause, took his own forces and went off.'[22]

This defection would have hit Antonius hard for several reasons. In the first instance, it removed another 6,000 cavalry and 7,000 infantry from his invasion force. However, again it was the wider implications that had the greatest impact, part psychological and part logistical. Whilst Artavasdes did not defect to the Parthians, his withdrawal from the invasion of Parthia sent a clear message to all that this was not an all-conquering and unstoppable Roman host. Indeed, it implied just the reverse, that the whole expedition was folly and unlikely to succeed, again bolstering the Parthian position and weakening the Roman one.

However, the far more dangerous issue for Antonius was that Armenia was central to his whole invasion strategy, being critical to his supply line. With Armenia's retreat into neutrality, this supply line was thrown into doubt. It is unfortunate that the sources provide us with little detail on the Armenian retreat, as Artavasdes was clearly taking a dangerous path – and one which would later cost him dearly – in pulling out on the Romans and leaving them in the lurch. In Roman minds, you were either for them or against them, and with this withdrawal he was placing himself into the latter category. It would be tempting to speculate on whether Phraates had a hand in this 'defection' with promises of Parthian assistance in the face of any Roman retaliation.

Whilst conducting the siege of Praaspa, Antonius suddenly found his whole campaign unravelling and needing urgent action on his part. It seems that he was alerted by Statianus to the impending disaster and left the siege to rush to his aid:

'Antonius, on the other hand, although he hastened, at the first message sent to him by Statianus, to go to his assistance, was nevertheless too late, for he found nothing but corpses. On this account he felt afraid, but inasmuch as he fell in with no barbarian, he suspected that they had gone off somewhere in alarm, and so regained his courage.'[23]

Antonius was too late to save Statianus' force and apparently found no sign of the Parthian army, which had again utilized its speed and mobility to leave Antonius chasing shadows. With seemingly no enemy to fight, Antonius returned to the siege. This whole episode seems to highlight an intelligence deficit; with the Parthians knowing the location of the Roman forces, but the Romans chasing shadows. The Parthians had struck out of nowhere, destroyed a Roman army and then retreated out of sight, fighting a perfect hit-and-run campaign. The Roman forces, by contrast, seemed to have been unable to scout the Parthian army's location, putting themselves at a distinct tactical disadvantage.

7. The Battle of Praaspa

Shortly afterwards, we are not told when exactly, and with Antonius commanding the siege once more, the Parthian army made their reappearance, this time at the siege itself. What followed was the second battle of the conflict in the vicinity of Praaspa, though its exact location is not known. The subsequent battle highlighted the full strengths and weaknesses of the Roman position, and surviving accounts can be found in both Dio and Plutarch, though the latter has the greater detail:

'Hence, when he [Antonius] met them [the Parthians] a little later, he routed them, for as his slingers were numerous and could shoot farther than the archers, they inflicted severe injury upon all, even upon the men in armour; yet he did not kill any considerable number of the enemy, because the barbarians could ride fast.'[24]

'And now the Parthians presented themselves to the besiegers in brilliant array and threatened them insultingly. Antonius, therefore, not wishing that the inactivity of his army should confirm and increase among them consternation and dejection, took ten legions and three praetorian cohorts of men-at-arms, together with all his cavalry, and led them out to forage, thinking that in this way the enemy would best be drawn into a pitched battle.

'After advancing a single day's march, he saw that the Parthians were enveloping him and seeking to attack him on the march. He therefore displayed the signal for battle in his camp, and after taking down his tents, as though his purpose was not to fight but to withdraw, he marched along past the line of the barbarians, which was crescent-shaped. But he had given orders that when the first ranks of the enemy should appear to be within reach of his legionaries, the cavalry should charge upon them.

'To the Parthians in their parallel array, the discipline of the Romans seemed to beggar description, and they watched them marching past at equal distances from one another, without confusion, and in silence, brandishing their javelins. But when the signal was given, and the Roman horsemen wheeled about and rode down upon them with loud shouts, they did indeed receive their onset and repel them, although their foes were at once too close for them to use their arrows; when, however, the legionaries joined in the charge, with shouts and clashing of weapons, the horses of the Parthians took fright and gave way, and the Parthians fled without coming to close quarters.

'Antonius pressed hard upon them in pursuit and had great hopes that he had finished the whole war, or the greater part of it, in that one battle. His infantry kept up the pursuit for fifty furlongs, and his cavalry for thrice that distance; and yet when he took count of those of the enemy who had fallen or had been captured, he found only thirty prisoners and eighty dead bodies. Despondency and despair therefore fell upon all; they thought it a terrible thing that when victorious they had killed so few, and when vanquished they were to be robbed of so many men as they had lost at the waggons.'[25]

From these sources we can see that the Parthian army reappeared at the siege of Praaspa and then refused to give battle, forcing Antonius to take the bulk of his army – some ten legions – in pursuit. The Parthians, possibly commanded by Phraates himself, still obviously held the initiative in the war, with the Romans fighting a reactive campaign. On this occasion it seems that the Roman scouts had spotted the Parthian army in time and averted an attack on them whilst they were still marching.

Thus forewarned, Antonius was able to deploy his army's full strength and probably superior numbers, and seemed to have routed the Parthian cavalry. Plutarch's description shows that the Roman army's discipline allowed Antonius to bluff the Parthians and then catch them by surprise, negating the dreaded Parthian attacks from long range. Dio adds the further detail that Antonius, learning from Ventidius, had a significant force of slingers in his army, matching and it seems outclassing the Parthians when it came to their use.

Yet whilst on the face of it this second battle was a Roman victory, with the Parthians driven off, the reality was quite different. The Parthians had no intention of meeting Antonius in a set-piece battle, where he could utilise the greater power of his infantry, backed up by his slingers, and deliver the decisive victory which his campaign so desperately needed. Indeed, the Parthians only seem to have offered battle when they thought there was a possibility of attacking Antonius' army on the march. When the Romans formed up and moved towards them, covered by their own slingers, the Parthian forces withdrew, again leaving the Romans chasing shadows. Leaving only thirty prisoners and eighty dead, the Parthian cavalry army disappeared into the mountainous terrain, in what must have been a well-rehearsed manoeuvre. Antonius was left with nothing tangible achieved and had to return to the siege once more, leaving the initiative with the Parthian army and its guerrilla tactics.

8. The Next Clashes

Having achieved little chasing the Parthian army, Plutarch relates a third battle which took place soon afterwards. Having regrouped, Antonius' army set off back to the siege of Praaspa, but once again the Parthian army attacked them en-route:

'On the following day they packed up and started on the road to Phraata [a variant spelling of Praaspa] and their camp. As they marched, they met, first a few of the enemy, then more of them, and finally the whole body, which, as though unconquered and fresh, challenged and attacked them from every side; but at last, with difficulty and much labour, they got safely to their camp.'[26]

1. Bust of Cn. Pompeius Magnus.

2. Bust of C. Iulius Caesar.

3. Bust of M. Antonius.

4. Bust of M. Vipsanius Agrippa.

5. Prima Porta statue of Augustus.

6. Coin of Orodes II.

7. Coin of Pacorus.

8. Coin of Antonius.

9. Coin of Labienus.

10. Coin of Antonius and Cleopatra.

11. Coin of Artavasdes I of Media.

12. Coin of Artavasdes II of Armenia.

13. Coin of Augustus depicting the Parthian surrender of Roman standards.

14. Coin of Augustus depicting the Parthian Triumphal arch.

Again this clash seems to have been less a full-scale battle, than the Parthians harrying the Roman column, in a classic hit-and-run tactic guerrilla campaign. We have no details other than those presented above, nor any idea of Roman casualties. Having rejoined the siege, the Romans found themselves under attack once more, when the Parthian army attacked their positions:

> 'Then the Medes made a sally against their mound and put its defenders to flight. At this Antonius was enraged and visited those who had played the coward with what is called decimation. That is, he divided the whole number of them into tens, and put to death that one from each ten upon whom the lot fell.'[27]

Antonius now found himself pinned down by the Parthian army, which was able to attack his positions seemingly at will, leaving him trapped in the siege.

9. Antonius' Stalingrad – The Siege of Praaspa

This failure to bring the Parthians to battle and deliver the critical blow left Antonius' campaign in disarray. He was committed to a siege, despite having lost his siege engines and, more importantly, lost control of the countryside around the city. With the Parthian army roaming at will between him and Armenia, he faced being cut off from his supply lines, a problem exacerbated by the retreat of his Armenian allies. Antonius' glorious invasion had become ground down in a protracted siege which sapped at his army's strength the longer it went on; his own Stalingrad in many ways.

Antonius was faced with two equally unpalatable options. He could withdraw from the siege, retreat back into Roman territory for the winter and regroup. The clear danger with this would have been the long retreat that it would entail, with a large Parthian army between him and safety to harry him at every opportunity. Furthermore, the logical route of retreat would be back into Armenia, but he could not be sure of the reception he would get from his now unwilling ally, Artavasdes II. There was even the possibility that Artavasdes could turn his neutrality into Parthian support and turn on the Roman army.

The second equally unpalatable option was to continue the siege and hold off the Parthian attacks long enough to capture the city, establish a winter base and then try to secure his supply lines back into Roman territory. The danger of this tactic was that his army was being worn down by Parthian attacks on two fronts: sorties from the city and attacks on his outer defences by the roaming Parthian cavalry. Aside from the Parthian attacks, the other key factor was his supplies, or lack of them, with the Parthian army cutting off a clear supply line to Armenia and harrying any foraging parties he sent out. Antonius' army's strength was being sapped daily and it would be a race to see which force collapsed quicker, the one defending the city or that attacking it. By this point, the balance of power had swung clearly in favour of the Parthians and their guerrilla tactics, with the Roman invasion blunted and in danger of being routed.

Faced with these two equally unpalatable options, Antonius chose the latter and stuck to the siege, rather than face an ignominious withdrawal. Yet effectively it was he who found himself under siege, with Parthian forces harrying him from both sides. Dio provides a detailed description of the practical issues faced by Antonius in maintaining his siege:

'So he proceeded again against Praaspa and besieged it, though he did no great injury to the enemy; for the men inside the walls repulsed him vigorously, and those outside would not readily join in battle with him. But he lost many of his own men in searching for and bringing in provisions, and many by his own discipline. At first, as long as they could get their food from somewhere in the neighbourhood, they were sufficient for both undertakings, being able not only to carry on the siege but also to secure their supplies in safety. When, however, all the supplies at hand had been used up, it was their experience that if only a few men were sent anywhere, they would not only fail to bring any provisions, but would perish as well, whereas if many were sent, they would be leaving the wall destitute of besiegers and meantime would lose many men and many engines at the hands of the barbarians, who would make a sortie against them.

'For this reason, Antonius gave all his men barley instead of wheat and destroyed every tenth man in some instances; and, in short, although he was supposed to be the besieger, he was enduring the hardships of the besieged. For the men within the walls kept a close watch for opportunities to make sallies; and those outside not only grievously beset the Romans who remained about the city, as often as they became separated, accomplishing this by making a sudden charge and wheeling about again in a short time, but also in the case of those who foraged for provisions, while they did not trouble them on their way out to the villages, yet they would fall upon them unexpectedly when scattered on their way back to camp.'[28]

The Romans found themselves facing a protracted siege, likely to continue throughout the winter, with shortages of food and constant attacks from the front and rear. The possibility of defeat was looming for Antonius. Even if he could have sent word back into Roman territory to organise a relief force, there would have been no chance of one due to the time it would take to assemble – having gathered such a formidable army in the first place – and the difficulties of invading Parthia, via Armenia, in the depths of winter and facing a potentially hostile Armenian army, never mind the Parthian forces.

10. An Outbreak of Peace – Negotiations for a Truce

Yet it seems that Phraates also had concerns about the war. First and foremost he too had supply and morale issues to consider, especially when it came to maintaining such a large force of cavalry in the field during the oncoming winter:

'Phraates, too, knew that his Parthians were able to do anything rather than to undergo hardships and encamp in the open during winter, and he was afraid that if the Romans persisted and remained, his men would desert him, since already the air was getting sharp after the summer equinox.'[29]

The Parthians would have needed significant supplies of food for the riders and horses of their army, and though Phraates had far more secure supply lines, his army would still have to gather food from farther and farther away from Praaspa. Furthermore, whilst Phraates clearly had the upper hand and had effectively placed the Roman army itself under siege, his cavalry was designed for a hit-and-run campaign. His problem was that to defeat the Romans he would, sooner or later, need to commit to a set-piece battle, which would favour the Romans. Thus, Phraates changed his tactics and opened up negotiations with Antonius, from a position of strength, offering a desperate man a lifeline:

> 'Those of the Parthians who were most acquainted with the Romans attacked them less vigorously in their forays for provisions and other encounters, allowing them to take some things, praising their valour, and declaring that they were capital fighting men and justly admired by their own king. After this, they would ride up nearer, and quietly putting their horses alongside the Romans, would revile Antonius because, when Phraates wished to come to terms and spare so many such excellent men, Antonius would not give him an opportunity, but sat there awaiting those grievous and powerful enemies, famine and winter, which would make it difficult for them to escape even though the Parthians should escort them on their way. Many persons reported this to Antonius, but though his hope inclined him to yield, he did not send heralds to the Parthians until he had inquired of the barbarians who were showing such kindness whether what they said represented the mind of their king.
>
> 'They assured him that it did, and urged him to have no fear or distrust, whereupon he sent some of his companions with a renewed demand for the return of the standards and the captives, that he might not be thought altogether satisfied with an escape in safety. But the Parthian told him not to urge this matter, and assured him of peace and safety as soon as he started to go away.'[30]

Antonius, a man whose patience, as we have seen, was notoriously short, was offered a glimmer of hope with a negotiated truce whereby he could withdraw peacefully back into Roman territory, recover over the winter and plan a fresh invasion. It is at this point that alarm bells should have been ringing for the Romans. Why would any enemy allow the invading force to withdraw gracefully so they could regroup and attack the following year? Furthermore, the man they were negotiating with was Phraates, who had ascended the throne by murdering his father and thirty of his siblings and had a track record of treachery and 'machiavellian' politics.

However, Phraates had Antonius over a barrel and he knew it. His army was bleeding its strength into the dust to take the royal city of Media that didn't even contain the king. Even if he took the city, he would still be deep in enemy territory with no clear supply lines and with a marauding Parthian army in the interior. The city had little intrinsic value, other than containing the royal residence and probably the treasury. It would have occurred to Antonius and his commanders that at some point they may have to retreat back to Armenia anyway, and at least this offer allowed a chance of doing so peacefully. Even if there was treachery, then this truce would allow them a head start. Furthermore, Antonius would have had to consider the morale of his men. One unit had already had to be decimated for poor discipline, and with the onset of winter, dwindling food and a seemingly endless siege, it would be a question of when, not if, discipline broke amongst the other units. For those reasons, Antonius accepted the lifeline being offered by Phraates and ordered the Roman withdrawal, in return for nothing more concrete other than Phraates' word of safe conduct.

Summary

How can one sum up the disaster that was the Roman invasion of Parthia in 36 BC? Perhaps the biggest surprise is how quickly the whole venture unravelled, given the amount of time and planning that had gone into it. Antonius had assembled the largest Roman invasion force ever seen in the East, with upwards of eighteen legions, augmented by large numbers of cavalry and slingers, to negate the Parthian military strengths. He had chosen to invade from 'friendly' territory to maintain a good supply chain and adopted a cautious approach to reduce the Parthian territory of Media-Atropatené and then advance deeper into the Parthian Empire, rather than adopt Crassus' invasion route of making straight for the Parthian capital.

The campaign swung on two key decisions; one made by each of the leaders. The first seemingly came from Phraates, when he chose to lead the

Parthian army and adopt a hit-and-run campaign in Media-Atropatené. Phraates makes an interesting compromise between his father Orodes and elder brother Pacorus. Orodes preferred to sit in the Parthian court and allow his generals to do the fighting, whilst Pacorus always seemed to favour a bold strategy of attack. Phraates seemingly chose a middle ground between the two. Although the Roman invasion army of 53 BC had been destroyed in a set-piece battle, every encounter since had ended badly for the Parthians, with the Romans having clearly evolved their tactics to negate the Parthian cavalry and archery attack, notably by using slingers. Thus, Phraates adopted a hit-and-run campaign, utilising the greater mobility of a cavalry-only force.

The other key element of this was to take the fight to the Romans in Media rather than assemble an army deeper in Parthia and await Antonius' advance. He did not allow the Romans to build up momentum, either militarily or politically. These tactics may have been forced upon him by the circumstances of his weak political position, facing internal opposition from the Parthian nobility, having seized the throne in a bloody coup. Whilst we have no surviving Parthians source for this, his opponents may have been waiting for the first sign of weakness – a defeat or a reticence to defend Parthia – to oust him. Whatever the cause, by advancing into Media to harry the Romans, it gave him the opportunity to take advantage of Roman tactical errors, which brought about victory in the short term.

The second key decision came from Antonius, with his desire to attack the city of Praaspa immediately. Had the Median king been in the city and had it fallen quickly, then it would have been judged a sound tactic. Unfortunately for Antonius, the king wasn't in the city and it had been prepared for a long siege. Even then, the decision may not have been disastrous, but for the key mistake of separating his forces and taking the bulk of his army to Praaspa, leaving just two legions behind to guard the siege train. Had he been aware of the Parthian army's location, shadowing his flank, then surely he wouldn't have taken this decision.

We can lay another charge at Antonius, that of splitting his army and haring off to attack a city which he knew little about, without being aware that a Parthian army numbering in the tens of thousands was within a few days' march. This and the lack of awareness of the readiness of Praaspa to withstand a siege smack of impatience and a lack of good intelligence. Ultimately, Antonius' rashness cost him, and a massive Roman invasion of Parthia became bogged down in a seemingly unwinnable siege of a minor city, forcing Antonius to contemplate a humiliating withdrawal under guarantee of safety from the notoriously untrustworthy Parthian king.

Chapter Eight

The Roman Invasion of the Parthian Empire II (The Retreat)

With the onset of winter 36 BC, M. Antonius found himself facing a critical period. It was clear that his invasion of Parthia had failed, largely due to his own rashness and Phraates' superior strategy. He now had to extricate a large Roman and allied army from Media-Atropatené and back into friendly Roman, or pro-Roman, territory, facing the dual threat of hunger and Parthian attacks. Dio and Plutarch preserve accounts of what was to become one of the most famous of all Roman military retreats, which must stand on a par with some of the most notorious in history. Of the two accounts, Plutarch's has the most detail and must have originated from a now-lost eyewitness account (see Chapter Two).

1. The Withdrawal from Praaspa

Antonius first action lifted the siege of Praaspa, which, according to Dio, he seems to have done before agreeing the truce with Phraates:

'[Antonius] withdrew without destroying any of his implements of siege, just as if he were in friendly territory. When Antonius had done this and was awaiting the truce, the Medes burned his engines and scattered his mounds.'[1]

But no sooner had Antonius lifted the siege, then the defending Median forces attacked and destroyed the Roman siege fortifications, a far from auspicious start to the withdrawal. Yet it seems that the main Roman army itself was unmolested, and Antonius was left with the crucial decision of which route to take back to Armenia, bearing in mind the need for provisions and fodder for such a large army and not wishing to expose himself to any potential Parthian traps. In this decision he was aided by a pro-Roman from the native Amardi peoples, who lived to the south of the Caspian Sea:

'As he was about to lead his army back by the road over which it had come, which ran through a level country without trees, a man of the Mardian race, who had great familiarity with the Parthian habits, and had already shown himself faithful to the Romans in the battle over the engines of war, came to Antonius and urged him in his flight to keep close to the hills upon his right, and not to expose an encumbered army of legionaries to so large a force of mounted archers, in bare and extended tracts; this was the very thing, he said, which Phraates had designed when he induced him by friendly conferences to raise the siege; he himself, he said, would conduct the army by a way that was shorter and furnished a greater abundance of provisions.

'On hearing this, Antonius took counsel with himself. He did not wish to have the appearance of distrusting the Parthians, now that a truce had been made, but since he approved of the shorter road and of having their march take them past inhabited villages, he asked the Mardian for a pledge of his good faith. The Mardian offered to let himself be put in fetters until he should bring the army safely into Armenia, and he was put in fetters, and led them for two days without their encountering trouble.'[2]

Apparently this local had assisted the Romans before, in the matter of the Parthian attack on the Roman siege train, but we are not told in what capacity. Upon his advice and apparent warnings of Parthian treachery, which the Romans must have been expecting, Antonius changed his proposed route and selected a shorter one, skirting the mountains, which provided him with the protection of rougher ground to avoid being encircled by Parthian mounted archers, as of course happened at Carrhae. This route also apparently provided more supplies for his army. Intriguingly, we will never know whether this offer of assistance was genuine or was a double bluff on the part of Phraates, leading the Romans into a trap by warning them of Parthian treachery. Nevertheless, the choice of a route that went via rougher terrain was a sound one and would play to Roman strengths.

2. The Parthian Ambush (Days 1–3)

Given both his military position and his natural disposition, it was inevitable that Phraates would renege on his offer of safe conduct for Antonius and his army. In fact, given the situation it was the only logical action to take. The Roman invasion of 36 BC had only been blunted due to tactical error on the part of its commander, and the assembled Roman army still represented a clear existential threat to the Parthian Empire and Phraates' throne. If they were allowed to regroup in Armenia, then they would return stronger the following year and there was no guarantee that Phraates could capitalise on any more of Antonius' mistakes. Sooner or later, the Parthians would be forced to face the Romans in battle and defeat could have spelt the end of everything, undoing the whole fragile rule of Phraates.

We don't know whether the Amardi guide Antonius was using led him into a trap, or whether the more mobile and fast-moving Parthian army, discerning Antonius' route, got ahead of him and had time to prepare an ambush. In any event they did not attack Antonius immediately on his withdrawal from Praaspa, realising that the Romans would be on guard and expecting treachery, so left it until the third day when the Romans were beginning to relax:

'But on the third day, when Antonius had put the Parthians entirely out of his thoughts and was marching along in looser order because of his confidence, the Mardian noticed that a dike of the river had been recently torn away, and that the stream was flowing out in great volume towards the road over which their march must be made. He comprehended that this was the work of the Parthians, throwing the river in their way to obstruct and delay the Roman march, and urged Antonius to look out and be on his guard, as the enemy were near.

And just as Antonius was setting his legionaries in array and arranging to have his javelineers and slingers make a sally through them against the enemy, the Parthians came into view and began to ride around the army in order to envelop and throw it into confusion on all sides. Whenever the Roman light-armed troops sallied out against them, the Parthians would inflict many wounds with their arrows, but sustain yet more from the leaden bullets and javelins of the Romans, and therefore withdraw. Then they would come up again, until the Celts, massing their horses together, made a charge upon them and scattered them, so that they showed themselves no more that day.'³

The Parthians launched a swift assault on the Romans, aiming to utilise their superior archery. The warning provided by the Amardi guide does seem to rule out treachery, but then the Parthians were able to set up the trap remarkable quickly and we cannot rule out his leading Antonius into it. Regardless of the origins of the attack, the Parthians were unable to defeat the Romans in open battle due to the modified tactics of the Roman units they were facing.

Once again, the Parthian archery attack, which had proved so effective at Carrhae, was matched and negated by the Roman use of cavalry and the long-range weapons of their javelineers and slingers. The Celts mentioned were most likely Galatians, a Roman allied kingdom from Asia Minor (see Map 4) who were Gallic by origin, having settled there in the early third century BC following a migration. Thus, the Parthians were not able to inflict widespread casualties on the Romans with their archery, and were forced to retreat rather than engage at close quarters.

3. Ongoing Hit and Run Clashes (Days 4–7)

With the original ambush defeated and the Roman column intact, the next few days followed a familiar pattern, with the Parthian army continuing their hit-and-run tactics and the Romans making steady progress:

'Having thus learned what he ought to do, Antonius covered not only his rear, but also both his flanks, with numerous javelineers and slingers, led his army in the form of a hollow square, and gave orders to his horsemen to rout the enemy when they attacked, but after routing them not to pursue them further. Consequently, the Parthians, during four successive days, suffered greater loss than they inflicted, became less eager, and made the winter an excuse for thoughts of going away.'⁴

The Romans came under regular lightning attacks for the next four days, but with their flanks and rear protected by javelineers and slingers, and with a cavalry outer guard, the bulk of the army was protected and the balance of power began to shift in Antonius' favour. It was now the Parthians who were being ground down and suffering the heavier casualties.

4. The Battle of Flavius Gallus (Day 8)

It was perhaps against this rising tide of optimism that one of Antonius' military tribunes, Flavius Gallus, proposed a bolder course of action. Believing that the Parthians were weakening, he suggested to Antonius that upon the next Parthian attack, rather than fall back and draw them onto the main body of the legionaries, in particular the slingers and javelineers, he would stand his ground against the Parthians, inflict greater casualties on them and hopefully drive them off once and for all. Such a tactic would have appealed to Antonius, whose impatience in military matters seems time and to again come to the fore. Antonius agreed to Gallus' plan, despite the inherent risk involved and the success of their defensive strategy:

> 'On the fifth day, however, Flavius Gallus, an efficient and able soldier in high command, came to Antonius and asked him for more light-armed troops from the rear, and for some of the horsemen from the van, confident that he would achieve a great success. Antonius gave him the troops, and when the enemy attacked, Gallus beat them back, not withdrawing and leading them on towards the legionaries, as before, but resisting and engaging them more hazardously.'[5]

However, no sooner had Gallus engaged the Parthians than he began to get cut off from the main body of the Roman army, with the Parthians slowly enveloping him:

> 'The leaders of the rearguard, seeing that he was being cut off from them, sent and called him back; but he would not listen to them. Then, they say, Titius the Quaestor laid hold of his standards and tried to turn them back, abusing Gallus for throwing away the lives

of so many brave men. But Gallus gave back the abuse and exhorted his men to stand firm, whereupon Titius withdrew. Then Gallus forced his way among the enemy in front of him, without noticing that great numbers of them were enveloping him in the rear. But when missiles began to fall upon him from all sides, he sent and asked for help.

'Then the leaders of the legionaries, among whom was Canidius [Crassus], a man of the greatest influence with Antonius, are thought to have made no slight mistake. For when they ought to have wheeled their entire line against the enemy, they sent only a few men at a time to help Gallus, and again, when one detachment had been overcome, sent out others, and so, before they were aware of it, they came near plunging the whole army into defeat and flight. But Antonius himself speedily came with his legionaries from the van to confront the fugitives, and the third legion speedily pushed its way through them against the enemy and checked his further pursuit.'[6]

The Romans were thus able to salvage something from this clash with the Parthians, but only in terms of rescuing the units that had been cut off. Plutarch records the toll of this confrontation on the Romans:

'There fell no fewer than three thousand, and there were carried to their tents five thousand wounded men, among whom was Gallus, who was pierced in front by four arrows. Gallus, indeed, did not recover from his wounds.'[7]

The Roman suffered some 8,000 casualties, 5,000 of whom were wounded and would have to continue to march, or be driven, in the retreat through Media towards Armenia. We are not given any casualty figures for the Parthians, but as they were mounted and able to retreat, we can assume that they numbered only in the hundreds. Once again, we see the disastrous result of the Romans splitting their forces in a rash engagement with the mobile Parthian cavalry army.

The defensive strategy might have struck Antonius and his commanders as being 'un-Roman', but it seemed to have been working. The Roman army was retreating through hostile country and facing a highly mobile cavalry-based army. While rushing forward to engage them at close quarters may have been a great display of Roman *virtus*, it was unsound tactically. Not only did the plan fail, but it gave the Parthians a morale-boosting success, whilst saddling the Romans with 5,000 wounded men on a forced march through hostile territory, slowing them down further.

5. The Battle of the Testudo (Day 9)

The Parthians were so boosted by this victory that they massed in even greater numbers, sensing the chance for a decisive blow against the Romans:

> 'The enemy, however, who had been already worn out and inclined to abandon their task, were so elated by their victory, and so despised the Romans, that they even bivouacked for the night near their camp, expecting very soon to be plundering the empty tents and the baggage of runaways. At daybreak, too, they gathered for attack in far greater numbers, and there are said to have been no fewer than forty thousand horsemen, since their king had sent even those who were always arrayed about his person, assured that it was to manifest and assured success; for the king himself was never present at a battle.'[8]

The Parthians massed nearly their full number of 40,000 cavalry for an attack on Antonius' army. Plutarch not only presents us the size of the Parthian force, but also the informs us that Phraates himself was in the vicinity but did not actually lead his army into battle. They attacked the Roman army as it was climbing down from a height, as related by Plutarch and Dio:

> 'However, as the Romans were descending some steep hills, the Parthians attacked them and shot at them as they slowly moved along. Then the shield-bearers wheeled about, enclosing the lighter armed troops within their ranks, while they themselves dropped on one knee and held their shields out before them. The second rank held their shields out over the heads of the first, and the next rank likewise. The resulting appearance is very like that of a roof,

affords a striking spectacle, and is the most effective of protections against arrows, which glide off from it. The Parthians, however, thinking that the Romans dropping on one knee was a sign of fatigue and exhaustion, laid aside their bows, grasped their spears by the middle and came to close quarters. But the Romans, with a full battle cry, suddenly sprang up, and thrusting with their javelins slew the foremost of the Parthians and put all the rest to rout.'[9]

'One day, when they fell into an ambush and were being struck by dense showers of arrows, they suddenly formed the testudo by joining their shields, and rested their left knees on the ground. The barbarians, who had never seen anything of the kind before, thought that they had fallen from their wounds and needed only one finishing blow; so, they threw aside their bows, leaped from their horses, and drawing their daggers, came up close to put an end to them. At this the Romans sprang to their feet, extended their battle-line at the word of command, and confronting the foe face to face, fell upon them, each one upon the man nearest him, and cut down great numbers, since they were contending in full armour against unprotected men, men prepared against men off their guard, heavy infantry against archers, Romans against barbarians. All the survivors immediately retired, and no one followed them thereafter.'[10]

Antonius had his first victory of the retreat, thanks to the Roman tactic of using the *testudo* (tortoise). Not only did this protect the Romans from the Parthian arrows, but apparently, as they hadn't seen it before, it fooled the Parthian cavalry into putting aside their bows and attacking at close quarters, which brought them face-to-face in combat with the better-equipped and trained Roman legionaries. For the first time in this whole year's warfare, the Romans and Parthians fought at close quarters, which concluded with a Roman victory. Dio continues his narrative with a description of the Roman *testudo*, which is worth quoting in full:

'This testudo and the way in which it is formed are as follows. The baggage animals, the light-armed troops, and the cavalry are placed in the centre of the army. The heavy-armed troops who use the oblong, curved, and cylindrical shields are drawn up around the outside, making a rectangular figure; and, facing outward and holding their arms at the ready, they enclose the rest. The others, who have flat shields, form a compact body in the centre and raise their shields over the heads of all the others, so that nothing but shields can be seen in every part of the phalanx alike and all the men by the density of the formation are under shelter from missiles. Indeed, it is so marvellously strong that men can walk upon it, and whenever they come to a narrow ravine, even horses and vehicles can be driven over it. Such is the plan of this formation, and for this reason it has received the name testudo, with reference both to its strength and to the excellent shelter it affords. They use it in two ways: either they approach some fort to assault it, often even enabling men to scale the very walls, or sometimes, when they are surrounded by archers, they all crouch together, even the horses being taught to kneel or lie down, and thereby cause the foe to think that they are exhausted; then, when the enemy draws near, they suddenly rise and throw them into consternation.'[11]

It is interesting to speculate upon why Antonius had not used the tactic before during the retreat. Perhaps we can see it as a response to the failure of Gallus' tactics the previous day: if attack hadn't worked, then try defence. With an additional 5,000 wounded, more defensive tactics would certainly have been called for.

6. A March of Attrition (Day 10 onwards)

The Battle of the Testudo seems to have swung the momentum back in Antonius' favour. We are not told the number of Parthian casualties – which must only have been recorded by the Parthians themselves – yet it could easily have been in the region of several thousand. Nevertheless, with an army of 40,000 cavalry at his disposal, Phraates was far from defeated. What this battle did prove to both sides was that neither could defeat the other, with the retreat seemingly evolving into a regular pattern. Plutarch reports that there were further Parthian attacks, but that they were all met in a similar manner, with the Romans adopting a *testudo*: 'This happened also on the following days as the Romans, little by little, proceeded on their way.'[12]

On these occasions, and now familiar with the tactic, the Parthians did not fall into the same trap of engaging the Romans at close quarters, and so would attack, shower them with arrows, and then break off. However, if Antonius had found a formula to negate the Parthian attacks, he still had to contend with the twin issues of hunger and disease, with the army carrying an increasing number of wounded. Plutarch provides a description of the hardships the Romans faced:

'Famine also attacked the army, which could provide itself with little grain even by fighting and was not well furnished with implements for grinding. These had been abandoned, for the most part, since some of the beasts of burden died, and the others had to carry the sick and wounded.

'Resorting, therefore, to vegetables and roots, they could find few to which they were accustomed, and were compelled to make trial of some never tasted before. Thus, it was that they partook of a herb which produced madness, and then death. He who ate of it had no memory, and no thought of anything else than the one task of moving or turning every stone, as if he were accomplishing something of great importance. The plain was full of men stooping to the ground and digging around the stones or removing them; and finally, they would vomit bile and die, since the only remedy, wine, was not to be had. Many perished thus, and the Parthians would not desist, and Antonius, as we are told, would often cry: "O the Ten Thousand!" thereby expressing his admiration of Xenophon's army, which made an even longer march to the sea from Babylon, and fought with many times as many enemies, and yet came off safe.'[13]

7. Ambush and Treachery

Having failed to defeat the Romans by force of arms, it seems that Phraates fell back on his tried and trusted tactic of deception. Up until now the Romans, advised by the Mardian guide, had stuck to the mountainous routes and avoided the open plains, negating the strengths of the Parthian cavalry. It seems that Phraates now came up with a ploy designed to draw the Roman army out of the mountains and into the plains, giving him one last chance to destroy the Romans before they made the relative safety of Armenia. To do this he needed to convince the Romans that he posed them no further threat:

> 'And now the Parthians, unable to throw the army into confusion or break up its array, but many times already defeated and put to flight, began once more to mingle peaceably with the men who went out in search of fodder or grain, and pointing to their unstrung bows would say that they themselves were going back, and that this was the end of their retaliation, although a few Medes would still follow the Romans one or two days' march, not molesting them at all, but merely protecting the more outlying villages. To these words they added greetings and acts of friendliness, so that once more the Romans became full of courage, and Antonius, when he heard about it, was more inclined to seek the plains, since the way through the mountains was said to be waterless.'[14]

'Phraates clearly hoped to play on Antonius' lack of patience and desire to reach the safety of Armenia, convincing him that the Parthians had given up on the war and wanted nothing more than to see him leave Media. Whether Antonius would have fallen for this we will never know, but Phraates' plan was undermined by the continued rivalries at the Parthian court, with the Parthian noble Monaeses entering the stage once more:

> 'But as he was about to do this, there came a man to the camp from the enemy, Mithridates by name, a cousin of the Monaeses who had been with Antonius and had received the three cities as a gift. Mithridates asked that someone should come to him who could speak the Parthian or Syrian language. So, Alexander of Antioch came to him, being a close friend of Antonius, whereupon Mithridates, after explaining who he was, and attributing to Monaeses the favour now to be shown, asked Alexander if he saw a range of lofty hills on beyond. Alexander said he did see them. "Under those hills," said Mithridates, "the Parthians with all their forces are lying in ambush for you. For the great plains adjoin these hills, and they expect that you will be beguiled by them into turning in that direction and leaving the road through the mountains. That road, it is true, involves thirst and hard labour, to which you are

now accustomed; but if Antonius proceeds by way of the plains, let him know that the fate of Crassus awaits him.'"[15]

Monaeses was able to warn Antonius that it was a Parthian ambush. He would have had to be back in the Parthian king's favour to have this knowledge, and this probably does place him as being with the Parthian army. Though he seems to have been reconciled to Phraates, he clearly believed that this was not part of a change of heart by Phraates, but was borne out of the necessity of having a united front in the face of a Roman invasion. Had Phraates' plan succeeded, with the Roman army destroyed, then Phraates would have nothing to curb his natural – and bloody – instincts. It was in Monaeses' best interests that the Romans were not destroyed, and thus he courted both sides simultaneously. Having consulted with his Mardian guide and receiving similar advice, Antonius abandoned any notion of marching through the plains and stuck to the harder mountainous route for his army:

'After giving this information the man went away, and Antonius, who was much troubled by what he now heard, called together his friends and his Mardian guide, who was himself of the same opinion as their visitor. For he knew that even were there no enemy the lack of roads through the plains would involve them in blind and grievous wanderings, and he showed them that the rough road through the mountains had no other annoyance than lack of water for a single day. Accordingly, Antonius took this route and led his army along by night, after ordering his men to carry water with them.'[16]

Having realized that the deception had failed, the Parthian army set off into the mountains after the Romans, seemingly determined to bring them to battle:

'But word was at once brought to the Parthians that Antonius was advancing, and contrary to their custom they set out in pursuit while it was yet night. Just as the sun was rising, they came up with the rear-guard of the Romans, which was exhausted with sleeplessness and toil; for they had accomplished two hundred and forty furlongs in the night. Moreover, they did not expect that the enemy would come upon them so quickly and were therefore disheartened.'[17]

It seems the Parthian advance guard was able to surprise the Roman rearguard, and a skirmish followed. However, when the main Roman army was brought back, the Parthians withdrew, unwilling to fight the Romans at close quarters:

'[Antonius] called his men back from fighting and gave the signal for pitching the tents, that the soldiers might at least enjoy the shade a little. Accordingly, the Romans went to pitching their tents, and the Parthians, as their custom was, at once began to withdraw.'[18]

It was at this point that Monaeses tipped off Antonius once more about Parthian intentions, via his agent/cousin:

'At this point Mithridates came again, and after Alexander had joined him, he advised Antonius to let the army rest only a little while, and then to get it under way and hasten to the river, assuring him that the Parthians would not cross it, but would continue the pursuit until they reached it. This message was carried to Antonius by Alexander, who then brought out from Antonius golden drinking-cups in great numbers, as well as bowls. Mithridates took as many of these as he could hide in his garments and rode off. Then, while it was still day, they broke camp and proceeded on their march.'[19]

Thus, again duly warned of the Parthian plans, the Roman army set off once more for the distant river and what they hoped was safety. Unfortunately for Antonius, his army suffered an outbreak of indiscipline that night, caused seemingly by the gifts that Antonius had given to Mithridates. It appears that seeing a Parthian agent being given golden trinkets, whilst they had received nothing from the campaign, was the last straw for an unknown number of Antonius' soldiers, who attacked, robbed and killed anyone they could find who was carrying valuables, even attacking their own baggage train:

'The enemy did not molest them, but they themselves made that night of all other nights the most grievous and fearful for themselves. For those who had gold or silver were slain and robbed of it, and the goods were plundered from the beasts of burden; and finally, the baggage-carriers of Antonius were attacked, and beakers and costly tables were cut to pieces or distributed about.

'And now, since there was great confusion and straggling throughout the whole army (for they thought that the enemy had fallen upon them and routed and dispersed them), Antonius called one of the freedmen in his body-guard, Rhamnus by name, and made him take oath that, at the word of command, he would thrust his sword through him and cut off his head, that he might neither be taken alive by the enemy nor recognized when he was dead.'[20]

The Roman army collapsed into indiscipline, murder and chaos, apparently brought about by the growing sense of injustice amongst the rank and file at having received so little reward from a campaign that had promised so much, along with the apparent closeness of safety. However, it seems that order was soon restored, especially once it was determined that there was no Parthian attack. Fortunately for the Romans, the Parthians were not made aware of this collapse into indiscipline, otherwise they would have surely taken advantage and pressed home an attack. Nevertheless, this incident does show the near state of collapse that Antonius' retreating army was in.

8. The Final Battle (Days 21–27)

With the Romans preparing to cross the river, the Parthians had time for one last attack, clearly hoping to take advantage of any disruption this operation caused to the Roman army:

'Day was already dawning, and the army was beginning to assume a certain order and tranquillity, when the arrows of the Parthians fell upon the rear ranks, and the light-armed troops were ordered by signal to engage. The men at arms, too, again covered each other over with their shields, as they had done before, and so withstood their assailants, who did not venture to come to close quarters. The front ranks advanced little by little in this manner, and the river came in sight. On its bank Antonius drew up his sick and disabled soldiers across first. And presently even those who were fighting had a chance to drink at their ease; for when the Parthians saw the river, they unstrung their bows and bade the Romans cross over with good courage, bestowing much praise also upon their valour. So, they crossed without being disturbed and regrouped themselves, and then resumed their march, putting no confidence at all in the Parthians.'[21]

Surprisingly, we are not told why the Parthians made such an arbitrary decision not to pursue the Roman army beyond this unnamed river. The decision must have been taken and agreed some days before, in order for Monaeses and Mithridates to be able to betray this fact to the Romans. In terms of location, all we know is that it was some six days' march away from the Median border with Armenia. The decision can perhaps be interpreted as a sign of dissension within the Parthian ranks. Militarily, it seems that they were now convinced that they could not defeat the Romans in close combat, as the 'Battle of the Testudo' had ably demonstrated. Furthermore, Phraates' plan to lure the Romans into the plains had failed, so there must have been many in the Parthian command who had come to the conclusion that it was time to give up on the pursuit and accept the escape of the Roman army. Ultimately, we must assume that the decision had been ratified by Phraates himself, unless he was once again losing control of the Parthian nobility.

Plutarch continues with the final few days of the Roman retreat from Media:

'And on the sixth day after their last battle with them they came to the river Araxes, which forms the boundary between Media and Armenia. Its depth and violence made it seem difficult of passage; and a report was rife that the enemy were lying in ambush there and would attack them as they tried to cross. But after they were safely on the other side and had set foot in Armenia, as if they had just caught sight of that land from the sea, they saluted it and fell to weeping and embracing one another for joy. But as they advanced through the country, which was prosperous, and enjoyed all things in abundance after great scarcity, they fell sick with dropsies and dysenteries.'[22]

9. The Aftermath – The Retreat from Armenia

Thus ended one of the most epic military retreats in history, certainly one on a par with the retreat of the Spartan 10,000 recorded by Xenophon. We must assume that accounts of the retreat were written, but given that it was a disastrous Roman campaign and the fact that it was led by Antonius – soon to be vilified in Roman history – these never received the widespread acclaim as that of Xenophon. Plutarch provides a summary which show the Roman losses from the campaign:

> 'There Antonius held a review of his troops and found that twenty thousand of the infantry and four thousand of the cavalry had perished, not all at the hands of the enemy, but more than half by disease. They had, indeed, marched twenty-seven days from Phraata, and had defeated the Parthians in eighteen battles, but their victories were not complete or lasting because the pursuits which they made were short and ineffectual.'[23]

The retreat had lasted for twenty-seven days, during which the Romans fought numerous battles or skirmishes against the Parthians, all the time whilst dealing with hunger, thirst and disease, resulting in some 24,000 dead. Yet the Romans had only reached the territory of Armenia, their erstwhile ally, not Roman territory proper, and Plutarch reports that many in the army wanted to regroup and attack the Armenian King Artavasdes for his treachery in retreating unilaterally following the destruction of the Roman siege train. Yet given the state of the Roman army, it clearly was in no condition to fight a fresh campaign and continue to fight its way through Armenia.

Artavasdes must have been in something of a quandary. Having deserted Antonius, he must have been hoping that the Parthians would 'finish the job' and ensure that Antonius never returned from Parthia. Unfortunately for him, Antonius emerged from Parthia with a reduced and battered Roman army, but still one capable of defeating his forces should he attempt to complete what the Parthians had started. He therefore had to allow the Romans to pass through Armenia unmolested and must have acquiesced to the Roman army seizing supplies as it did so. He must also have known that once the Romans had retreated from Armenia there would be a reckoning for his treachery, though perhaps he thought he could bargain or pay his way out of any retribution. If he made that assumption, later events proved him to be terribly wrong. Yet as Plutarch points out, although the Roman army was free from military attack and would have been able to forage and pillage the Armenian towns and villages, the continued retreat was not without its hardships and dangers:

'But now, hastening on through much wintry weather, which was already at hand, and incessant snow-storms, he lost eight thousand men on the march. He himself, however, went down with a small company to the sea, and in a little place between Berytus and Sidon, called White Village, he waited for Cleopatra to come; and since she was slow in coming he was beside himself with distress, promptly resorting to drinking and intoxication, although he could not hold out long at table, but in the midst of the drinking would often rise or spring up to look out, until she put into port, bringing an abundance of clothing and money for the soldiers. There are some, however, who say that he received the clothing from Cleopatra, but took the money from his own private funds, and distributed it as a gift from her.'[24]

The final death toll from the retreat was some 32,000 men. The remnants of the army wintered in a port and were resupplied from Ptolemaic Egypt. The campaign of 36 BC had thus ended with the remnants of the Roman army reaching safe territory again, having suffered a disastrous campaign and harrowing retreat.

Summary

Although the campaign had been a disaster for Antonius and a clear Parthian victory, it was not one that would determine the outcome of the war itself.[25] Unlike the Carrhae campaign, the bulk of the Roman army had successfully withdrawn back into Syria and the Roman commander, who controlled the whole of the Eastern Republic and its allies, was still alive. For the war to end, Phraates needed to remove Antonius, and in this he had failed. As Antonius had so publicly demonstrated, with the wealth of Egypt behind him and the manpower resources of the Eastern Republic and its allies, he could soon rebuild his army and launch a fresh invasion.

The retreat had shown both the strengths and weaknesses of the Parthians. Whilst they were able to inflict heavy casualties on the retreating Roman army, they did not have the military capability to destroy it. Notable victories came only through surprise attacks and poor Roman tactics. However, once the Romans were fully committed to a defensive strategy, as exemplified by the use of the *testudo*, then they were able to withstand the Parthian attacks and inflict serious casualties on them. Furthermore, although Antonius had suffered the treachery of his Armenian allies, Phraates' campaign had been undermined at the end, when Antonius looked like he would escape, by treachery from within his own noble command staff, in the form of Monaeses and probably others.

The year 36 BC closed with a stalemate in the East. Antonius had been bloodied but not beaten. We cannot help but contrast this to the situation in the Western Republic, where the civil war between the Triumvirs and the Pompeian faction had reached a decisive conclusion. Under command of M. Vipsanius Agrippa, the Triumviral forces had defeated those of Sex. Pompeius and recaptured the island of Sicily, forcing Pompeius to flee to the East (and Antonius).

Octavianus, thanks to his able general, had now established complete control of the Western Republic, having also double-crossed his Triumviral colleague M. Aemilius Lepidus, who found himself without political position or military forces, although he maintained his religious position of Pontifex Maximus. Ironically, Rome now had only two Triumvirs: one (Octavianus) who was now master of the Western Republic and the other (Antonius) who had just suffered a defeat at the hands of a powerful rival and was stuck in a seemingly unwinnable war.

Section IV

Stalemate (36–30 BC)

Chapter Nine

Consolidation and Civil War (36–35 BC)

1. Re-establishing Control of the Eastern Republic

For Antonius, the winter of 36/35 BC gave him a chance to regroup, regain control over the Eastern Republic and reconsider his strategy. Although Octavianus had been victorious in the West, relations between the two men were still cordial and the Western Republic itself was still recovering from seven years of warfare and food shortages. Octavianus would need time to rebuild the West. He chose to channel his military energies into consolidating and expanding Rome's empire in the West with a war of conquest in Illyria to secure his eastern flank. Furthermore, the two Triumvirs were still tied by a bond of marriage – Antonius having married Octavianus' sister – so a lull in the civil wars fell over the whole Roman Republic.

This would have provided Antonius with the time he needed to reassert his control of the Eastern Republic and regain the initiative. His powerbase was still a strong one as he had the whole resources of Rome's eastern provinces and their allies to call on; the richest in the ancient world. Although his invasion of Parthia had been a disaster, he had extricated three-quarters of his army and shown that the Parthians could be beaten in close combat.

Furthermore, there was no danger of a renewed Parthian invasion. Despite beating off the Roman attack on Parthia, Phraates had seen all too readily that engaging the Romans at close quarters could easily lead to defeat. The Parthian victories had come when they struck fast and hard, using their superior cavalry numbers, and usually when they had numerical superiority, notably with the destruction of the two legions of Oppius Statianus. Phraates, though he had fought an excellent defensive campaign, was not cut from the same cloth as his older brother Pacorus. He also had more pressing concerns in Parthia, such as keeping his throne secure and suppressing internal dissension brought about by his bloody accession to it. Whilst it seems that Antonius' invasion of Parthia had temporarily united the Parthian ruling elites, the removal of this immediate Roman threat would clearly test this solidarity. Thus, even though Phraates had clearly won the previous campaign it was his position, not that of Antonius, which seemed the weaker.

Yet Antonius was potentially facing enemies on two fronts. To the east was the Parthian Empire, with which he was at war, albeit with both sides taking stock after suffering defeated invasions. To the north-east lay the Kingdom of Armenia, nominally a Roman ally, but one which seems to have thrown off its pro-Roman stance and adopted a position of neutrality, supporting neither side. To the west lay the Western Roman Republic led by Antonius' Triumviral colleague, Caesar Octavianus, who after eight years had finally united the region under his rule. The remnants of the Pompeian faction had been driven out of the Western Republic and were sailing eastwards, possibly bringing the civil war with them. Given this potential dual threat, Antonius took a number of measures to secure his control of the Eastern Republic.

With Antonius wintering on the Syrian coast and then making his way to Alexandria, he ensured that he had a group of competent commanders distributed about the Eastern Republic. On the eastern frontier was P. Canidius Crassus, perhaps the most capable general under his command, who had subdued Armenia in 37 BC. We have no record of him holding a formal governorship, but he seems to have been stationed with a portion of the Roman army on the Romano-Parthian frontier, presumably to head off or deter any renewed Parthian invasion, however unlikely. Such a move would be prudent from an Armenian point of view as well as a Parthian one, given that Artavasdes II was now proving to be an unreliable ally. Further to the south, command of Syria fell to another experienced commander, M. Munatius Plancus, one of the Consuls of 42 BC. Antonius seems to have appointed a certain Q. Dellius as special envoy to the Judean court, to represent his interests with the newly appointed Herodian monarchy.

Further to the north-west, command of the Roman provinces of Bithynia and Pontus were still under the control of another long-standing commander, Cn. Domitius Ahenobarbus, who had been governor there since 40 BC and had accompanied Antonius on his invasion of Parthia. Ahenobarbus now resumed his rule of these provinces, securing Anatolia. Further east came C. Furnius, governor of Asia, whilst Greece and Macedonia were commanded by an unknown Antonine governor.

2. The Reorganization of the East – 36/35 BC

Having re-secured his grip on the Roman provinces of the Eastern Republic, Antonius turned his attentions to the client kingdoms of the East, undertaking a wholesale reorganization. Given his role as a Triumvir, it was within his powers to deal with the rulers of the client kingdoms in the region as he saw fit, although these acts would eventually need ratification by the Senate and People of Rome. There is much uncertainty over the timings of this reorganisation, but Dio clearly places it after Antonius' return from the failed invasion of Parthia and thus places it in late 37 or early 36 BC. This seems to be a sensible time for the reorganisation of the client kingdoms, given Antonius' issues with the loyalty of the King of Armenia and his need to reassert his control of the Eastern Republic.

The first stage of this restructuring was to appoint a new King of Galatia (see Map 4). The kingdom, a long-standing Roman ally, had been ruled since 63 BC by its king, Deiotarus, who had been able to keep his crown by successfully changing sides in the various conflicts which made up the Third Roman Civil War, but died c.40 BC of old age and apparently without a legitimate successor. In his place Antonius elevated the son of Deiotarus' former co-ruler, Brogitarius, a man named Amyntas, to be the new king. Amyntas had been a long-standing ally of Antonius ever since changing sides from the Brutus-Cassian faction before the Battles of Philippi, whilst in command of a Galatian army. Thus, Antonius elevated to kingship a long-standing ally and a man he could trust. He extended the territories of Galatia by adding the regions of Lycaonia and parts of Pamphylia.

In Cappadocia however, Antonius went one stage further and actually overthrew the serving king, Ariarathes X, and the ruling dynasty. There are no surviving sources which inform us why Antonius did so and, according to Valerius Maximus, had him executed,[1] but he clearly came to suspect his loyalty and that of his family. Cappadocia joined Judea in being client kingdoms whose ruling dynasties were overthrown by Antonius. In his place he elevated a man named Archelaus, whom Dio discusses thus: 'This Archelaus belonged on his father's side to those Archelauses who had contended against the Romans, but on his mother's side was the son of Glaphyra, a courtesan.'[2]

By mentioning Archelaus' mother's profession, Dio was drawing a link to the reason he was appointed by Antonius. The fame of Glaphyra is such that she is mentioned by both Appian and Martial as being a woman who attracted Antonius' favour, with the former stating:

'In Cappadocia, for example, between Ariarathes and Sisina [Archelaus], awarding the Kingdom to Sisina, on account of his mother, Glaphyra, who struck him as a beautiful woman.'[3]

It has been argued that it was Glaphyra who was the architect of this move, acting as a woman determined to rule through her son.[4] Given the few surviving sources we have, we will never know the full story behind this decision, but the outcome was clear: another native dynasty had been overthrown and replaced with a new one loyal to Antonius himself.

Antonius' reorganisation not only concerned the major kingdoms in the region, as Dio provides us with the example of Lysanias, ruler of a small kingdom near Mount Hermon, between Syria and Judea. According to Dio, Antonius had previously elevated this man to rule the region, but now had him executed for suspected collusion with the Parthians: 'In the districts both of Malchus and of the Ituraeans, for he executed Lysanias, whom he himself had made king over them, on the charge that he had favoured Pacorus.'[5]

Thus, we can see that Antonius, in the wake of the failed invasion of Parthia and the betrayal of the King of Armenia, engaged in a wholescale reorganisation of the client kingdoms of the East in an attempt to ensure their loyalty to him personally. No doubt there will have been other examples which have not survived in our few remaining sources. Antonius also seems to have given some of the territory confiscated from these kings to his own children, pre-empting a more famous distribution of territories still to come (see Chapter Ten).[6]

As their recent history had shown, these client kings, regardless of who put them on their thrones, needed to have flexible loyalties when it came to both the Romans and the Parthians. Many had only survived by professing loyalty to whichever power had the nearest army, be it Roman or Parthian, and would continue to do so. History proved this to be the case, as both Amyntas and Archelaus outlasted Antonius' rule in the East and found accommodation with the new regime, though ultimately for nought. In both cases, upon their deaths, their kingdoms were annexed by Rome (in 25 BC and AD 17 respectively).[7]

The one client king which Antonius had not yet dethroned for his disloyalty was Artavasdes, the King of Armenia, who had deserted Antonius at the siege of Praaspa. However, he was not as defenceless as those whose kingdoms lay within Roman territory and it would need a military campaign to remove him.

3. Antonine Propaganda and Relations with Rome

With his provinces militarily secured, Antonius took steps to try to secure his political position in Rome, the ultimate source of his political power. To those ends, he sent dispatches to the Senate and People concerning his expedition into Parthia, but apparently concealing the nature of his reversals and losses. However, this seems to have met with little success as word of the retreat reached Rome anyway, no doubt spread by stories from the survivors to their relatives in Rome:

'The Romans at home were not ignorant of anything that had taken place, not because he told them the truth in his dispatches (for he concealed all his reverses and in fact described some of them as just the opposite, making it appear that he was meeting with success), but because rumour reported the truth and Caesar and those with him investigated it carefully and discussed it. They did not, however, yet expose the situation to the public, but instead offered sacrifices and held festivals.'[8]

Officially at least, Antonius' campaign was not acknowledged as the disaster it had been, even though the rumours abounded. This did not put Antonius on the back foot as officially having been defeated by the Parthians, and thus maintained his standing. Whilst Octavianus was taking great pains to be seen to be treating his colleague fairly and not highlighting his military shortcomings, it seems that he was not above making life difficult for Antonius. To that end he encouraged his sister Octavia – Antonius' Roman wife – to head up a delegation from Rome:

> 'For she was bringing a great quantity of clothing for his soldiers, many beasts of burden, and money and gifts for the officers and friends about him; and besides this, two thousand picked soldiers equipped as praetorian cohorts with splendid armour. These things were announced to Antonius by a certain Niger, a friend of his who had been sent from Octavia, and he added such praises of her as was fitting and deserved.'[9]

Although the fresh forces, provisions and monies would be a welcome sight, that of his Roman wife was another matter. Their marriage, like most Roman aristocratic ones, was a political alliance, but unlike most, Antonius had also married the Egyptian Pharaoh Cleopatra and had three children with her. Whilst the latter marriage had no standing in Roman law, it did leave him vulnerable in the eyes of Roman public (and Senatorial) opinion on two fronts. Firstly, it allowed rumours to spread that he was being manipulated by a 'foreign' ruler. Secondly, it was an insult to his Roman wife and her family, and in this case her brother, none other than Caesar Octavianus himself. Plutarch reports both factors at some length, and Antonius had to order his wife to progress no further than Athens, to ensure that his two wives did not meet and matters escalate:

> 'But at Rome Octavia was desirous of sailing to Antonius, and Caesar gave her permission to do so, as the majority say, not as a favour to her, but in order that, in case she were neglected and treated with scorn, he might have plausible ground for war. When Octavia arrived at Athens, she received letters from Antonius in which he bade her remain there and told her of his expedition.'[10]

Barring Octavia from the East seemed to be the lesser of two evils for Antonius; better than her meeting Cleopatra. Aside from the personal aspect, each of his wives represented a key pillar of his powerbase. Whilst technically his command of the Eastern Republic came from a grant of power from the People and endorsed by the Senate, his position in Rome greatly depended upon his alliance with Octavianus, due to the latter's proximity to the Senate and Assemblies. Key to this alliance was Octavianus' sister, as a public symbol of their association. However, his powerbase in the East greatly depended on the ability to tap into the resources of Ptolemaic Egypt, commanded by Cleopatra. Antonius' current position depended on balancing both wives and ensuring no offence or public affront was given to either. His two wives represented the dual and increasingly complicated nature of his current position: both Roman commander (and Triumvir) and eastern (Ptolemaic) ruler in his own right. Antonius must have realised that sooner or later he would not be able to maintain this balancing act and would have to choose one role or the other.

4. Civil War Reignited – Pompeius and Antonius

In the short term his balancing act continued and peace was maintained with his Triumviral colleague in the West. However, a new threat emerged from the West, and one which Octavianus had a hand in. In ending the civil war in the Western Republic, Octavianus had defeated Pompeius and finally captured his powerbase of Sicily. Yet he had not captured the man himself, who was now forced to flee to the East, the powerbase of his deceased father, now controlled by Antonius. Octavianus had thereby achieved a bonus; not only had he secured control of the Western Republic, but he had sent his rival in the East a problem which he would need to deal with.

It is only Appian who provides any detail on Pompeius' activities in the East and the brief ignition of a fresh civil war. Here we can see the complexities of the various shifting factions and powerbases at play in the Mediterranean. At face value, Pompeius was an enemy of the Triumvirate and so, being an enemy of Octavianus, should have been one of Antonius. Yet as we have seen, Antonius and Octavianus were at best temporary allies, having gone to war with each other on at least two separate occasions (43 and 41/40 BC). As Appian points out, Pompeius may have expected a friendlier welcome in the Roman East, especially given his role as son of Pompeius Magnus, former patron of the region. However, Antonius was now at war with the Parthians, who, having lost Labienus, would possibly be amenable to gaining a new Roman ally. So Pompeius arrived in the East with various opportunities:

> 'Pompeius, fleeing from Sicily to Antonius, stopped at the Lacinian promontory and robbed the rich temple of Juno of its gifts. He landed at Mitylene and spent some time at that place, where his father, when at war with Caesar, had bestowed him with his mother, while still a boy, and after his defeat had joined him again. As Antonius was now waging war in Media against the Medes and the Parthians, Pompeius decided to entrust himself to Antonius on his return. When he heard that Antonius had been beaten, and this result was more than confirmed by reports, his hopes were once more revived, and he fancied that he might succeed Antonius if the latter were dead or share his power if he returned. He was continually thinking of Labienus, who had overrun Asia not long before.
>
> 'While he was in this frame of mind the news reached him that Antonius had returned to Alexandria. Scheming for both objects, he sent ambassadors to Antonius ostensibly to place himself at the latter's disposal and to offer himself as a friend and ally, but really to get accurate information about Antonius' affairs. At the same time, he sent others secretly to the princes of Thrace and Pontus, intending, if he should not obtain what he desired from Antonius, to take flight through Pontus to Armenia. He sent also to the Parthians, hoping that, for the remainder of their war against Antonius, they would be eager to receive him as a general, because he was a Roman, and especially because he was the son of Pompeius the Great. He refitted his ships and drilled the soldiers he had brought in them, pretending at one time that he was in fear of Octavianus, and at another that he was getting ready to assist Antonius.'[11]

Appian here sums up the various permutations which offered themselves to Pompeius: alliance with Antonius, alliance with the less pro-Roman client kingdoms (Thrace, Pontus and Armenia) or alliance with Parthia against Antonius. Antonius too faced a dilemma. On the one hand Pompeius was a dangerous enemy, not only because of his war with Octavianus, but more importantly his connections to the East and the danger that he too could ally with Parthia and undermine Antonius' control of the Eastern Republic, from within and without. As we have seen, Antonius had good cause to suspect the loyalties of many in the Eastern Republic, even without the arrival of a new and charismatic figurehead.

Wintering in Alexandria, news reached Antonius that Pompeius and his small fleet had entered the waters of the Eastern Republic. In response, he assigned M. Titius to command a fleet to intercept him, whilst keeping an open mind about the latter's intentions:

'He [Antonius] ordered the latter to take ships and soldiers from Syria and to wage war vigorously against Pompeius if he showed himself hostile, but to treat him with honour if he submitted himself to Antonius.'[12]

If nothing else, Antonius had to divert resources away from the war in the East to ensure that another one did not break out on his western flank. This clearly showed that Antonius had not made up him mind whether to treat Pompeius as a valuable ally in a fight with Octavianus or a dangerous enemy in a war with Parthia. Pompeius, it seems, kept his options firmly open and sent messengers to both the Alexandrian and Parthian courts, expressing friendship and offering his services. Appian preserves what purports to be their message to Antonius, though as always, we must question whether their words are accurate. However, even if these were not the actual words, we can assume that the tone and arguments they used were authentic. The message they brought was that Pompeius was presenting himself as an ally against the rise of a tyrant in the West, none other than Octavianus Caesar:

'You [Antonius] are now the only remaining one who stands between him and the monarchy that he longs for: indeed, he would already have been at blows with you, had not Pompeius stood in the way.'[13]

Pompeius offered himself as an ally for Antonius in the upcoming conflict with Octavianus, which many in the Republic would have been predicting and even offering Antonius a narrative for the war: preventing Octavianus from becoming a tyrant. Unfortunately for Pompeius his messengers to the Parthian court were captured by Antonius' men – though by what means we are not told – and also brought to the Alexandrian court, presumably along with their message of friendship and offer of services to the Parthians.

We must assume that Antonius was not shocked by this, and that both men continued to dance round each other. Even though Antonius had the stronger position and clearly realized the danger that Pompeius could cause him, this had to be weighed against the use that Pompeius could be, both in reconciling the provinces and kingdoms of the East to his rule and in any future war in the West. If the two men united, it would look as though it was a war to prevent a tyranny from being established in the Western Republic rather than just a falling out amongst Caesarean Triumvirs.

However, this lack of clarity from Antonius over whether Pompeius was an ally or an enemy created uncertainty amongst his own commanders, presenting an opportunity for Pompeius. With Titus not yet having reached the western edges of the Eastern Republic, Pompeius was allowed to make landfall, along with his forces, in the province of Asia, governed by the Antonine commander C. Furnius:

> 'In the meantime, Furnius, who was governing the province of Asia for Antonius, had received Pompeius when he arrived, as he was behaving quietly; since Furnius had not sufficient force to prevent him and did not yet know Antonius' mind. Seeing Pompeius drilling his troops, he mustered a force from the provincials and hastily summoned Ahenobarbus, who had command of an army in the vicinity, and also Amyntas from the other side. They responded promptly, and Pompeius complained against Furnius for regarding him in the light of an enemy when he had sent ambassadors to Antonius and was waiting for an answer from him.'[14]

Without clear orders, Furnius had to call on Ahenobarbus, who was governing the Roman province of Bithynia and Pontus, and the newly appointed King of Galatia to supply forces to match those of Pompeius. But despite having mustered an army, they could not use it against Pompeius without explicit instruction from Antonius, or even Titius, ceding the initiative further to Pompeius. Seeing a build-up of Antonine forces against him, Pompeius chose to negotiate from a position of strength and set about entrenching his position in Asia, first by treachery and then by force:

> 'While he [Pompeius] was saying this, he was meditating the project of seizing Ahenobarbus, with the connivance of Curius, one of Ahenobarbus' officers, intending to hold that general as a valuable hostage to exchange for himself in case of need. The treachery was discovered and Curius was convicted before the Romans present and put to death. Pompeius put to death his freedman Theodorus, the only person who was privy to the plan, believing that he had divulged it. As he no longer expected to conceal his projects from Furnius, he possessed himself of Lampsacus by treachery, a city which contained many Italians, placed there as colonists by Iulius Caesar. These Italians he induced to enter his military service by large bounties. Having now two hundred horse and three legions of infantry, he attacked Cyzicus by land and sea. He was repulsed on both sides, because Antonius had a force, although not a large one, in Cyzicus, that was guarding some gladiators whom Antonius supported there. So Pompeius retired to the harbour of the Achaeans and collected provisions.'[15]

In a short space of time, and exploiting the indecision of the Antonine forces, Pompeius had recruited a sizeable army and started seizing territory for himself. Antonius soon found that in addition to his ongoing war with Parthia to the east, he now had an escalating civil war in the west of his territories.

5. The Battle of the Scamandrian Plain (36 BC)

Even with overtly hostile acts being perpetrated by Pompeius, the Antonine forces were still seemingly handicapped by not knowing the wishes of Antonius, in a manner similar to that experienced in 41 BC during the civil war between Octavianus and L. Antonius.[16] All Furnius felt he was able to do was to use this combined Bithynian/Galatian force to shadow and harry Pompeius where he could. Again, though, this ensured that Pompeius had the initiative, and he chose to use it by attacking Furnius' force:

> 'Furnius did not begin hostilities, but he continually camped alongside of Pompeius with a large body of horse and prevented his foe from foraging or winning the cities to his side. As Pompeius had no cavalry, he assaulted the camp of Furnius in front and, at the same time, sent a force secretly around to his rear. Furnius accordingly directed his forces against Pompeius' front attack, but he was driven out of his camp by the force in his rear. Pompeius pursued his men and killed many as they fled over the Scamandrian plain, which was saturated with recent rains. Those who were saved withdrew for the time to a place of safety, as they were not fit for battle.'[17]

The first battle in the renewed civil war between Pompeius and Antonius was a resounding victory for Pompeius. We are not told the casualties on either side, but it is clear that Pompeius had the upper hand in Asia by the end of 36 BC. This was reinforced by a naval victory by Pompeius' fleet over the local forces at the 'Harbour of the Achaeans' on the Asian coast off the Troad.[18] Pompeius, temporarily, had both military and naval superiority in Asia. It seems that the Bithynian/Galatian force of Furnius was not destroyed, but was in no position to openly contest Pompeius.

6. A Question of Resources

Nevertheless, whilst Pompeius held a temporary dominance in Asia, his longer-term position was still a precarious one. Asia, although a rich province, was never known as a stronghold of Roman military power. To the west lay Macedonia and its armies, under the control of Antonius' unnamed governor, whilst to the east lay the Roman powerbases of Syria and Egypt, with the bulk of Rome's eastern forces. Furthermore,

Antonius had dispatched M. Titius with a force to intercept Pompeius, and they were making their way from Syria.

Whilst Pompeius may temporarily have had the largest military force in Asia Minor, unless he could link up with potential allies, he faced being isolated. The greatest possible allies would certainly have been the Parthian Empire, but as we have seen, his earlier emissaries to the Parthian court had been intercepted. Armenia may have been willing to support him, but would not risk sending forces across Roman-controlled Asia Minor, especially with Roman forces on its borders. There may have been other native rulers and peoples who were sympathetic to his cause, but none would rush to support him until he looked like being a clear winner.

Another key problem Pompeius faced was that he had been able to take advantage of the indecision on the part of Antonius' commanders, having no clear orders to oppose him until his intentions were known. Having restarted the civil war, it was now clear that his intentions were hostile and that he could be treated as an enemy to be crushed. Furthermore, his previous strength lay in his navy and his ability to move quickly by sea, but now he was having to pursue a land-based strategy, partly due to his loss of naval superiority after being defeated at Sicily.

Appian highlights another clear military deficiency which Pompeius suffered from, namely a lack of cavalry: 'Pompeius, deficient in cavalry, and thus crippled in procuring supplies.'[19] Pompeius seemed to be suffering from the same problem which Antonius faced in his retreat from Media, namely, how to keep an army provisioned when in hostile territory. We must also assume that the remnants of Furnius' army were still shadowing Pompeius' forces and harrying them whenever they went foraging for supplies. Pompeius also apparently had a plan to secure the services of the fresh cavalry being sent to Antonius from Rome – along with his wife Octavia – but his emissaries carrying the monies were intercepted by the unnamed governor of Macedonia. Given that this was the second time his emissaries had been intercepted whilst on clandestine business, we must question whether Pompeius was suffering from someone leaking information to Antonius.

The beginning of 35 BC saw Pompeius advance from Asia and into Bithynia, capturing the key cities of Nicea and Nicomedia and their resources. However, this proved to be the high point of his campaign as the greater resources of Antonius began to be brought to bear against him, with reinforcements arriving from both the West and the East:

> 'But Furnius, who was camping not far away from him, was reinforced, at the beginning of spring, first with seventy ships that had come from Sicily, which had been saved from those that Antonius had lent to Octavianus against Pompeius; for after the close of the war in Sicily Octavianus had dismissed them. Then Titius arrived from Syria with one hundred and twenty additional ships and a large army; and all these had landed at Proconnesus [the island of Marmara].'[20]

Pompeius now faced two of Antonius' commanders – Furnius and Titius – both of whom had reinforced armies. It was clear that he had lost his naval superiority, and even if he had chosen flight, there were no potential allies to whom he could sail. So he gambled on fighting a land war, destroying the remnants of his fleet:

> 'So Pompeius became alarmed and burned his own ships and armed his oarsmen, believing that he could fight to better advantage with all of his forces combined on land.'[21]

It is possible that Pompeius had in mind a continued march eastward towards either Armenia or Parthia, but he faced a superior Antonine force to his north and west, as well as all the Antonine forces still on the Parthian/Armenian border and in Syria proper. Whilst Pompeius still believed that he could prevail, or at least fight his way to safety, his remaining supporters clearly did not, and soon started to defect to Antonius' side:

> 'Cassius of Parma, Nasidius, Saturninus, Thermus, Antistius, and the other distinguished men of his party who were still with him as friends, and Fannius, who held the highest rank of all, and Pompeius' father-in-law, Libo, when they saw that he did not desist from war against superior forces even after Titius, to whom Antonius had given entire charge, had arrived, despaired of him, and, having made terms for themselves, went over to Antonius.'[22]

7. Unnamed Night Battle

Despite these losses, Pompeius continued his march eastwards, further into Bithynia, which Appian informs us was with the intention of reaching Armenia, and then possibly Parthia. He was pursued by the armies of Furnius and Titius, along with the Galatian King Amyntas. Despite this, Pompeius managed to engineer another victory by attacking his pursuers at night in a surprise raid on their camps:

> 'One night as he marched out of his camp quietly, Furnius and Titius followed him, and Amyntas joined in the pursuit. After a hot chase they came up with him toward evening, and each encamped by himself around a certain hill without ditch or palisade, as it was late, and they were tired. While they were in this state, Pompeius made a night attack with 300 light troops and killed many who were still asleep or springing out of bed. The rest took to disgraceful flight completely naked. It is evident that if Pompeius had made this night attack with his entire army, or if he had followed up energetically the victory he did win, he would have overcome them completely. But, misled by some evil genius, he let slip these opportunities also, and he gained no other advantage from the affair than to penetrate farther into the interior of the country.'[23]

Pompeius was able to put his pursuers to flight, but could not end their pursuit. Appian is being particularly harsh on him here. Had he attacked in larger numbers, then he surely would have alerted his enemies to their presence and thus lost the element of surprise. Furthermore, though we are not given any numbers for the respective armies, Pompeius' forces must have been vastly outnumbered by this point, reducing his ability to do anything more than buy time. However, having retreated further eastwards, his opponents clearly learned their lesson, were able to corner him and began to starve him out:

> 'Titius and Furnius pursued him, and overtaking him at Midaeum in Phrygia, surrounded him.'[24]
> 'His enemies, having formed a junction, followed him and cut him off from supplies, until he was in danger from want. Then

he sought an interview with Furnius, who had been a friend of Pompeius Magnus, and who was of higher rank and of a more trustworthy character than the others.'[25]

This personal connection came to nought, as Furnius followed his orders stating that Titius was Antonius' appointed representative in this matter and not he and that Pompeius should surrender to Titius. Appian adds at this point that Titius had been captured by Pompeius' forces in the civil war in the West and had been spared by him.[26] Faced with the unappetising prospect of surrendering to Titius, Pompeius tried one last stratagem:

> 'When night came Pompeius left the customary fires burning, and the trumpets giving the usual signal at intervals through the night, while he quietly withdrew from the camp with a well-prepared band, who had not previously been advised whither they were to go. He intended to go to the sea-shore and burn Titius' fleet, and perhaps would have done so had not Scaurus deserted from him and communicated the fact of his departure and the road he had taken, although ignorant of his design. Amyntas, with fifteen hundred horse, pursued Pompeius, who had no cavalry. When Amyntas drew near, Pompeius' men passed over to him, some privately, others openly. Pompeius, being almost entirely deserted and afraid of his own men, surrendered himself to Amyntas without conditions, although he had scorned to surrender to Titius with conditions.'[27]

Thus, his final stratagem failed due to treachery from within his dwindling band of supporters, leaving Pompeius with only two options: suicide or surrender. Interestingly, he chose the latter, clearly hoping that he may still be able to come to some arrangement with Antonius. In this, however, he was mistaken, as he was handed over to Antonius' emissary M. Titius, transferred to the city of Miletus and then quietly murdered. At the time, it was far from clear – perhaps deliberately so – who had given the order, and it remains so today:

'This he [Titius] did either on his own account, angry at some former insult, and ungrateful for the subsequent kindness, or in pursuance of Antonius' order. Some say that Plancus, not Antonius, gave this order. They think that Plancus, while governing Syria, was authorised by letters to sign Antonius' name in cases of urgency and to use his seal. Some think that it was written by Plancus with Antonius' knowledge, but that the latter was ashamed to write it on account of the name Pompeius, and because Cleopatra was favourable to him on account of Pompeius Magnus. Others think that Plancus, being cognisant of these facts, took it upon himself to give the order as a matter of precaution, lest Pompeius, with the co-operation of Cleopatra, should disturb the auspicious respect between Antonius and Octavianus.'[28]

Ultimately Antonius would not have been aggrieved to see the back of Pompeius, who was a clear threat to his control of the Eastern Republic and his war against the Parthians. He may have been useful in the longer term in a future war against Octavianus, but in the short term he was too much of a danger. So Pompeius was removed from the equation and Antonius' hands were left relatively clean of the bloody deed. With Pompeius dead and the civil war in the East extinguished, Antonius could turn his full attention to the lapsed war against the Parthians.

8. A Tale of Two Artavasdes

Even prior to the arrival of Pompeius in the East, before Antonius could begin a fresh campaign against the Parthians, he needed to deal with the issue of Artavasdes II, King of Armenia, who had abandoned him during the invasion of Media and seemingly was attempting to be as neutral as possible when it came to Rome and Parthia. As we have seen, Armenia was key to any campaign against Parthia which intended to use the northern route to invade, the other being across the Euphrates.

Artavasdes had clearly hoped that by abandoning Antonius in Media it would lead to his death and defeat, and that he would be able to use the ensuing chaos to reassert Armenian independence from both empires. Antonius' successful retreat from Media put paid to that plan, leaving him to face Antonius' wrath once the latter had recovered sufficiently. It was also clear that he could expect no help from Parthia, with Phraates readying his empire for another expected Roman invasion. We do not know whether he began negotiations with Antonius, perhaps with the offer of a substantial donation to the Antonine cause. Even if he had, since his return from Media, Antonius had hardened his policy on the running of the Eastern Roman Republic and exerted a far closer control on his 'allies'. Furthermore, a short military campaign would have been ideal preparation for the new invasion army he was raising.

Before he assembled a fresh army for an invasion of Armenia, Antonius received word from the other Artavasdes, the King of Media and a Parthian ally, about a potential defection to Rome. According to both Plutarch and Dio, the defeat of Antonius' invasion had brought about a reversion to character for the Parthian King Phraates, who set about alienating his closest allies once more, as Plutarch and Dio relate:

> 'And now the king of the Medes had a quarrel with Phraates the Parthian; it arose, as they say, over the Roman spoils, but it made the Mede suspicious and fearful that his dominion would be taken away from him. For this reason, he sent and invited Antonius to come, promising to join him in the war with his own forces. Antonius, accordingly, was in high hopes. For the one thing which he thought had prevented his subjugation of the Parthians, namely, his lack of a large number of horsemen and archers on his expedition, this he now saw supplied for him, and he would be granting and not asking a favour. He therefore made preparations to go up again through Armenia, effect a junction with the Mede at the river Araxes, and then prosecute the war.'[29]

> 'For this he placed no small hope in the Mede, who in his anger against Phraates because he had not received from him many of the spoils or any other honour and in his eagerness to punish the Armenian for bringing in the Romans had sent Polemon to him requesting his friendship and alliance. Antonius was apparently so exceedingly delighted over the affair that he both made terms with the Mede and later gave Polemon Lesser Armenia as a reward for his mission.'[30]

Phraates had managed to once again alienate his allies and divide the united front that had been able to defeat the previous Roman invasion. Antonius had the prospect that Media, the gateway into the Parthian Empire, for which he had fought so determinedly in 36 BC, would now fall to him without a fight. Here we see another native ruler having to switch allegiances between the two expanding empires to maintain his independence. In a nice historical parallel, whilst Artavasdes II of Armenia had defected from Antonius, Artavasdes I of Media had now defected to him.

For Antonius, this meant that the tactical advantages had switched back in his favour. All that was required was to subdue Armenia and then link up with the Median king, and he now had an open route into the Parthian Empire. Dio reports that Antonius at first tried subterfuge to capture the Armenian king:

'First, then, he summoned the Armenian to Egypt as a friend, in order that he might seize him there without effort and make away with him; but when the king suspected this and did not respond to the summons, he plotted to deceive him in another fashion. He did not openly become angry with him, lest he should alienate him, but in order that he might find him unprepared, he set out from Egypt as if to make another campaign against the Parthians at this time.'[31]

It is not surprising that Artavasdes did not fall for Antonius' obvious trap, especially given the manner in which other client kings had been treated. Nevertheless, Antonius spent the rest of 35 BC assembling a fresh eastern army with which to invade Armenia and link up with his new Median ally.

Summary

As we can see, 35 BC was a year of consolidation for Antonius following his disastrous invasion of Parthia the previous year. Yet whilst we can question Antonius the general, Antonius the ruler was clearly of a different calibre. The shock of the defection of the Armenian king at such a crucial time seems to have clarified Antonius' thoughts towards ruling the Eastern Republic, the bulk of which lay outside of direct Roman control. Rome had provinces in the West (Macedonia/Greece and Asia), two provinces in Asia Minor (Bithynia–Pontus and Cilicia) and Syria in the East (see Map 4). The rest of the territories lay in the control of client kingdoms, whose allegiance to Rome – or to Antonius himself – was only as solid as their conviction that Rome was the stronger power.

Antonius' defeat in 36 BC, no matter how he dressed it up, combined with the open defection of Armenia, brought this conviction of Rome's strength into question. A range of Rome's allies in the East therefore received new rulers, notably Galatia and Cappadocia. This policy seemed to pay dividends when Antonius' control of the Eastern Republic was challenged by Sex. Pompeius, calling on the personal connections of many of the region's rulers to his late father. Yet most of the men who had sworn allegiance to Pompeius Magnus – in the name of Rome – had been replaced by men (and women) loyal to Antonius. It was only Antonius' indecision over whether Pompeius was more use to him as an ally against Caesar Octavianus than as a dead enemy that allowed Pompeius to seize the military advantage. Once Antonius and his lieutenants had determined on war, then the greater resources of Antonius were brought to bear and Pompeius' civil war was crushed.

Having re-established greater control of Rome's Eastern Republic, Antonius received a bonus in the defection of the King of Media to his side, which removed a major obstacle in his invasion of the Parthian Empire and potentially swung the balance of the war back in his favour. Thus Antonius' position in the winter of 35/34 BC was far stronger than that of 36/35 BC, a strength which would lead Antonius to make some fundamental changes to the nature of his rule in the East and see the rise of a new hybrid empire.

Chapter Ten

The Rise and Fall of the
Antonine Empire (34–30 BC)

For Antonius, 34 BC opened with him holding a Consulship (albeit *in absentia*) which he formally resigned after just one day in office, demonstrating the lip-service that the Triumvirs showed to the traditional Roman constitution.[1] Nevertheless, Antonius ensured that one of his supporters, L. Sempronius Atratinus, was chosen in his place, so he still had lieutenants protecting his interests in Rome: the ultimate source of his position in the East.

With matters in Rome settled, Antonius once more turned his attention eastward to his preparations for renewal of the war with Parthia. With the defection of the King of Media to his side, Antonius only faced one obstacle to a renewed invasion of Parthia, namely Armenia and its King Artavasdes II, who two years before had betrayed him during his previous invasion of Media.

1. The Armenian War (34 BC)

Having failed to lure Artavasdes II out of Armenia on a pretext, Antonius went to Armenia himself, along with his army. Still wishing to avoid a military confrontation, he sent his emissary, Q. Dellius, ahead on the pretext of discussing a marriage alliance between Artavasdes' daughter and one of Antonius' Egyptian sons, Alexander. Having reached Nicopolis, Antonius once again summoned Artavasdes to discuss the next invasion of Parthia, but again Artavasdes refused, clearly aware of the danger. Dellius was again dispatched to the Armenian court, whilst Antonius and his army invaded Armenia and made for the city of Artaxata.

Having resisted Antonius for so long, it being nearly eighteen months since his betrayal, seeing the Roman army invade Armenia finally forced Artavasdes to make a choice: either fight, submit or flee to Parthia. Having disregarded the option of fighting what would have been a hopeless battle against the Romans, and seeing no hope of Parthian reinforcements, Artavasdes chose the lesser of the various evils and set off for Antonius' camp. Dio writes:

'In this way he [Antonius] succeeded in inducing him [Artavasdes] to come into his camp, after a long time, partly by using the king's associates to persuade him, and partly by using his own soldiers to terrorize him, and by writing and acting toward him in every way precisely as he would toward a friend. Thereupon he arrested him, and at first kept him without fetters and led him around to the various forts where the king's treasures were deposited, in the hope that he might secure them without a struggle.'[2]

Thus, another native client king fell to Antonius, payback for his desertion during the invasion of Media. On this occasion, however, the Armenians attempted to fight back and maintain their independence:

'When, however, the keepers of the gold would pay no heed to the king, and the Armenian citizens who bore arms chose Artaxes, the eldest of his sons, king in his stead, Antonius bound him [Artavasdes] in silver chains; for it was unseemly, apparently, that this man who had been king should be bound in fetters of iron.

   'After this Antonius occupied the whole of Armenia, taking some of the people peaceably and some by force; for Artaxes withdrew and went to the Parthian King, after fighting an engagement and suffering defeat.'[3]

Armenia was subdued by force once more, clearly unable to resist the Roman army in the region. We have no other details of the fighting, other than this brief mention of a battle fought between Artaxes – the king's son and pretender – and Antonius' forces. Having been defeated, Artaxes fled Armenia to the Parthian court, which now had its own pretender to the Armenian throne.

   After a short conflict, Antonius had subdued Armenia, carried its king off in chains and was able to link up with King Artavasdes of Media, clearing the way for his anticipated invasion of Parthia. This alliance was cemented with the betrothal of the Median king's daughter to Antonius' son Alexander. The only downside for Antonius was the creation of a pretender to the Armenian throne, who now resided in the Parthian court. The current king, Artavasdes II, and his remaining family were carried as prisoners to Alexandria, leaving no ruling family at all in Armenia. With a pretender to the throne being shielded by Parthia, Artavasdes seems to have remained King of Armenia, albeit a captive one. Having secured Armenia, however, Antonius returned to Egypt rather than press home his attack on Parthia:

'After accomplishing these things Antonius betrothed to his son the daughter of the Median King with the intention of making him still more his friend; then he left his legions in Armenia and went once more to Egypt, taking the great mass of booty and the Armenian [king] with his wife and children.'[4]

This failure to press home his tactical advantage in the war with Parthia seems odd at first, but Antonius had more important matters to attend to with regard to his position in the East.

2. An Alexandrian Triumph

Though hardly a major victory, Antonius used the Armenian campaign as an excuse to celebrate a unique Romano-Alexandrian Triumph, which he in turn used as a launchpad for his most ambitious policy decision yet, one which was a turning point in the history of the Eastern Roman Republic. Antonius, having very publicly celebrated a Romanesque Triumph, not in Rome, but in Alexandria, the de-facto capital of his Eastern Republic, provided everyone with a very public notice of the fusion of eastern and western traditions that were the hallmark of Rome's Eastern Republic under Antonius:

'Sending them with the captives ahead of him into Alexandria in a kind of triumphal procession, he himself drove into the city upon a chariot, and he not only presented to Cleopatra all the other spoils but brought her the Armenian [king] and his family in golden bonds. She was seated in the midst of the populace upon a platform plated with silver and upon a gilded chair.'[5]

3. From Republic to Empire

Yet the Triumph was merely the prelude to a much greater piece of theatre. Having established himself publicly as a conquering general, Antonius used the Triumph to unveil what would be an epoch-defining moment in the history of the Mediterranean.

Throughout his stewardship of Rome's Eastern Republic, Antonius faced one fundamental problem: the very nature of his power relied upon having been granted a Triumviral command by the Senate and People of Rome, albeit at sword point. Every war he fought, every king he deposed, was done – theoretically – in Rome's name, and in this he was no different from any other Roman commander exercising his imperium, though he and his colleague Octavianus had been granted a new office, that of Triumvir, with superior power to all others. Yet the role of Triumvir had been created for the emergency period in 43 BC when the Republic was being wracked by multi-factional civil wars.

Even with complete control of a purged Senate and a threatened People, the grant of Triumviral power had to be time-limited, with the current term ending in 32 BC, having been last renewed for five years in 37 BC (see Chapter Six). This grant of office could theoretically be renewed again and again, for the rest of Antonius' life, yet even if the Triumvirs agreed this between themselves, there would always be opposition by the Senate and People to perpetual rulers, as Caesar himself had discovered to his cost. This was especially the case given that the emergencies which had led to the creation of this office were now resolved. Ironically, it had been Antonius himself who had ensured this, by his execution of Sex. Pompeius. The Roman world was now at peace with itself, and both Triumvirs were intent on expanding Rome's empire; Octavianus in mainland Europe (notably Illyria) and Antonius in the East.

Furthermore, there was absolutely no guarantee that Octavianus would agree to a Triumviral extension and a perpetuation of the split of the Republic between the two men. Whilst Antonius certainly had a sizeable following in the Senate to look after his interests, physical control of Rome and Italy fell to Octavianus, and at any time Antonius could find the legal basis of his rule removed. To add to this dilemma was the fact that even if peace with Octavianus was maintained and the Triumviral office extended, this would still only leave Antonius as a general of Rome.

It is an interesting point to note that Antonius and Octavianus were both de-facto rulers of the two greatest states in the Mediterranean, yet legally were nothing more than officers of the Senate and People, so they found themselves in the same position that Caesar had before them. If anything, this position was worse for Antonius, who had been based in the East for the last eight years, and his de-facto capital, Alexandria, was the seat of one of the three great Hellenistic monarchies, and was not only founded by Alexander the Great, but was custodian of his body, and therefore his legacy. Thus, Antonius had the daily trappings and power of a Hellenistic monarch, but not the legal basis of one. Added to this was the fact that he was fast creating his own dynasty, with a Hellenistic queen for a wife, three royal children – one of whom was even named Alexander – and a royal stepson. The East had an Antonine dynasty in all but name.

Antonius clearly had no intention of ever returning to Rome and retiring to private life, as many of his illustrious predecessors had. Furthermore, as the disaster of 36 BC had shown, his conquest of Parthia could not be accomplished quickly and creating a new eastern empire would probably take up the rest of his lifetime; by 34 BC Antonius was already 49 years old. For all these reasons, Antonius had clearly used the previous year to think through his constitutional position and plan for the future. In 34 BC, pre-empting Octavianus and his constitutional settlement by some seven years, Antonius unveiled his constitutional blueprint for converting his stewardship of Rome's Eastern Republic into a new Antonine Empire; a fusion of eastern and western traditions, much as Alexander the Great's empire had been. Just as Caesar – and shortly Octavianus himself – had to grapple with, Antonius could not outright declare himself king, having to make allowances for Roman Republican sensibilities, both back home and amongst his own supporters. Thus, he was awarded no new titles or powers, but his Egyptian queen consort and their children and stepchildren were:

218 Rome and Parthia: Empires at War

'After this Antonius feasted the Alexandrians, and in the assembly made Cleopatra and her children sit by his side; also, in the course of his address to the people he commanded that she should be called Queen of Kings, and Ptolemy, whom they named Caesarion, King of Kings. And he then made a new distribution of provinces, giving them Egypt and Cyprus in addition; for he declared that in very truth one was the wife and the other the son of the former Caesar, and he professed to be taking these measures for Caesar's sake, though his purpose was to cast reproach upon Caesar Octavianus because he was only an adopted and not a real son of his. Besides making this assignment to them, he promised to give to his own children by Cleopatra the following districts: to Ptolemy, Syria and all the region west of the Euphrates as far as the Hellespont; to Cleopatra, Cyrenaica in Libya; and to their brother Alexander, Armenia and the rest of the countries east of the Euphrates as far as India; for he even bestowed the last-named regions as if they were already in his possession.'[6]

'For after filling the gymnasium with a throng and placing on a tribunal of silver two thrones of gold, one for himself and the other for Cleopatra, and other lower thrones for his sons, in the first place he declared Cleopatra Queen of Egypt, Cyprus, Libya, and Coele Syria, and she was to share her throne with Caesarion. Caesarion was believed to be a son of the former Caesar, by whom Cleopatra was left pregnant. In the second place, he proclaimed his own sons by Cleopatra Kings of Kings, and to Alexander he allotted Armenia, Media and Parthia (when he should have subdued it), to Ptolemy Phoenicia, Syria, and Cilicia. At the same time, he also produced his sons, Alexander arrayed in Median garb, which included a tiara and upright head-dress, Ptolemy in boots, short cloak, and broad-brimmed hat surmounted by a diadem. For the latter was the dress of the kings who followed Alexander, the former that of Medes and Armenians. And when the boys had embraced their parents, one was given a bodyguard of Armenians, the other of Macedonians. Cleopatra, indeed, both then and at other times when she appeared in public, assumed a robe sacred to Isis, and was addressed as the New Isis.'[7]

At a stroke, a new empire arose in the east (see Map 10), that of the Antonine dynasty.[8] His Egyptian wife Cleopatra and their four children and stepchildren were now given rule over all of Rome's eastern empire beyond Asia Minor. Cleopatra VII was reconfirmed as Pharaoh of Egypt, ruling jointly with her (and Caesar's) son Ptolemy XV (Caesarion). Egypt had the Roman province of Cyprus – annexed from the Ptolemies in 58 BC – restored to its rule. The Roman province of Cyrene – annexed from the Ptolemies in 74 BC – was given to Antonius' daughter Cleopatra Selene II to rule. The Roman provinces of Syria and Cilicia were given to Antonius' youngest son Ptolemy Philadelphus, whilst Antonius' oldest son, Alexander Helios, received Armenia, Media and Parthia to rule, though Parthia obviously had yet to be conquered.

The two sources differ when it comes to the title of King of Kings, the old title for the Persian emperor, the supreme ruler of the world. The title itself is believed to have originated much earlier than the Persians, with the Assyrian Empire, though it is most noted for its usage in the First Persian Empire. Following the fall of Persia, the title had been appropriated first by the Seleucids, then the Parthians under Mithradates I, and most recently the Armenian King Tigranes II, each trying to legitimize their conquests and empire by claiming the universal title of the Persians.

It is clear that Antonius tapped into this mythos by appropriating it from the Parthians and using it for his own dynasty, a clear, and provocative, statement that his dynasty was now the inheritors of both the Alexandrian and the Persian Empires, and that the day of the Parthians had passed. Where the sources differ is on the identity of who Antonius gave the title to. In Plutarch's account, Antonius strangely bestows the title on both his sons, Alexander and Ptolemy, each now with an empire either side of the Euphrates, ironically still being used as a dividing line. Yet Dio states Antonius bestows the title of King of Kings on Ptolemy Caesarion, Caesar's son.

This difference is an important one, certainly in symbolic terms. If we are to follow Dio, then Antonius is making a very bold claim by stating that Caesar's son is the supreme ruler, albeit one without much of an empire, being only co-ruler of Egypt and Cyprus, with his mother, who became Queen of Kings; an interesting female version of the ancient title. Thus Ptolemy Caesarion became a figurehead for the new dynasty, the son of Caesar and inheritor of the Alexandrian legacy, yet one without any practical power, which would be held by his stepbrothers, who would rule the two largest empires of the East. Caesar's son is merely a figurehead, whilst the real power stays within Antonius' own flesh and blood.

If we are to follow Plutarch, however, then Ptolemy Caesarion is relegated to being co-ruler of Egypt whilst his stepbrothers both become King of Kings, a sharing of the title which rather renders it nonsensical. Aside from this, bestowing the title on Ptolemy Caesarion makes greater sense in terms of Antonius' relationship with his partner, brother-in-law and greatest rival, Caesar Octavianus, who had only risen to power due to his being Caesar's Roman heir, yet he was only his legally adopted son, not his natural one. Though Caesarion had no legal standing in Roman law, being born a bastard – albeit a royal one – being the natural born son of the now deified Caesar was a clear challenge to the legally adopted son of Caesar back in Rome. If Caesarion was of superior status to Octavianus, then Octavianus' claim to power was theoretically diminished. By proclaiming to the world that Ptolemy Caesarion, his stepson, was the King of Kings, he was elevating him above Octavianus.

At the head of this new dynasty was Antonius himself, who strangely was theoretically now shorn of most of his power. Whilst he was still a fully appointed Triumvir of Rome, if we accept the widest extent of this reorganisation (see below) then he only had command of the Roman province of Macedonia (and Greece). He was, however, still commander of all the Roman legions stationed in his family's empire. Yet whilst his Roman status was diminished, in theory, he officially married – or confirmed his marriage[9] – to Cleopatra, which whilst it again held no standing in Roman law, made a clear statement about Antonius' long-term intentions. He now became the official consort to the Queen of Kings and stepfather to the King of Kings, with three regal children, all of whom were only infants.[10] Thus Antonius had a clear role to play as regent for his children's empires.

We must clarify exactly which Roman provinces were in the scope of this reorganisation. Certainly Cyrene, Cyprus, Cilicia and Syria were all named, but crucially Dio asserts that all territories up to the Hellespont were given to Ptolemy Philadelphus. Though not named, this would include the Roman provinces of Asia and Bithynia-Pontus. Critically, this would mean that the clock had been turned back a century – to the 130s BC – and that Rome held no territory west of the Hellespont. The Middle East would be dominated by a series of four new powers: two huge empires either side of the Euphrates, from the Hellespont to the Euphrates and then from the Euphrates to the Indus, supported by two lesser kingdoms in the south, Egypt (and Cyprus) and Cyrenaica, which had the potential to expand into Roman Africa.

Thus one of Rome's commanders had disposed of most of Rome's eastern empire at a stroke and turned the Roman Republic into only a western-based (European-centric power) accomplishing by decree what every Hellenistic power had been trying to achieve since the days of Antiochus the Great (see Chapter One). The legal basis for this transfer of Rome's empire in the East was Antonius' own Triumviral power, granted by the Senate and People of Rome, with full powers to make treaties and deal with territories overseas as he wished. Whilst clearly the Senate and People had not conceived that a Roman commander would use this power to dispose of Rome's own empire to his family, in practice there was little that could be done.

Although in theory he had not elevated his own position, nor taken the title of king, he had dismembered Rome's eastern empire, something which Mithridates VI of Pontus and the Parthians had been trying to accomplish for several decades, and created a new empire in its place: the Antonine one. We have to question whether he hoped that the rest of the Roman oligarchy would accept this course of action. From a financial standpoint alone, the riches of the East would no longer flow into Rome's coffers, but those of Alexandria, though this must have been the practice for the last eight years. In effect, Antonius was making permanent the partition of Rome's empire into two separate entities: a Western Republic ruled from Rome and an Eastern Empire ruled from Alexandria, pre-empting the permanent split between the Eastern and Western Roman Empires by some four centuries.

Whilst in practice Rome's empire had been separated into two for nearly a decade, the illusion of unity had been maintained. This impression had now been shattered, and even though he must have known that it would lead to war with the Western Republic, he may have hoped that Octavianus would be content with just ruling in the West. In the short term this tactic seemed to work, and Antonius sent the Senate notice of his actions, to be ratified before the People of Rome:

'Not only did he [Antonius] say this in Alexandria, but he sent a despatch to Rome as well, in order that it might secure ratification also from the people there. None of these despatches, however, was read in public; for Domitius and Sosius were Consuls by this time, and being extremely devoted to him, refused to publish them to all the People, even though Caesar urged it upon them. But, although they prevailed in this matter, Caesar won a victory in his turn by preventing any of Antonius' despatches regarding the Armenian king from being made known to the public; for he not only felt pity for the prince, inasmuch as he himself had been secretly in communication with him for the purpose of injuring Antonius, but he also grudged Antonius his Triumph.'[11]

Antonius' own allies in Rome thought it prudent not to put the matter before the People, all too aware of the public backlash he would face, which Antonius himself seemed to be unaware of. However, Octavianus' focus was on the military conquest of Illyria and expanding Rome's empire in mainland Europe, rather than confronting Antonius in the East.

4. Armenia, Media and Parthia (33 BC)

With that being the case, Antonius resumed his interest in a fresh invasion of Parthia in conjunction with King Artavasdes of Media. Despite campaigning in Armenia early in 34 BC, he does not seem to have undertaken a fresh campaign until the following year:

'Antonius, accordingly, was in high hopes. For the one thing which he thought had prevented his subjugation of the Parthians, namely, his lack of a large number of horsemen and archers on his expedition, this he now saw supplied for him, and he would be granting and not asking a favour. He therefore made preparations to go up again through Armenia, effect a junction with the Mede at the river Araxes, and then prosecute the war.'[12]

Throughout 35 and 34 BC and all these events, there is one noticeable absence; that of Parthia itself. Despite their victory in 36 BC in repelling the Roman invasion, we hear almost nothing about their activities in the following years. Whilst we always have to acknowledge the absence of any native sources, and the Roman sources' focus on internal politics between Antonius and Octavianus, Parthia's apparent passivity in relation to Antonius' actions in these two years is interesting and perhaps revealing. It has already been noted that the King of Media himself had fallen out with the Parthian king in the immediate aftermath of their victory over Antonius, yet there are other references to events in Parthia, and in particular with reference to the Parthian King Phraates himself:

'Phraates, upon this success, becoming still more insolent, and being guilty of many fresh acts of cruelty, was driven into exile by his subjects.'[13]

'… putting off the Mede until the summer season, although Parthia was said to be suffering from internal dissensions.'[14]

Thus, it seems that Phraates had used his victory over the Romans to strengthen his position at home and turned his focus inwards on those he perceived to be his enemies within the Parthian nobility. Yet rather than using this victory to enforce his position as a victorious, and thus legitimate, Parthian king – much as his father had done in the wake of the victory at Carrhae – it seems to have given him free licence to persecute his enemies. The unity brought about by the Roman invasion seems to have shattered and Parthia appears to have collapsed, if not into outright civil war, then into a major political crisis, all of which took its focus off events in the west and the threat from Rome.

Whilst we hear that the Parthian court gave shelter to the son of the Armenian king, there was no attempt to restore him by force or to bring the Median King Artavasdes back into the Parthian fold, nor repay him for his defection to the Romans. Thus, once again, Rome (and Antonius) had an excellent opportunity, brought about by the weak Parthian monarchy, to take advantage and overcome Parthia once and for all. Yet Antonius too must have had one eye on internal issues, and his campaign of 33 BC did not reach Parthia proper. His army once more passed through Armenia to the border with Media, now a Roman ally:

'Antonius meantime had marched as far as the Araxes, ostensibly to conduct a campaign against the Parthians, but was satisfied to arrange terms with the Median king. They made a covenant to serve each other as allies, the one against the Parthians and the other against Caesar, and to cement the compact they exchanged some soldiers, the Mede received a portion of the newly-acquired Armenia, and Antonius received the king's daughter, Iotape, to be united in marriage with Alexander, and the military standards taken in the battle with Statianus.'[15]

Therefore, whilst Antonius certainly made progress with his eastern design, the war with Parthia dragged on, with neither side seeming willing to commit wholeheartedly to it, given their own internal dissensions. Antonius returned to Roman territory once more, having achieved a notable propaganda coup by recovering the Roman standards lost in 36 BC during the defeat of Oppius Statianus. He also secured a marriage for his son Alexander, whom he had crowned as King of Armenia and Media, to the daughter of the current King of Media, ensuring a joining of the royal families, and going some way to reassuring Artavasdes as to his family's future in the Antonine Empire.

Furthermore, with the transfer of soldiers to Artavasdes, he seems to have left him in command of the war against Parthia in Antonius' absence, almost as a legate. Thus, we can see that in the Antonine Empire, command of Roman soldiers was being delegated to non-Romans and native rulers were acting as legates to Antonius. It is also clear that Armenia itself continued to suffer under Antonius' rule, with portions of it being given to Artavasdes and becoming part of Media. The region of Lesser Armenia was given to another client of Antonius', named Polemon, to rule as its king.[16]

With one eye on events in Rome and relations between himself and Octavianus, Antonius would not commit wholeheartedly to an invasion of Parthia but preferred to have his proxy fight the war for him. Given the state of Parthia at the time, this might have seemed a sensible compromise, but ultimately this failure to capitalise on Parthian weakness would undermine the whole Roman war effort.

5. A Tale of Two Civil Wars – The Roman Civil War in the East (32–30 BC)

Yet by the year 32 BC, both great empires once again stood on the brink of civil war, offering each the possibilities for changing the balance of the ongoing war for domination in the East. Of the two it seems that it was the Romans who collapsed into renewed civil war first, though the exact timing of the subsequent Parthian Civil War remains unknown (see below). It will be a never-ending debate as to whether the two Triumvirs and their respective Republics would have ever been able to peacefully co-exist, but it seems clear that the two men had different goals.

Octavianus appears to have harboured the more traditional desire for a unified Republic, ruled from Rome and controlled by himself (albeit behind the scenes). This unified Republic would be bolstered with a massive imperial expansion programme in mainland Europe, to finally provide Rome with defensible European borders, perhaps fulfilling the expansion programme begun by his adopted father. Antonius, on the other hand, seems to have harboured no thoughts about ruling the Western Republic, but had clearly set his sights on the East and the recreation of the empire of Alexander the Great. Yet, despite this desire for peaceful co-existence with the Western Republic, it was Antonius' actions in transferring the majority of Rome's eastern provinces to his family that made war between the two Republics inevitable. No Roman would have been able to stand for the loss of the bulk of Rome's eastern provinces beyond Asia, especially to form the core of a new imperial dynasty.

Ultimately, we will never know whether Antonius realised the effect this would have in Rome, especially having spent the bulk of the last decade at the imperial court in Alexandria. As we have already seen, it is clear that Antonius' own supporters in Rome could not bring themselves to publicly support such a move. Nevertheless, in Antonius' mind it seems to have been clear that the time for a clean break from Rome was upon him, and that he believed that he had outgrown the Republic and needed to break away and create his own dynastic empire. He may have hoped that he could have avoided war with Octavianus and the Western Republic, especially with so many supporters in the Senate, or at least delayed it for a while. Yet when war came, he seemed to have been more than prepared.

As 32 BC unfolded, it was clear that an irrevocable breach between the two men and their Republics was developing. The year opened with both Consuls being leading men from Antonius' faction; Cn. Domitius Ahenobarbus and C. Sosius, both veterans of Antonius' eastern wars. Both men went on the attack against Octavianus, and only the intervention of a Tribune (Nonius Balbus) prevented Sosius from bringing proposals against him. We must assume that such a brazen, and perhaps surprising, attack on Octavianus in the heart of his own powerbase was an Antonine tactic, not to facilitate civil war but to force Octavianus to the negotiating table. Twice already these two men had been to the brink of civil war (43 and 41–40 BC), and on both occasions they had struck a deal. If this was Antonius' tactic, then he must have hoped that in return for abandoning moves against him in the Senate and Assemblies, Octavianus would agree to support his eastern settlement.

If this was Antonius' plan, then it backfired spectacularly. Octavianus countered this political attack by seizing control of the Senate with a body of soldiers and armed supporters, which forced the Consuls and a number of Antonius' other supporters to flee Rome and then Italy and head eastwards. When news of this reached the East, Antonius convened his own Senate to discuss war with Octavianus, upon which a number of his officers quit and fled westwards to Rome, including several senior commanders. He also seems to have formally divorced his Roman wife, Octavia, the sister of Octavianus.

It was two of these defecting officers – none other than M. Titius[17] and L. Munatius Plancus – who supplied Octavianus with the final piece of information which he could use to inflame Roman public opinion. Against all custom and practice, he seized Antonius' will from the Vestal Virgins and revealed its contents in public, confirming that Antonius had decreed that he was to be buried in Alexandria:

'This caused the Romans in their indignation to believe that the other reports in circulation were also true, to the effect that if Antonius should prevail, he would bestow their city upon Cleopatra and transfer the seat of power to Egypt. And they became so angry at this.'[18]

Thus, with Antonius' supporters in the Senate having fled and the Roman People inflamed, Octavianus called for, and had passed, a vote for war against Cleopatra (though not Antonius), ensuring that he was not technically calling for a renewal of a civil war, but a foreign war against the Ptolemaic Empire, primarily to recover Rome's 'lost' eastern empire:

'For they voted to the men arrayed on his side pardon and praise if they would abandon him, and declared war outright upon Cleopatra, put on their military cloaks as if he were close at hand, and went to the Temple of Bellona, where they performed through Caesar (Octavianus) as fetialis all the rites preliminary to war in the customary fashion. These proceedings were nominally directed against Cleopatra, but really against Antonius.'[19]

The full scope of the war falls outside the remit of this work, but we need to consider the implications for the East. With Rome having declared war on Cleopatra – and by implication her children, both Caesar's and Antonius' – Antonius and his Roman supporters now found themselves on the wrong side of a declaration of war by the Senate and People of Rome. Likewise, Antonius' client kings now had to declare either for Rome or for Cleopatra (Antonius), though a number wisely chose to remain neutral. Nevertheless, Antonius seized the initiative and moved the bulk of his military forces to the most western part of his Republic, namely Macedonia and Greece, and thus poised on Italy's borders.

Throughout the whole of the Third Roman Civil War (from 49 BC), Greece had proved to be the preferred theatre for Roman civil warfare, sitting halfway between the Western and Eastern Republics: in 48 BC, when Caesar held the West and Pompeius the East, and again in 42 BC, when the Triumvirs held the West and the Brutan-Cassian faction the East. Thus, for the third time in two decades, armies from the two Republics faced each other in Greece.

It is interesting to discuss each side's objectives. For Octavianus it was the defeat of Antonius and Cleopatra, and the conquest and reincorporation of the provinces of the Eastern Republic, along with the annexation of Ptolemaic Egypt. We can question whether the opposite was the case for Antonius.

He certainly needed victory over Octavianus (and his general Agrippa) and to re-establish control over the Senate and People of Rome, and at the very least reverse the declaration of war against Cleopatra. Rather than incorporating the whole of the Western Republic into his embryonic Antonine Empire, he would most likely have settled for keeping the two entities separate, albeit securing the Senate and People's approval for his eastern dynastic reorganisation and ensuring his faction kept control of the key organs of Republican government. Dio reports that Antonius swore the following:

> 'As for Antonius, he on his part swore to his own soldiers that he would admit no truce in the war he waged, and promised in addition that within two months after his victory he would relinquish his office and restore to the senate and the people all its authority; and it was with difficulty, forsooth, that certain persons prevailed upon him to postpone this act to the sixth month, so that he might be able to settle the public business at his leisure.'[20]

Furthermore, control of Rome would also allow Antonius to tap into the greater manpower resources of the Western Republic to underwrite his wars of eastern conquest. Thus, one protagonist was fighting to unify the Mediterranean and reorientate it to the west, whilst the other was fighting to ensure a permanent division of the Mediterranean and reorientate it eastwards. We can therefore see what made the ensuing Battle of Actium so vital for the history of the Roman Republic and Mediterranean, split between East and West.

Again, even though Antonius took the advantage and chose Greece to be his battleground, it was the Western Republic that was in the stronger position. In the two previous clashes between the Eastern and Western Republic in this Third Civil War period, both had been won by the leaders of the Western Republic. Control of Italy meant that they could utilize the near unlimited manpower resources of Italy and Spain, which provided the bulk of the Roman professional army. Thus the Western Republic could field far more integrated armies than those constructed from the various provinces and client kingdoms of the East; Dio reports that there was even an Arabian contingent as part of Antonius' army.[21] They also had the advantage of far shorter supply lines from the heartland of their powerbase.

On this occasion the decisive battle took place on the sea, on 2 September 31 BC, and was won by the Western Roman navy commanded by Octavianus' key lieutenant, M. Vipsanius Agrippa, the man who had done so much to win the civil war against Sex. Pompeius. Again, as noted before, Antonius had no such key general to fall back upon. Ventidius' fate after his return from Rome is unknown, but he is believed to have died by this point. Furthermore, the Western Republic had the advantage that they could concentrate all their military forces on this conflict, whilst Antonius was still at war with the Parthian Empire and was forced to recall forces from the eastern front to support the western one (with ultimately disastrous consequences – see below).

The result of the Battle of Actium is well known, a victory for Agrippa (and Octavianus) and a defeat for Antonius and Cleopatra.[22] For the third time in a row, the Western Republic had defeated the Eastern one. Yet although it was a victory for Octavianus, it is often overlooked that the battle did not end the war. It was Antonius' own subsequent actions that turned a defeat into a disaster. Having been defeated at sea, Antonius turned southwards and retreated, leaving his land army, said to be some nineteen legions strong (with 12,000 cavalry), still in Greece.[23] Antonius' army, commanded by P. Canidius Crassus, found itself abandoned by its leader.

Nevertheless, Crassus could have tried to salvage the situation and if not engage Octavianus, then at least march the army back into Asia or Syria, the heartlands of the Eastern Republic, and defend the region against an Octavianus advance. Instead, he too fled for Egypt, allegedly at night, leaving the army behind. Unsurprisingly, abandoned by their commander, the whole army surrendered to Octavianus. Thus defeat turned into disaster and the Eastern Republic now lay defenceless, and open to attack, from both west and east.

Antonius initially retreated to Cyrenaica, where he had a number of legions stationed under the command of one of his legates, L. Pinarius Scarpus. Unfortunately, Scarpus, having heard of the defeat at Actium, switched sides and declared for Octavianus, forcing Antonius back to Alexandria.

Unsurprisingly, having defeated Antonius' fleet and more importantly captured his entire army, Octavianus marched into Asia, dismantling the Antonine Empire piece by piece, one province and client kingdom at a time:

> 'Caesar now punished the cities by levying money and taking away the remnant of authority over their citizens that their assemblies still possessed. He deprived all the princes and kings except Amyntas and Archelaus of the lands which they had received from Antonius, and he also deposed from their thrones Philopator, the son of Tarcondimotus, Lycomedes, the king of a part of Cappadocian Pontus, and Alexander, the brother of Iamblichus. The last-named, because he had secured his realm as a reward for accusing Caesar, he led in his triumphal procession and afterwards put to death. He gave the kingdom of Lycomedes to one Medeius, because the latter had detached the Mysians in Asia from Antonius before the naval battle and with them had waged war upon those who were on Antonius' side. He gave the people of Cydonia and Lampe their liberty, because they had rendered some assistance; and in the case of the Lampaeans he helped them to found anew their city, which had been destroyed.'[24]

By the end of 31 BC, the Antonine Empire had collapsed under assault on two fronts. In the West, Octavianus took control of Macedon, Greece, Asia, Bithynia, Cilicia, Syria and the client kingdoms, including Judea. In the East, the Parthians had taken advantage of the Roman Civil War and had overrun Media and Armenia (see below). By the beginning of 30 BC, the new Antonine Empire, a fusion of Roman and Ptolemaic, which had dreams of emulating that of Alexander the Great, was reduced to just the core possession of Egypt. As Dio describes, Antonius and Cleopatra found their allies swiftly deserting them and escape routes being cut off:

'While these negotiations were proceeding, the Arabians, instigated by Quintus Didius, the governor of Syria, burned the ships in the Arabian Gulf which had been built for the voyage to the Red Sea, and the peoples and princes without exception refused their assistance to Antonius. Indeed, I cannot but marvel that, while a great many others, though they had received numerous gifts from Antonius and Cleopatra, now left them in the lurch.'[25]

6. The Roman Invasion of Egypt (30 BC)

With the loss of the eastern provinces and the potential escape down the Red Sea denied to them, Antonius committed himself to a defence of Egypt. Potentially there was at least one other avenue open to him, and Cleopatra, and that would have been to seek sanctuary at the Parthian court. Yet even if Antonius could have reconciled himself to such a reversal of fortune, there was the issue of how he was going to reach Parthia itself. Antonius and Cleopatra both sent embassies to Octavianus hoping for a negotiated settlement, but all were rebuffed. Thus Antonius chose Egypt to make a last stand.

Octavianus approached Egypt from two directions: he personally led the main Roman army overland through Syria and Judea, whilst a legate, C. Cornelius Gallus, took command of Scarpus' forces in Cyrene and approached from the west. To escape this pincer movement, Antonius chose to attack the nearer (and smaller) force, Gallus' army travelling down the coast of Egypt from Cyrene:

The Battle of Paraetonium (30 BC)

Gallus' forces had captured the Egyptian port of Paraetonium, and Antonius chose to march there, principally hoping to turn the army back to his cause:

'[Antonius] proceeded against Gallus, in the hope of winning over the troops without a struggle, if possible, inasmuch as they had been with him on campaigns and were fairly well disposed toward him, but otherwise of subduing them by force, since he was leading against them a large force both of ships and of infantry. Nevertheless, he was unable even to talk with them, although he approached their ramparts and raised a mighty shout; for Gallus ordered his trumpeters to sound their instruments all together and gave no one a chance to hear a word. Moreover, Antonius also failed in a sudden assault and later suffered a reverse with his ships as well. Gallus, it seems, caused chains to be stretched at night across the mouth of the harbour under water, and then took no measures openly to guard against his opponents but contemptuously allowed them to sail in with perfect immunity. When they were inside, however, he drew up the chains by means of machines, and encompassing their ships on all sides, from the land, from the houses, and from the sea, he burned some and sank others.'[26]

Antonius had to retreat back to Alexandria, his offensive campaign at an end. At the same time, Octavianus reached the Egyptian port of Pelusium in the Nile Delta, which controlled access to Egypt from the east, and thus closed the pincer movement. Being surrounded by two armies, Antonius chose to launch one final campaign and attacked Octavianus as he approached Alexandria from the east.

The Battle of Alexandria (30 BC)
According to Dio:

'At the news concerning Pelusium Antonius returned from Paraetonium and went to meet Caesar in front of Alexandria, and attacking him with his cavalry, while the other was wearied from his march, he won the day. Encouraged by this success, and because he had shot arrows into Caesar's camp carrying leaflets which promised the men six thousand sesterces, he joined battle also with his infantry and was defeated.'[27]

Thus, despite some initial success, Antonius was again ultimately defeated by Octavianus. The final act came when his remaining naval and cavalry forces deserted him for Octavianus, after which Antonius retired to the Ptolemaic imperial palace and committed suicide, followed a few days later by Cleopatra:

'At daybreak, Antonius in person posted his infantry on the hills in front of the city and watched his ships as they put out and attacked those of the enemy; and as he expected to see something great accomplished by them, he remained quiet. But the crews of his ships, as soon as they were near, saluted Caesar's crews with their oars, and on their returning the salute changed sides, and so all the ships, now united into one fleet, sailed up towards the city prows on. No sooner had Antonius seen this than he was deserted by his cavalry, which went over to the enemy, and after being defeated with his infantry he retired into the city.'[28]

Thus Ptolemaic Egypt, the last of the successor kingdoms to Alexander the Great, was conquered and annexed by Octavianus, and with it fell the fledgling Antonine Empire. More importantly for Rome, the two Republics – Western and Eastern – were united once more, almost for the first time since the beginning of the Third Civil War. With it the focus of Roman power and attention moved back westwards from Alexandria to Rome, and became more European-focused rather than Near Eastern.

7. The Bloody Aftermath

The deaths of Antonius and Cleopatra did not bring an immediate end to the bloodshed, as there were still a number of scores to be settled. The fates of the rest of the Antonine dynasty were mixed; those that posed a direct threat to Octavianus were murdered, the others spared:

'Of their children, Antyllus was slain immediately, though he was betrothed to the daughter of Caesar and had taken refuge in his father's shrine, which Cleopatra had built; and Caesarion while fleeing to Ethiopia was overtaken on the road and murdered. Cleopatra was married to Juba, the son of Juba; for to this man who had been brought up in Italy and had been with him on campaigns, Caesar gave both the maid and the kingdom of his fathers, and as a favour to them spared the lives of Alexander and Ptolemy. To his nieces, the daughters whom Octavia had had by Antonius and had reared, he assigned money from their father's estate.'[29]

The two most notable casualties were M. Antonius Antyllus (the Roman son and legal heir of M. Antonius) and Ptolemy Caesarion (Ptolemy XV), Caesar's natural son and Octavianus' stepbrother (by adoption), and the recently acclaimed King of Kings. Both were young men, and in themselves neither constituted an immediate danger to Octavianus' position. However, Antyllus, as Antonius' legal heir, would inherit more than just his father's wealth, but all of his political support and thus be a beacon for those surviving supporters of Antonius, many of whom had been pardoned, and so was a potential rival to Octavianus in Rome.

If Antyllus posed a danger to Octavianus in Rome, then Caesarion was a threat to him in the East. Not only was he Caesar's natural-born son – albeit illegitimate in Roman law – but he was the last crowned Pharaoh of Egypt and the King of Kings. Both of these statuses, biological and regal, ensured that Octavianus could not allow him to live. Whilst Rome had military control of Egypt, the clear danger was that Ptolemy Caesarion could flee and find sanctuary and be used as a rival to Octavianus; the most obvious refuge being the Parthian court of Phraates. As we have seen (Chapter One), this region had a history of Roman hostages escaping their comfortable captivity and making their way back to the East. So even if Caesarion had been housed in Rome, there was always the danger that he would escape to the East and be a focal point for anti-Roman and anti-Octavian sentiment, especially if he was backed militarily by the Parthians. Octavianus could take no chances, and therefore had him murdered.

By contrast, Antonius' three Egyptian children, all crowned heads of Ptolemaic/Antonine possessions, were surprisingly spared. All three were apparently transported as Octavianus' 'guests' back to Rome. Of the three, it is Antonius' daughter Cleopatra Selene II whose fate is best recorded, married off to Juba II, King of Numidia and the Mauri in North Africa, ruling as a consort of a Roman client king.

The fate of her two brothers is rather more obscure. Despite the surviving sources recording Octavianus' mercy in not murdering Antonius' two Egyptian sons, both crowned heads of (mostly fictitious) eastern empires, they soon disappear from history and are never heard of again, which is most surprising given their heritage. This clearly raises the prospect that Octavianus' show of clemency was just that, a show, and that once matters had quietened down, then both princes – one around 10 years old, the other 6 – were quietly disposed of, rather in the manner of the more famous 'princes in the tower' (Octavianus was even their stepuncle).

Though their royal titles were only ever theoretical ones, in the wrong hands (such as the Parthians) either could have been used as a figurehead to rally anti-Roman opposition, lead an army or rule as a puppet. Thus, again, it made cold logical sense to dispose of both princes. Perhaps key to their initial survival was their age. Antyllus and Ptolemy Caesarion were both old enough to be considered men – each was 17 – and therefore it may have been more allowable for them to be murdered. Alexander and Ptolemy, by contrast, were mere children, so their public murders may have offended Roman sensibilities.

Aside from his Egyptian family and Antyllus, Antonius had a number of other children by his various wives (five in total). Nothing is known of the children of his first marriage, and a daughter from his second settled in the East, marrying a rich Greek ally of Antonius, Pythodoros. Both husband and wife seem to have survived the fall of her father. The only other child we know of was another son, Iullus Antonius, younger brother of Antyllus.

Unlike his elder brother, he returned to Rome when his father divorced his step-mother (Octavia) and so was not in the East when it fell to Octavianus. It may have been this lack of connection to his father and his age – 13 in 30 BC – that ensured his survival. He surprisingly become part of the imperial inner circle, marrying one of Octavianus' nieces and his own stepsister (daughter of his father's fourth wife), who had also been the wife of M. Vipsanius Agrippa. He reached the Consulship in 10 BC but committed suicide in 2 BC when charged with treason against Augustus, being a lover of Augustus' daughter Iulia, another of Agrippa's wives. His initial survival seems to have been an attempt by Octavianus to demonstrate his mercy.

Perhaps the most famous of these others were his two children by Octavia, Octavianus' own sister, who fortunately for them were daughters, both named Antonia, elder and younger. As Octavianus' nieces, they became part of the wider 'imperial' family. They too had the experience of growing up knowing that their uncle had caused the death of their father.

Both were married off, with the youngest Antonia marrying Octavianus' stepson Nero Claudius Drusus, and becoming mother to the famous Germanicus and the Emperor Claudius, grandmother to the Emperor Caius (Caligula) and great grandmother to the Emperor Nero. Her sister, the elder Antonia, married into the distinguished Republican family, the Domitii Ahenobarbi, with her husband rising to be Consul in 16 BC. She too, however, was related to a later emperor, being a grandmother of the Emperor Nero (born a Domitius Ahenobarbus).

Whilst many supporters of Antonius had switched sides to Octavianus and were pardoned,[30] there were some who were not so lucky and were swiftly butchered. Orosius tells us that three other Romans met their deaths on Octavianus' orders: P. Canidius Crassus, Q. Ovinius[31] and C. Cassius Palmensis, the latter of whom was recorded as the last surviving murderer of Caesar.[32]

6. The Romano-Median Parthian War (32–31 BC)

Whilst the civil war campaigns and the Battle of Actium and subsequent invasion of Egypt are both well-known and well-documented, the same cannot be said of the other war which was raging at this time in the East, between the Parthians and the Antonine commander Artavasdes I of Media. Having been put in command of the eastern war and bolstered by a contingent (of unknown size) of Roman and allied troops, it seems that Artavasdes took the offensive and launched an attack into Parthia proper. Thus the war which had been in abeyance since Antonius' retreat from Media in 36 BC started anew. The problem we have is that this war is virtually ignored in the surviving Roman sources, who are all too busy focussing on the Roman Civil War. A major stage in the Second Romano-Parthian War is virtually unrecorded to a modern audience, depriving us of a vital stage of the conflict. All we do have is a reference by Dio:

> 'The Mede at first, by employing the Romans as allies, conquered the Parthians and Artaxes who came against him; but as Antonius summoned back his own soldiers, and moreover retained those of the king, the latter was in turn defeated and captured, and so Armenia was lost together with Media.'[33]

It is from this small excerpt that we must try and reconstruct a whole campaign. Nevertheless, with Media as a launchpad for the Romano-Media invasion of Parthia, and a secured Armenia behind them, this invasion seemed to meet with much more success than Antonius' in 36 BC. This showed that the Romans had clearly learned their lesson and were able to take the war to the Parthians. The Parthians and Phraates must have been well aware of the treachery of Artavasdes, but seem to have been unable to mount a preventative expedition earlier than 32 BC.

We unfortunately do not know who struck first, whether the Parthians mounted a pre-emptive strike to deter an invasion or they sat back and waited for the Roman invasion. Unfortunately the Dio reference is too vague and can be interpreted both ways. What we do know is that the exiled Armenian king, Artaxes (his father Artavasdes II still being a prisoner in Alexandria), was leading at least part of the Parthian army that fought Artavasdes of Media.

We don't know what role Phraates himself played in this campaign, but we must assume that he held a similar position as in the Antonine invasion and was present on the campaign, but allowed a proxy or proxies (including Artaxes) to command the actual fighting, much as Artavasdes of Media had done in the earlier invasion. The early stage of the war saw the Parthians defeated and the Romano-Median army presumably advancing into Parthian territory proper, though by what route is lost to us. We can roughly date this early phase to 32 BC.

However, once again the distraction of a civil war disputed the war between these two empires, decisively in this case. With war in the West looming, Antonius had to recall some or all of the Roman and allied forces which he had given to Artavasdes. Given the distance that they would have to travel to reach Macedonia, and the size of Antonius' existing army, this was a spectacularly short-sighted decision and one which fundamentally altered the course of the war. Without these forces, which must have been the finest quality of Artavasdes' army, if not the most numerous, the Romano-Median attack stalled and was then decisively routed. It is possible that Antonius was buoyed by the success of Artavasdes in his communications to him, but whilst fighting a war on two fronts, Antonius fatally undermined the strength of the eastern front to shore up the western one, with the net result that both fronts were overwhelmed, as the additional forces proved to be of no use in a naval battle in Greece.

This is a clear failure of strategy on Antonius' part. Had he kept the Roman forces on the eastern front, then Artavasdes could have continued his push into Parthia and at least secured his gains. This would have presented Antonius with additional options following his defeat at Actium and the collapse of the western front. As it turned out, both fronts collapsed at the same time and by 31 BC the Parthians had overrun both Media and Armenia and installed Artaxes on the Armenian throne, actually extending their territory farther than it had been in 36 BC. Faced with an advancing Roman army to his west, Antonius had no eastern provinces to fall back to. Had he still held Armenia and Media, and perhaps some additional Parthian territories, he could have retreated eastwards and consolidated, the region being far more difficult to reach than Alexandria. Whether he would have sacrificed Egypt, or have been allowed to, was another matter. Nevertheless, he would have been in a far stronger position to perhaps bargain with Phraates to either allow the Romano-Median army to march west to reinforce him or even provide Parthian forces to come to his assistance. As it was, with Parthia ascendant in the East, he had nothing to bargain with and Parthia could consolidate its gains in relative peace, at least in the short term.

Summary

The end of 30 BC saw another decisive turn in the Second Romano-Parthian War, with a second Roman (Romano-Median) invasion of Parthia being comprehensively defeated. On this occasion the defeat was so serious that the Parthians were able to overrun the barely defended Roman client kingdoms of Media and Armenia. Yet the Parthians had achieved this greatly by the absence of opposing forces, with the Roman Civil War raging in the West. However, with the fall of Egypt, the Parthians were no longer facing a disunited and distracted Antonine Empire, but a freshly united Roman Republic, with Egypt and the East being occupied by large Roman armies commanded by the sole ruler of Rome, Caesar Octavianus, son of the man who had committed himself to the conquest of Parthia and the East.

Section V

Waiting for Augustus (30–20 BC)

Chapter 11

Waiting for Augustus (30–20 BC)

1. A Tale of Two Civil Wars – The Parthian Civil War (31–29 BC)

As had been common in this period, neither Rome nor Parthia were able to hold an advantage over the other for long, and this proved to be the case for the Parthians at this time. Having scored notable victories in the East over the Romano-Median forces and retaken both Media and Armenia, they too collapsed into a fresh civil war. Thus, as one civil war ended in the West, another began in the East. Again, details are scant, but it seems from various sources that Phraates, whose rule had never been secure, had been challenged, or even overthrown, by one of his generals, Tiridates, who installed himself on the Arsacid throne as Tiridates II:

'It seems there had been dissension among the Parthians and a certain Tiridates had risen against Phraates.'[1]

'During his absence, the Parthians had made one Tiridates king.'[2]

'The perilous Parthians pitiably fight each other.'[3]

Other than the above, we have little in terms of surviving sources which detail the origins of the latest Parthian Civil War. However, as we have seen, Phraates' grip on the throne had never been secure, coming to power in a bloody coup against his father Orodes II in the wake of the Parthian defeat at Gindarus. Whilst technically an absolute monarch, the Parthian kings – at least from the first century BC onwards – had always needed to rule with the consent of the Parthian nobility, whom Phraates consistently alienated. Once again it seems that with the imminent danger of Roman invasion removed, Phraates lapsed into his old absolutist ways, and this time paid the price.

We know next to nothing about his successor, Tiridates, though it has been suggested that he was a Parthian general, perhaps one who led the victorious campaign in Media and Armenia.[4] We are also unclear on whether he was of the Arsacid line, or from an unrelated family. We certainly know that Tiridates was able to seize the Parthian court and the royal family, including one of Phraates' sons. Phraates himself was able to evade capture and fled eastwards to the Scythian tribes which bordered the Parthian Empire in the east, where he set about gathering a Scythian army to reclaim his throne.

In terms of the ongoing Romano-Parthian War, the pendulum had seemingly swung in favour of the Romans once more. On the face of it, the Roman Civil War had been won and the Republic reunified under one ruler, who had huge numbers of men under arms and was currently occupying Alexandria, having annexed the wealth of the Ptolemaic Empire to Rome once and for all. By contrast, the Parthian Empire had collapsed into civil war, with a usurper occupying the throne and the unseated monarch in the East raising an army of Scythian horsemen to reclaim his throne.

2. Octavianus and the Parthian Civil War (29 BC)

The chronology of the subsequent civil war in Parthia and the Roman involvement is confused by our having two surviving accounts, both of which depict similar events – Tiridates fleeing to Roman territory and seeking assistance from Octavianus – but each dated to a different period. The first comes from Dio and places these events in 29 BC, when Octavianus was still in the East, settling affairs in the aftermath of his victory over Antonius:

'It seems there had been dissension among the Parthians and a certain Tiridates had risen against Phraates; and hitherto, as long as Antonius' opposition lasted, even after the naval battle, Caesar [Octavianus] had not only not attached himself to either side, though they sought his alliance, but had not even answered them except to say that he would think the matter over. His excuse was that he was busy with Egypt, but in reality, he wanted them in the meantime to exhaust themselves by fighting against each other. But now that Antonius was dead and of the two combatants Tiridates, defeated, had taken refuge in Syria, and Phraates, victorious, had sent envoys, he entered into friendly negotiations with the latter; and, without promising to aid Tiridates, he permitted him to live in Syria. He received from Phraates one of his sons by way of conferring a favour upon him, and taking him to Rome, kept him as a hostage.'[5]

Yet Justin, based on the works of Pompeius Trogus, depicts a similar account, but by this time Augustus (as he had become) was fighting a war in Spain (see below).[6] Taking into account the overall accuracy of the two sources, it is all too tempting to believe that they are both describing the same event and that Justin (or Pompeius Trogus) has confused his dates. Yet moving aside from these two accounts, we find that Tiridates was issuing coins at Parthian mints until 25 BC. There is also the work by Isidore of Charax (the 'Parthian Stations'), which refers to the war between Tiridates and Phraates, which can be dated to c.26 BC.

We have to conclude that there were two phases to this latest Parthian Civil War. The first ended with Phraates being restored to his throne by a Scythian army, and with Tiridates fleeing to Octavianus in Syria for Roman assistance in his 'restoration' to the throne. Thus, once again, the Romans gave sanctuary to one participant in a Parthian Civil War; a useful strategic asset, if they needed to put a pro-Roman monarch on the Parthian throne.

3. Octavianus and the Roman Civil War (29–27 BC)

Yet, despite the advantageous strategic position the Romans found themselves in with regard to their Parthian neighbours, no further Roman attack was forthcoming. Whilst the Parthians may have been weakened by their civil war, it was the Roman Civil War which occupied Octavianus, not the Parthian one. Historiography, both modern and ancient, would like to neatly end this Third Roman Civil War in 31 BC with the Battle of Actium; a view which Octavianus himself would have encouraged. Yet Roman civil wars, at least in the Republican period, were seldom ended on the battlefield. Actium was the third of the 'great' civil war battles (the others being Pharsalus and Philippi), yet victory in these previous battles had not brought the winners anything more than temporary dominance in the ongoing civil war. Even after the conquest of Egypt and the deaths of Antonius and Cleopatra (and Caesarion), Octavianus had only gained temporary dominance of the Republic. His former Triumviral colleague Lepidus still lived, though in exile, and a new generation of Roman commanders were making names for themselves, most notably Octavianus' friend M. Vipsanius Agrippa and the young M. Licinius Crassus, grandson of the Triumvir.

Although Octavianus may have gained temporary military control of a now-unified Roman Republic, his overall position was far from secure. For one thing, he was currently at the far eastern edge of the Republic and thus far away from the centre of power, the Senate and People of Rome, who bestowed legitimacy and legality to whomever they selected. For another, Octavianus' Triumviral power had expired, which left him with only a Proconsular command of the war against Cleopatra, a war which by late 30 BC had ended. So despite being the (temporarily) undisputed warlord of the Republic, paradoxically he held little official power.

Critically, he clearly had no mandate from either the Senate or People to invade Parthia and continue the war. More important, however, was the fact that he clearly lacked the desire to do so, as at this time his prime concern must have been the conversion of his victory in the East into a lasting domination of the Republic. The priority for Octavianus was to settle maters in the East temporarily, to allow him to turn his attentions back to Rome.

4. Octavianus' Eastern Settlement – Parthia

Octavianus seems to have brought about a truce in the ongoing war with Parthia. He had an excellent bargaining chip in the form of the now-deposed Parthian King Tiridates, who resided in Syria under Roman protection, from which he seems to have plotted a further attack on the Parthian throne, albeit without Roman forces. Nevertheless, the Parthians had still been able to extend their empire to include Armenia, as a client kingdom, and had annexed the kingdom of Media-Atropatené. Dio reports that some form of truce was established, based on the status quo:

'Tiridates, defeated, had taken refuge in Syria, and Phraates, victorious, had sent envoys, he entered into friendly negotiations with the latter; and, without promising to aid Tiridates, he permitted him to live in Syria. He received from Phraates one of his sons by way of conferring a favour upon him, and taking him to Rome, kept him as a hostage.'[7]

Thus this status quo was maintained, with Parthia keeping the kingdoms of Armenia and Media and a temporary truce established between the two empires, allowing each ruler to secure their own positions without external interference. Nevertheless, this appears to have been nothing more than a temporary solution for both sides. Furthermore, Octavianus not only had a son of the Parthian king as hostage – though we are unclear how many sons Phraates had – he also had important hostages/refugees from Armenia and Media:

'Of his own accord he restored Iotape to the Median king, who had found an asylum with him after his defeat; but he refused the request of Artaxes that his brothers be sent to him, because this prince had put to death the Romans left behind in Armenia.'[8]

Thus, Octavianus had the exiled King of Media and a number of Armenian princes enjoying his hospitality in the Roman East, available to be used in any campaign to recover these territories.

5. Octavianus' Eastern Settlement – the Client Kings

We have seen to what lengths Antonius went to secure the loyalty of the region's client kingdoms, overthrowing established ruling dynasties and replacing them with new ones loyal to him and his family. Yet it was hardly surprising that these new dynasties soon abandoned this loyalty to the Antonines and threw in their lot with Octavianus, once the result of Actium had been confirmed:

'Caesar [Octavianus] now punished the cities by levying money and taking away the remnant of authority over their citizens that their assemblies still possessed. He deprived all the princes and kings except Amyntas and Archelaus of the lands which they had received from Antonius, and he also deposed from their thrones Philopator, the son of Tarcondimotus, Lycomedes, the king of a part of Cappadocian Pontus, and Alexander, the brother of Iamblichus. The last-named, because he had secured his realm as a reward for accusing Caesar, he led in his triumphal procession and afterwards put to death. He gave the kingdom of Lycomedes to one Medeius, because the latter had detached the Mysians in Asia from Antonius before the naval battle and with them had waged war upon those who were on Antonius' side.'9

Therefore, once again the cites and kingdoms of the Middle East were reorganized by a victorious Roman oligarch. Yet despite the number of changes, the three most important kings held on to their thrones: Amyntas I of Galatia, Archelaus I of Cappadocia and, perhaps most infamously, Herodes I of Judea. Herodes had actually been fighting a war of his own, against the Nabatean Arabs (32–30 BC) and had thus been defending Rome's south-eastern border against Arabia, and not therefore taking up arms against Octavianus. It was during this war that he had finally seized his chance and murdered his predecessor as King of Judea, Hyrcanus II, the last king of the Hasmonean dynasty, perhaps to ensure that there was no rival who could be installed by Octavianus as an alternative ruler of Judea.

For Herodes there was the additional bonus that the Ptolemaic dynasty of Egypt, long-term opponents of Judean independence and power, had been removed. Perhaps recognizing the need for a strong power in the southern Levant, as a bulwark to the new Roman province of Egypt, Octavianus not only confirmed Herodes as King of Judea (with some interesting religious ramifications), but enlarged the Kingdom of Judea itself:

'He did not only bestow other marks of honour upon him, but made an addition to his kingdom, by giving him not only the country which had been taken from him by Cleopatra, but besides that, Gadara, and Hippos, and Samaria; and moreover, of the maritime cities, Gaza and Anthedon, and Joppa, and Strato's Tower. He also made him a present of four hundred Gauls [Galatians] as a guard for his body, which they had been to Cleopatra before.'[10]

Thus, with Egypt annexed, Rome's eastern provinces restored and the loyalty of the client kingdoms reaffirmed, not to mention a temporary truce with Parthia in place, Octavianus left the East for Rome and, for him, the more important business of securing his political control of the Roman Republic. This was a task initially accomplished by 27 BC with his first constitutional settlement, finally bringing about an end to the Third Roman Civil War.[11]

6. Augustus and the East – The Parthian Civil War (26–25 BC)

With political control of the Roman Republic, Octavianus – who by 27 BC had adopted another new identity, that of Augustus, the Republic's benevolent First Citizen (at least in Augustan propaganda) – turned his attention to Rome's empire. In the years that followed he began on a massive expansion of the empire, particularly in mainland Europe, with ad-hoc expansion being replaced by an overall grand design, guided by imperial necessities of trade and security. Yet Augustus' initial focus was not in the East, but the North and the West.

On the face of it, the lull in the Romano-Parthian War continued, with Parthia still holding Armenia and Media, whilst the Romans held Asia Minor, Syria and, most importantly of all, Egypt.[12] Yet as we have seen throughout this war, open conflict between Roman and Parthian forces had been interspersed with wars fought by proxies, whether it be Q. Labienus in 40 BC or Artavasdes of Media in the late 30s. This again seems to have been the case in c.26 BC when the exiled Parthian king, Tiridates II, previously a guest of Augustus in Roman Syria, seems to have launched an invasion of the Parthian Empire down the Euphrates. We only have one brief mention of this in the surviving sources (supported by some numismatic evidence), coming from the Greek travel writer Isidore of Charax:

'Beyond is an island in the Euphrates; there was the treasure of Phraates, who cut the throats of his concubines, when Tiridates who was exiled, invaded the land.'[13]

Tiridates seems to have launched a surprise invasion of Parthia, catching Phraates off guard, so much so that he fled, having murdered his own harem, displaying typical Phraatrean ruthlessness. We must assume that Tiridates launched his assault from Roman territory and headed straight down the Euphrates, presumably making for the Parthian capital of Ctesiphon. We have no other sources which provide any further details on the war which followed, but we can assume from the time that Tiridates had to mint his own coins once more, that he briefly resumed control of at least a portion of the Parthian Empire.

The question we must ask ourselves, however, is what role the Romans played in this invasion? We know that, at the time, Augustus himself was campaigning in Spain, and we have no references to any Roman forces being involved. However, if, as likely, Tiridates did invade the Parthian Empire from Syria, he must have done so with the tacit blessing of the Roman governor, even if he had not amassed a large force, and it is highly unlikely that any Roman governor would do so without Augustus' blessing.[14]

We are drawn to the conclusion that Tiridates' invasion of Parthia was done with the knowledge and blessing of the Romans, and most probably Augustus himself. Such a move can be seen to make perfect strategic sense. Augustus was not in a position to attack Parthia, being tied up with his wars in the West, and thus, as Antonius had done just a few years before, he utilised a local proxy to do it for him. At worst, Tiridates would be defeated but having weakened Phraates' rule further and with Augustus not directly implicated. At best, Phraates would be overthrown and a pro-Roman Parthian king would ascend the throne, bringing Parthia into Rome's orbit.

As it was, Tiridates fared no better the second time in his war against Phraates, and early successes were soon turned into defeat, with Phraates again seemingly relying upon his Scythian allies to protect his throne. We must assume that Tiridates did not possess sufficient forces to match the Phraates' Scythians. Both Dio and Justin report the outcome:

'During his absence, the Parthians had made one Tiridates king, who, when he heard of the approach of the Scythians, fled with a great body of his partisans to Caesar, who was then carrying on war in Spain, taking with him, as a hostage for Caesar, the youngest son of Phraates, whom, being but negligently guarded, he had secretly carried off. Phraates, on hearing of his flight, immediately sent ambassadors to Caesar, requesting that his slave Tiridates, and his son, should be restored to him. Caesar, after listening to the embassy of Phraates, and deliberating on the application of Tiridates (for he also had asked to be restored to his throne, saying that Parthia would be wholly in the power of the Romans, if he should hold the kingdom as a gift from them), replied that he would neither give up Tiridates to the Parthians, nor give assistance to Tiridates against the Parthians. That it might not appear, however, that nothing had been obtained from Caesar by all their applications, he sent back to Phraates his son without ransom, and ordered a handsome maintenance to be furnished to Tiridates, as long as he chose to continue among the Romans.'[15]

'Thus, when Tiridates in person and envoys from Phraates came to settle their mutual recriminations, he brought them before the Senate; and afterwards, when the decision of the question had been referred to him by that body, he did not surrender Tiridates to Phraates, but sent back to the latter his son whom he had once received from him and was keeping, on condition that the captives and the military standards taken in the disasters of Crassus and of Antonius should be returned.'[16]

Thus, once more, Tiridates fled to Roman territory, again with a son of Phraates in captivity. As always, we must watch out accidental duplications in our differing sources with regard to the finer details, but it seems that Augustus again gave Tiridates sanctuary and a pension, in Roman territory, perhaps away from the Parthian frontier on this occasion. We certainly hear no more of Tiridates after this final defeat. On this occasion, however, Augustus maintained scrupulous constitutional niceties and referred the matter to the Senate, with it being perhaps the first time that Parthian envoys had been to Rome. Furthermore, this seems to have been the first mention by Rome and Augustus of the return of the Roman standards lost by Crassus and Antonius (though those of Statianus were returned by the Median king in the 30s BC).

Phraates had been able once more to cling onto his throne, but it was a timely reminder from Augustus and Rome that his position was not a strong one. Whilst he could use his Scythian allies to fight in Parthia and overwhelm a weaker opponent, could he utilise them in a defence of Parthia from a full Roman invasion? Having again restored a temporary treaty between the two empires, Augustus resumed his conquest of Spain. However, in the years which followed, Augustus' attention and subsequent Roman military activity increasingly turned eastwards.

7. Augustus' Other Eastern Wars

i) The Arabian War (26–25 BC)

The Arabian War was the first aggressive war of expansion in the East during Augustus' rule. Its objective was seemingly not to acquire territory, but to secure control of the trade routes between Egypt and India by ensuring Rome's military domination of the southern Arabian Peninsula, in what is now Yemen. The whole campaign showed the importance of annexing Ptolemaic Egypt to Rome's empire. Outside of the Mediterranean world there was a well-established network of trade routes spanning from China to India and then into the Near East, the two principal routes overland (the famous silk road) or across the Indian Ocean and up the Red Sea.[17] The problem for Rome (prior to the final civil war) was that the land route was controlled by the Parthian Empire, whilst the sea route was dominated by the Ptolemaic Empire. Whilst control of the land route was still outside of Roman control, with the annexation of Egypt, Rome now had direct access to the maritime trading network which spanned the ancient world.

Yet control of Egypt did not mean control of the Red Sea, and in particular the tribes of the southern Arabian Peninsula had the prime strategic position to intercept merchant shipping and engage in piracy. Thus, if Rome was to make the most of access to these trade routes then these tribes needed to be brought under Roman control (whether direct or indirect). These lands also had a potential economic as well as a strategic value.[18] To those ends, Augustus ordered a 10,000-strong force to cross from Egypt to southern Arabia. Although this move sounds strategic sense in itself, we can also view it in terms of the ongoing war with Parthia, and it can be seen as an outflanking manoeuvre, giving Rome access to the Indian Ocean and bypassing the Parthian Empire. Command of the expedition was given to the Prefect of Egypt, C. Aelius Gallus, a friend of the geographer Strabo, who produced an account of the Arabian War, taken from Gallus himself:[19]

'It was his [Augustus'] intention either to conciliate or subdue the Arabians. He was also influenced by the report, which had prevailed from all time, that this people were very wealthy, and exchanged their aromatics and precious stones for silver and gold, but never expended with foreigners any part of what they received in exchange. He hoped to acquire either opulent friends, or to overcome opulent enemies. He was moreover encouraged to undertake this enterprise by the expectation of assistance from the Nabataeans, who promised to co-operate with him in everything …[20]

'… he [Gallus] constructed a hundred and thirty vessels of burden, in which he embarked with about ten thousand infantry, collected from Egypt, consisting of Romans and allies, among whom were five hundred Jews and a thousand Nabataeans, under the command of Syllaeus.'[21]

Gallus' army included a contingent of allied forces from Judea and Nabataea. Their main target was the Sabaean kingdom. Unfortunately for Gallus, the Nabataeans and Syllaeus, the official envoy of the Nabataean King Obodas III, seemingly had no intention of allowing the Romans to expand their powerbase into the Arabian Gulf, and Syllaeus, acting as a guide, did his best to hamper the expedition. Despite some initial successes against poorly equipped natives and their cities, the heat and disease set in and forced Gallus to retreat back to Nabataea, a march which saw the vast majority of the army succumb to the elements and disease. According to Roman sources, this disastrous retreat was caused by the treachery of Syllaeus, but that may well be the Romans looking for a scapegoat.

After eighteen months, and with the majority of his army dead, Gallus returned to Alexandria and then Rome in disgrace, with the expedition a disaster. Whilst Rome still had access to the maritime trading routes of the ancient world, it never managed to secure a presence in the southern Arabian Peninsula or the Indian Ocean. Nevertheless, as McLaughlin reports, the expedition did weaken the Sabaean kingdom, allowing it to be overrun by its neighbours, who studiously paid token homage to Rome.[22]

Syllaeus himself, though clearly acting on orders from his king, paid the price for the disaster:

'Syllaeus, the author of these disasters, was punished for his treachery at Rome. He affected friendship, but he was convicted of other offences, besides perfidy in this instance, and was beheaded.'[23]

The Nabataeans remained a client state of the Romans, defending Egypt and Syria from the Bedouin tribes of Arabia, until their annexation by the Emperor Trajan in AD 106/107.

ii) The Kushite War (c.25–23 BC)
It was Egypt again rather than Parthia which continued to dominate Augustus' strategic thinking and military attention. Exploiting the absence of the main Egyptian garrison (in Arabia), the neighbouring Nubian Kushite kingdom launched a massive invasion of southern Egypt, overwhelming the few remaining garrisons and sacking various cities and temples, most famously decapitating a statue of Augustus himself and carrying the head off to be buried in a Kushite temple at Meroe (it was not recovered until it was excavated in 1910 by British archaeologists: see images).[24] Again, Strabo preserves an account:

'The Ethiopians, emboldened in consequence of a part of the forces in Egypt being drawn off by Aelius Gallus, who was engaged in war with the Arabs, invaded the Thebais, and attacked the garrison, consisting of three cohorts, near Syene; surprised and took Syene, Elephantina, and Philae, by a sudden inroad; enslaved the inhabitants, and threw down the statues of Caesar.'[25]

In response, Augustus dispatched the new governor of Egypt, C. Petronius, with a fresh army to retaliate. Strabo gives an excellent account of the campaign:[26]

'But Petronius, marching with less than 10,000 infantry and 800 horse against an army of 30,000 men, first compelled them to retreat to Pselchis, an Ethiopian city. He then sent deputies to demand restitution of what they had taken, and the reasons which had induced them to begin the war. On their alleging that they had been ill treated by the nomarchs [provincial governors], he answered, that these were not the sovereigns of the country, but Caesar. When they desired three days for consideration, and did nothing which they were bound to do, Petronius attacked and compelled them to fight. They soon fled, being badly commanded, and badly armed; for they carried large shields made of raw hides, and hatchets for offensive weapons; some, however, had pikes, and others, swords. Part of the insurgents were driven into the city, others fled into the uninhabited country; and such as ventured upon the passage of the river escaped to a neighbouring island, where there were not many crocodiles on account of the current. Among the fugitives, were the generals of Candace, queen of the Ethiopians in our time, a masculine woman, and who had lost an eye. Petronius, pursuing them in rafts and ships, took them all and despatched them immediately to Alexandria. He then attacked Pselchis and took it. If we add the number of those who fell in battle to the number of prisoners, few only could have escaped.'[27]

Thus the Romans, operating further south than they ever had, were able to inflict a series of defeat on the Kushites, sacking cities and taking captives. The war dragged on until 23 BC, when the Kushites opened negotiations with Petronius and ambassadors were sent to Augustus in the East:

'In the meantime, Candace attacked the garrison with an army of many thousand men. Petronius came to its assistance and entering the fortress before the approach of the enemy, secured the place by many expedients. The enemy sent ambassadors, but he ordered them to repair to Caesar: on their replying, that they did not know who Caesar was, nor where they were to find him, Petronius appointed persons to conduct them to his presence. They arrived at Samos,

where Caesar was at that time, and from whence he was on the
point of proceeding into Syria, having already despatched Tiberius
into Armenia. The ambassadors obtained all that they desired, and
Caesar even remitted the tribute which he had imposed.'[28]

The Kushites had been brought into the Roman client system, and
Petronius was able to create a secure southern border for Egypt by
establishing a Roman fort at Premnis, between the First and Second
Cataracts of the Nile, on the site of an older Egyptian fort, securing
the route down the Nile into Egypt.[29] Nevertheless, we can see that the
annexation of Ptolemaic Egypt brought both great benefits and great
dangers to Rome. Control of Egypt brought direct access to the great
trading routes of the ancient world, removing a middleman and thus
increasing the flow of profits into Roman coffers.[30] Yet within just the
first decade of Roman possession of Egypt, Roman armies had been
dispatched into Southern Arabia and the Sudan. So whilst Rome's
formal empire did not expand, its informal network of client kingdoms
and spheres of influence did, stretching deep into Africa and Arabia.

In terms of the ongoing, but stalled, Parthian War, the important
aspect to note is that Augustus and Rome's attentions were on these
eastern matters, with campaigns in Arabia and the Sudan, rather than
on the Near East. When the latest Parthian Civil War ended in c.25 BC
and emissaries were sent by Phraates to Augustus, the Romans were too
preoccupied with matters further south to renew hostilities.

iii) The Annexation of Galatia (25 BC)
Another insight into Augustus' policy in the East came in 25 BC when
Amyntas I, king of the allied kingdom of Galatia in Asia Minor, died. As
we have seen, Amyntas had been an appointment of Antonius, and had
been one of only few Antonine client kings who survived Octavianus'
purges following Actium. Yet upon his death, Augustus seized the
opportunity to annex the kingdom and turn it into a Roman province:

'On the death of Amyntas he did not entrust his kingdom to the sons
of the deceased but made it a part of the subject territory. Thus,
Galatia together with Lycaonia obtained a Roman governor, and the

portions of Pamphylia formerly assigned to Amyntas were restored to their own district.'[31]

Augustus here began the policy of converting client kingdoms into Roman provinces, ensuring more direct Roman control of Asia Minor and the regions bordering the Parthian Empire, a policy continued piecemeal by his successors.

8. Augustus, the Sakan Embassies and a Second Front

In 26 BC, whilst Augustus was campaigning in Spain, he received a most unusual embassy:

> 'The reputation for prowess and moderation which he thus gained led even the Indians and the Scythians, nations known to us only by hearsay, to send envoys of their own free will and sue for his friendship and that of the Roman People.'[32]
>
> 'Meanwhile envoys from the Indians and Scythians, after crossing the whole world, finally found Caesar at Tarragona in Hither Spain.'[33]

India at the time was a patchwork of kingdoms and races, several of which in the Indus region were ruled by the Saka, the formerly nomadic raiders which had overrun the eastern Parthian Empire in the second century BC (see Chapter One). Though neither ancient source names the race or kingdom that these ambassadors represented, McLaughlin has argued that they came from the Saka kingdoms of the Indus, which at the time were under pressure from an advancing Parthian Empire, expanding eastwards towards the Indus.[34]

This embassy was followed by a second, in 22 BC, which reached him at Samos (see below):

> 'For a great many embassies came to him, and the people of India, who had already made overtures, now made a treaty of friendship.'[35]
>
> 'He says that at Antioch, near Daphne, he chanced to meet the Indian ambassadors who had been despatched to Caesar Augustus;

that the letter plainly indicated more than three ambassadors, but that only three had survived (whom he says he saw), but the rest, mostly by reason of the long journeys, had died; and that the letter was written in Greek on a skin; and that it plainly showed that Porus was the writer, and that, although he was ruler of six hundred kings, still he was anxious to be a friend to Caesar, and was ready, not only to allow him a passage through his country, wherever he wished to go, but also to co-operate with him in anything that was honourable.'[36]

It could be argued that the passage from Strabo which states that the unnamed Indian king would wish to cooperate with Augustus and allow him passage through his country could easily be read as offering a military alliance. McLaughlin argues that the king in question was Azes, the last of the great Sakan monarchs of the Indus kingdoms, and that he was offering Augustus an alliance against the Parthians. Thus the enemy of his enemy would hopefully become his friend.[37]

This is an intriguing suggestion that Augustus could have allied with an Indian king in an aggressive pact against Parthia and thereby open up an eastern front in the ongoing war. Whilst this is only speculation, it would add an intriguing aspect to Augustus' tactical thinking and perhaps help to apply pressure on the Parthian Empire, which potentially would find itself fighting a simultaneous war on two fronts; something that they had always suffered from (see Chapter One).

As it turned out, Augustus received the embassies and offers of friendship with courtesy, along with the exotic gifts they brought, but declined any alliance. Ironically, within a generation the Sakan kingdoms had been swept aside by the Parthians, but the region soon seceded from the Parthian Empire, under the command of a Parthian noble named Gondophares, who came from the Parthian noble family of Suren. Thus the descendants of the famous Surenas became kings in their own right in the Indo-Parthian kingdom (c.AD 19–240) and enemies of the Arsacid Dynasty.

9. Agrippa and the East (23 BC)

It was in 23 BC that we perhaps see a sign that Augustus' attention was turning once more to the Near East, with Augustus' deputy, and leading general, M. Vipsanius Agrippa, dispatched to the East to command Syria.

Many commentators, both ancient and modern,[38] have viewed this in terms of the struggle for the right to be seen as Augustus' successor, then being contested by Agrippa (his deputy) and M. Claudius Marcellus (Augustus' nephew and son-in-law). Some state that it was a voluntary exile, others that Augustus ordered him out of Rome to avoid a potential conflict between his two potential successors:

'When he [Augustus] recovered, therefore, and learned that Marcellus because of this was not friendly toward Agrippa, he immediately sent the latter to Syria, so that no occasion for scoffing or for skirmishing might arise between them by their being together. And Agrippa straightway set out from the city, but did not reach Syria; instead, acting with even more than his usual moderation, he sent his lieutenants thither, and tarried himself in Lesbos.'[39]

Given that all of these ancient sources were written after the event, and with the well-known and corpse-laden struggle for the imperial succession, it is not a surprise that every action is viewed through this lens. Yet in several respects we can also view this action in relation to the ongoing Romano-Parthian War. Firstly, as we have seen, it was around this period that Phraates emerged successful in the Parthian Civil War against Tiridates II, his Roman-backed opponent. So even if Augustus did want to remove Agrippa from Rome, dispatching his best general to Syria made excellent strategic sense.

Stationing Agrippa in Syria would serve several functions: it was a warning to Phraates not to renew hostilities and a reminder that Augustus had not forgotten the East, despite his military activities elsewhere. Furthermore, if Augustus was planning to visit the East himself to bring an end to the Romano-Parthian War, one way or another he would need someone on the ground whom he could trust to gather the necessary intelligence and make the necessary preparation. Viewed in these terms, it is therefore no surprise that Rome's leading general was dispatched to the East, as Magie points out, although Josephus paints a different picture and one not tainted by court politics: [40]

'Now Agrippa was sent to succeed Caesar in the government of the countries beyond the Ionian Sea, upon whom Herod lighted when he was wintering about Mitylene.'[41]

Magie further argues that one of Agrippa's roles was to open negotiations with the Parthians about the return of the lost standards.[42] As it turns out, Agrippa made it no further than the Greek island of Lesbos, preferring to rule Syria via legates. Once again, matters at Rome trumped those in the East. On this occasion it turned out that his caution was warranted, as events in Rome turned in his favour. Augustus had dropped dangerously ill, a situation which could have plunged the Republic back into civil war (echoing the situation in 44 BC where there were a number of men who could have claimed to be Caesar's successors, men such as Antonius, a contemporary, or Octavianus, a relative by blood). Some twenty years later, for Antonius and Octavianus, this could so easily have been Agrippa and Marcellus. As it turns out, Augustus survived the health scare, but it was Marcellus who died, of what was reported to be natural causes. This meant that Agrippa was now the clear successor to Augustus, a position Augustus himself confirmed when he recalled Agrippa to Rome and married him to his newly widowed daughter Iulia.

10. The End of the Second Romano-Parthian War (22–20 BC) – The Political Settlement

Augustus' health scare and the loss of his natural heir brought about a number of changes, the greatest being a new – and final – constitutional settlement in 23 BC, to secure his position in Rome.[43] With these matters settled, his thoughts do seem to have turned to the Near East and the war with Parthia. It may well have been that his brush with death brought about a period of introspection and realisation that the situation in the East remained the greatest unsolved issue of his rule.

As we have seen, in the intervening years, both empires had consolidated their positions. Phraates had ended the latest civil war and been restored to the throne, backed by an unknown number of Scythian tribes, though his opponent, Tiridates, and his own son remained in Roman hands. Yet during this period, the Romans had secured Ptolemaic Egypt, started to directly access the trade routes to India and China, and secured the submission of the neighbouring Kushite kingdom in the Sudan. Egypt was now clearly Roman and lost to Parthia – as was Judea – removing the last independent power in the region. After sixty years of warfare, starting in the 80s BC, only two powers remained – the Roman Republic and the Parthian Empire – with all other kingdoms having been reduced to the status of a province or client kingdom.

Having secured a new constitutional settlement in Rome and recalled Agrippa to Rome, Augustus left Rome in 22 BC and began a tour of the East, making his way via Greece. After wintering in Greece, during 21 BC he passed into Asia Minor and then into Syria on a grand tour, dispensing justice and settling local issues as he went:

> 'Thus, he instituted various reforms, so far as seemed desirable, and made donations of money to some, at the same time commanding others to contribute an amount in excess of the tribute. He reduced the people of Cyzicus to slavery because during a factious quarrel they had flogged and put to death some Romans. And when he reached Syria, he took the same action in the case of the people of Tyre and Sidon on account of their factious quarrelling.'[44]

By 21 BC, Augustus had reached Syria, not at the command of an army, though there were legions stationed there. Phraates would have been well aware of the impending approach of Augustus and must have been clearly wondering about his intentions towards Parthia. The lack of an army ruled out an immediate invasion, but the presence of Augustus himself could have meant that he was in the region to begin such preparations. It was at this point that Phraates 'blinked' in the standoff and offered terms to end hostilities. Several years earlier, Augustus had named his price for peace, and it was not land – having already conquered Egypt – but prestige.

Following both Crassus' and Antonius' failed invasions of the Parthian Empire, the Romans had lost a number of legionary standards, the very symbol of Roman martial pride, along with a significant number of Roman prisoners, most of whom seemed to have been quartered on the very eastern fringes of the Parthian Empire at Merv.[45] Roman rhetoric and poetry had long called for revenge for the losses at Carrhae and the death of Crassus, as best recorded by Propertius:

> 'Caesar, our God, plots war against rich India, cutting the straits,
> in his fleet, across the pearl-bearing ocean. Men, the rewards are

great: far lands prepare triumphs: Tiber and Euphrates will flow
to your tune. Too late, but that province will come under Ausonian
wands, Parthia's trophies will get to know Latin Jupiter. Go, get
going, prows expert in battle: set sail: and armoured horses do your
accustomed duty! I sing you auspicious omens. And avenge that
disaster of Crassus! Go and take care of Roman history!'[46]

The standards lost at Carrhae and those of Antonius thus took on a
symbolic status in Roman politics and society, which made their return
of central importance, far more than additional territories in the East.
Furthermore, if Parthia could be made to give them up, then it would not
only erase the bitter memories of the losses to Parthia, but act as a token
of submission, at least in Roman eyes. Phraates offered up what to the
Parthians were fairly meaningless trophies of bygone battles and hoped
to buy off Augustus from contemplating a renewal of the war:

'Meanwhile Phraates, fearing that Augustus would lead an
expedition against him because he had not yet performed any of his
engagements, sent back to him the standards and all the captives,
with the exception of a few who in shame had destroyed themselves
or, eluding detection, remained in the country. Augustus received
them as if he had conquered the Parthian in a war; for he took great
pride in the achievement, declaring that he had recovered without a
struggle what had formerly been lost in battle. Indeed, in honour of
this success he commanded that sacrifices be decreed and likewise a
Temple to Mars Ultor on the Capitol, in imitation of that of Jupiter
Feretrius, in which to dedicate the standards; and he himself carried
out both decrees. Moreover, he rode into the city on horseback and
was honoured with a Triumphal arch.'[47]

'Sometime after, when Caesar had finished the Spanish War, and
had proceeded to Syria to settle the affairs of the east, he caused
some alarm to Phraates, who was afraid that he might contemplate
an invasion of Parthia. Whatever prisoners, accordingly, remained
of the army of Crassus or Antonius throughout Parthia, were
collected together, and sent, with the military standards that had
been taken, to Augustus. In addition to this, the sons and grandsons

of Phraates were delivered to Augustus as hostages; and thus Caesar effected more by the power of his name, than any other general could have done by his arms.'[48]

Augustus was able to add another triumph to his record without even fighting a war. The return of the standards – and to a lesser degree the prisoners – became a major event in Rome, commemorated through public celebrations, buildings and coins (see images). Furthermore, in Roman eyes he had secured the submission of the King of Parthia and the whole Parthian Empire without having to risk another dangerous invasion.

11. The End of the Second Romano-Parthian War (20 BC) – The Military Settlement

Nevertheless, aside from all the pomp and celebrations we must ask ourselves what were Augustus' intentions for the East? Though far from an accomplished general himself, he was in the process of overseeing the largest expansion of Rome's empire that had ever been witnessed. By the end of his rule, Rome had annexed huge swathes of continental Europe, establishing the Danube as border between Rome and tribal Europe, along with a failed attempt to annex all the German tribes up to the Elbe, eventually retreating to the Rhine.

With the whole of the military resources of Rome's empire at his command and a firm control of Rome itself, he was in a position that exceeded any previous Roman general, including that of his adopted father. Furthermore, although he himself was not a great general, he had a wide range of able generals from which to choose, including the grandson of Crassus himself, M. Licinius Crassus, and his old ally – and now son-in-law – M. Vipsanius Agrippa, along with his stepson Ti. Claudius Nero (Tiberius).

Yet the fact remains that Augustus did not order the invasion of the Parthian Empire, nor its annexation, nor fulfil the ambitions of many Romans to take their empire to Bactria and even India. In this respect Augustus stood out as unusual, perhaps the only Roman oligarch not to be drawn in by the myths of Alexander the Great and his conquests and attempts at establishing a universal empire, which had so drawn in men such as Pompeius, Caesar and Antonius.

Nevertheless, even though there was no invasion of the Parthian Empire nor attempt at its annexation, before the year was out, Augustus did take more practical measures to ensure Roman military dominance of the region. As detailed earlier, amongst the many high-status refugees from the East who were sheltering under Augustus' protection were the family of the pro-Parthian ruler of Armenia and the sons of the King of Media-Atropatené, all of whom had been receiving a Roman education and upbringing. This policy paid off when the Armenians, clearly taking advantage of the presence of Augustus and the outbreak of peace between him and Phraates, revolted against their pro-Parthian King Artaxes, who had been installed in the wake of the Parthian victories in 32/31 BC (see Chapter Ten):

> 'And since the other Armenians had preferred charges against Artaxes and had summoned his brother Tigranes, who was in Rome, the emperor sent Tiberius to drive Artaxes out of the kingdom and to reinstate Tigranes. And although nothing was accomplished by Tiberius commensurate with his preparations, since before his arrival the Armenians slew Artaxes, yet he assumed a lofty bearing, especially after sacrifices had been voted to commemorate what he had done, as though he had accomplished something by valour.'[49]

Despite the Parthians returning the Roman legionary standards, or perhaps because they did, Augustus chose to demonstrably flex Roman power and ordered his stepson, Tiberius, to invade the Parthian client kingdom of Armenia and install a pro-Roman client king on the throne. Thus, ten years after Rome lost Armenia, it was returned to its earlier status as a Roman client kingdom. It is telling that Phraates and the Parthians did nothing to intervene, acknowledging through their inaction that they had no wish to resume or restart the war with Rome.

It may well have been at this time that the Romans installed a pro-Roman king on the throne of Media-Atropatené, the other major client kingdom overrun by the Parthians in 32/31 BC. Following the Parthian victory, the pro-Roman (and pro-Antonine) King Artavasdes I fled to

Roman territory and was replaced by a previously unknown, but pro-Parthian, relative, Asinnalus. Yet by 20 BC we see the son of the exiled Artavasdes installed on the throne of Media, ruling as Ariobarzanes II. When he was installed is not known, but it would be logical that it was done at the same time as a pro-Roman ruler was placed on the throne of Armenia.

By the end of 20 BC, not only had Augustus secured the return of the Roman legionary standards and the prisoners, but he had overturned the result of the last conflict fought between Rome and Parthia and placed pro-Roman rulers on the thrones of Armenia and Media-Atropatené, returning them to the Roman fold. Having accomplished all of this, Augustus signalled an end to the hostilities between the two powers and returned to Rome to celebrate his 'victory' over Parthia, reorganising more of the eastern provinces on the way:

> 'Therefore, he undertook no war, at any rate for the time being, but actually gave away certain principalities; to Iamblichus, the son of Iamblichus, his ancestral dominion over the Arabians, and to Tarcondimotus, the son of Tarcondimotus, the kingdom of Cilicia, which his father had held, except for a few places on the coast. These latter together with Lesser Armenia he granted to Archelaus, because the Mede, who previously had ruled them, was dead. To Herod he entrusted the tetrarchy of a certain Zenodorus, and to one Mithridates, though still a mere boy, he gave Commagene, inasmuch as its king had put the boy's father to death.'[50]

12. The End of the Second Romano-Parthian War (20 BC)

By the end of 20 BC, the second war between the Roman Republic and the Parthian Empire had been brought to a conclusion, albeit with a whimper not a bang. The war which had started with the Parthian invasion of the Near East and its attempted annexation, and had seen a counter Roman invasion of the Parthian Empire, ended with a de-facto agreement not to resume hostilities.

With the pendulum swinging back and forth between the two powers, by 20 BC the Romans clearly had the upper hand. The civil wars which had been so successfully exploited by the Parthians had been concluded, and now only one Roman held sway in the Republic. By contrast, although the latest Parthian Civil War had been won by Phraates, his position – and that of Parthia – were far less secure. He had seemingly been ousted from his throne twice in the last decade by his rival Tiridates, who was residing in comfortable exile at Rome's expense. All of the most recent conflicts with Rome had seen Parthian internal divisions exposed, fuelling plots against his rule, which had never been secure since his far more popular and able brother, Pacorus, had died fighting the Romans at the Battle of Gindarus.

Thus, it suited both Augustus and Phraates to end hostilities. Augustus could return to Rome and claim victory in the war and submission over the Parthians without ever having to risk a third Roman invasion of the Parthian Empire. Clearly, he judged the whole effort not worth it, both in terms of the possible territorial gains and the pursuit of the myth of Alexander the Great. Throughout his oversight of the Republic, Augustus seems to have aimed at securing defendable borders for Rome's empire and ending the exposure to the vast swathes of tribal Europe.[51] It is more than probable that he calculated that the annexation of the Parthian Empire would lead to the reverse and expose Rome to the vast swathes of tribal Asia. If nothing else, Phraates had proved that he could command the tribes of Scythia, who could sweep into Parthia at will. Parthian history had shown that the exposed eastern border was a constant danger (see Chapter One).

Augustus had resecured Roman dominance in the East, both by the de-facto ending of hostilities with Parthia and the ability to depict his actions as a victory back in Rome.[52] As always, there may well have been an element that he did not wish to be sucked into a long-term war in the East, allowing his enemies – or even his allies – at Rome time to undermine his position as Rome's *Princeps* (First Citizen).

For Augustus, it seems that Egypt was the real prize and that had already been secured, along with its wealth, food supply and access to the eastern trade routes. The Euphrates was now in reality the border between the two powers, though more in a sense of line of demarcation than a defensible border.[53] Furthermore, both Armenia and Media had been brought back into the Roman sphere of influence, reversing the

Parthian gains of the 30s BC. Thus for Augustus, and the Republic he spoke for, the war was at an end and they were the winners.

Phraates could also claim that he had at least not lost the war. For the price of a few trophies and prisoners, and two pro-Roman monarchs, the perpetual threat of Roman invasion had been ended, at least for his lifetime, and he could concentrate on securing his shaky rule of the Parthian Empire, itself riven by years of civil war. Nevertheless, although Parthia had not lost any territory – at least since before the war – this de-facto treaty ended the two-century westwards expansion of the Parthian Empire and its dream of recreating the Persian Empire of Darius the Great. The Mediterranean was now firmly in the control of the Romans, as was Egypt itself (see Map 11).

Summary – Shaping the Future; The End of Alexander's Dream

By 20 BC, the constant flux that the Middle East had experienced since the decline of the Seleucid Empire had come to an end. Despite the best efforts of each side, there was to be no new universal empire stretching from the Mediterranean to the Indus. The region was now divided between two great empires, those of Rome and Parthia, with the Euphrates as the dividing line. Yet we must be careful not to make too much of this division, as the peoples on either side still shared a common bond with their neighbours, regardless of whether they paid their tribute to Rome or to Ctesiphon. The trade routes that spanned the region continued, and if anything prospered now the two empires learned to co-exist with each other.

In the short term, the end of the Second Romano-Parthian War brought an end to sixty years of near continuous fighting: from the rise of the empires of Pontus and Armenia, to Rome's great eastwards expansion in the Great Eastern War (74–63 BC), the first clashes between the two empires in the First Romano-Parthian War (55–50 BC) and finally the titanic struggle of the Second Romano-Parthian War (40–20 BC). Time and again, cities and kingdoms were devastated by one side or the other, or even both, as the two empires marched their armies across the Near East and Asia Minor. The accommodation that Augustus and

Phraates reached brought an end to all this and allowed an outbreak of peace, which lasted nearly eighty years until the Third Romano-Parthian War in AD 58.

In the longer term, we can see that throughout their histories these two great powers had always been expanding towards each other, and in many cases mirroring each other's progress, both in the highs and lows they experienced. Between them they destroyed the old Hellenistic order that had sprung up from the destruction of the great Persian Empire and the collapse of its brief Alexandrian successor. In many ways this parallel process can be seen by the frequent Roman desire to see themselves as the inheritors of Alexander and his dream of westward expansion, contrasted with the frequent desire of the Parthians to see themselves as the inheritors of Darius and Xerxes and their eastward expansion.

In the end, neither power was to achieve its dream of inheritance. Augustus and most of his successors – excluding Trajan – gave up on the Alexandrian dream of eastern conquest, satisfied with control of the Mediterranean and in particular the prize of Egypt. Thirty years of warfare across two wars had left the Romans acutely aware of the disasters of Carrhae and Antonius' invasion, and that the conquest of Parthia was seemingly not worth the effort. Whilst the East had been central to Alexander, to those living in Rome, it was but on the fringes of their empire and consciousness.

Phraates and his successors also had to acknowledge the end of the dream of recreating the great Persian Empire. Though they claimed the ancient title of King of Kings, Egypt, Syria and Asia Minor were lost to the Romans. They too could point to the disaster at Gindarus and the death of Pacorus, up until which point the dream had seemed possible.

Nevertheless, the stalemate that both Augustus and Phraates accepted proved to be an incredibly durable one, ultimately lasting some 650 years, with periods of peace being broken by intermittent warfare. It is remarkable that this dividing line was maintained for such a long period, given the radical changes that each empire underwent. In Rome's case, the Republic evolved into an Empire and then an Eastern Empire with a new capital at Constantinople, coupled with a new universal religion. In the Parthian case, the Arsacid Dynasty was overthrown by a Sassanid one and the Parthian Empire became a reborn Persian one. Over 600 years later, these two powers engaged in another titanic struggle (AD 602–628) which briefly saw the Persian Empire annex Egypt and the whole Near East and Asia Minor. Yet this war too ended in a stalemate and a return to the borders agreed some 650 years earlier. Ultimately, however, neither empire would achieve their respective dream of recreating a universal empire – be it Persian or Alexandrian – as each fell victim to the rise of a third power, aided by the exhaustion of both Rome and Persia, and thus the ancient world did finally see the rise of a new universal empire, that of the Islamic Caliphate, which brought the ancient world to an end.

Rulers of the Eastern Kingdoms

Kings of Parthia (c.247–2 BC)

Exact dates for the majority of the Parthian kings are impossible to determine to the nearest year. Furthermore, there is still no certainty over the chronology of the first two Parthian kings and the role of the founder of the Dynasty, Arsaces. Thus modern scholarship has a number of different lists for the number and dates of the Parthian kings prior to the first century BC. Presented below are a traditional and modern interpretation of the ancient sources.

Traditional List[1]		Alternative List[2]	
Arsaces		Arsaces I	c.247–210
Tiridates	c.247–211	Arscaes II	c.210–185
Artabanus	c.211–191	Phriapatius	c.185–170
Priapatius	c.191–176	Arscaes IV	c.170–168
Phraates	c.176–171	Phraates I	c.168–165
Mithradates	c.171–138	Mithradates I	c.165–132
Phraates II	c.138–128	Phraates II	c.132–126
Artabanus II	c.128–124	Bagasis	c.126
Mithradates II	c.123–88	Artabanus I	c.126–122
Gotarzes	c.91–80	Arsaces X	c.122–121
Orodes I	c.80–76	Mithradates II	c.121–91
Sinatruces	c.76–70/69	Sinatruces	c.92–70/69
Phraates III	c.70/69–58/57	Gotarzes I	c.91–87
Mithradates III	c.58/57–55	Mithradates III	c.87–80
Orodes II	c.57–37	Orodes I	c.80– 5
Phraates IV	37–2	Arsaces XVI	c.78/77–62/61
		Phraates III	c.70/69–58
		Mithradates IV	c.58–55

Orodes II	57–37
Phraates IV	37–2
Tiradates	c.30–26

Kings of Macedon (336–147 BC)

Alexander III	336–323
Alexander IV	323–310
Philip III	323–317
Olympias	317–316
Cassander	315–297
Philip IV	297
Alexander V	297–294
Antipater I	297–294
Demetrius I	294–288
Pyrrhus	287–285
Lysimachus	287–281
Seleucus I	281
Ptolemy	281–279
Antigonus II	276–239
Demetrius II	239–229
Antigonus III	229–221
Philip V	221–179
Perseus	179–167

167 BC: Kingdom of Macedonia Abolished by Rome.

Andriscus	149–148

147 BC: Republics of Macedonia Annexed by Rome.

Seleucid Kings (c.311–64 BC)

From the foundation of the Seleucid Empire, following the death of Alexander the Great

Seleucus I	c.311–281
Antiochus I	281–261

Antiochus II	261–246
Seleucus II	246–226
Seleucus III	226–223
Antiochus III	223–187
Seleucus IV	187–175
Antiochus IV	175–164
Antiochus V	164–162
Demetrius I	162–150
Alexander I	150–145
Demetrius II	145–139 & 129–125
Antiochus VI	145–142
Antiochus VII	138–129
Cleopatra	126–123
Antiochus VIII	126–96
Seleucus V	126
Antiochus IX	114–95
Seleucus VI	95
Antiochus X	95
Demetrius III	95–88
Antiochus XI	95
Philip I	95–83
Antiochus XII	87
Philip II	83

83 BC: Seleucid Empire Annexed by Armenia.
Antiochus XIII   69–64

64 BC: Seleucid Empire Annexed by Rome.

Ptolemaic Pharaohs (c.304–30 BC)

From the foundation of the Ptolemaic Dynasty, following the death of Alexander the Great

Ptolemy I	c.304–283
Ptolemy II	285–246
Ptolemy III	246–221

Ptolemy IV	221–204
Ptolemy V	204–180
Ptolemy VI	180–145
Ptolemy VIII	170–163 & 145–116
Cleopatra II	170–164 & 163–116
Ptolemy VII	145
Cleopatra III	139–101
Ptolemy IX	116–107 & 88–81
Ptolemy X	107 – 88
Ptolemy XI	80
Ptolemy XII	80–58 & 55–51
Berenice IV	58–55
Archelaos	56–55
Ptolemy XIII	51–47
Cleopatra VII	51–30
Ptolemy XIV	47–44
Ptolemy XV (Caesarion)	44–30

30 BC: Kingdom of Egypt Annexed by Rome.

Antonine Dynasty (34–30 BC)

Cleopatra VII	Queen of Kings	34–30
Ptolemy XV (Caesarion)	King of Kings	34–30
Alexander Helios	King of Armenia, Media & Parthia	34–30
Cleopatra Selene II	Queen of Cyrenaica	34–30
Ptolemy Philadelphus	King of Syria, Phoenicia and Cilicia	34–30

30 BC: Kingdom of Egypt Annexed by Rome.

Kings of Epirus (307–233 BC)

Alcetas II	313–306
Pyrrhus I	307–302
Neoptolemos II	302–297
Pyrrhus I	297–272
Alexander II	272–255

Pyrrhus II	255–237
Ptolemy	237–234
Pyrrhus III	234
Deidamia	234–233

233 BC: End of Epirote Monarchy.

167 BC: Epirus Annexed by Rome.

Kings of Armenia (first century BC)

Tigranes I	123–95
Tigranes II (Great)	95–55
Artavasdes II	55–34
Artaxes II	33–20
Tigranes III	20–10

Kings of Bithynia (first century BC)

Nicomedes III	127–94
Nicomedes IV	94–74

74 BC: Kingdom of Bithynia Annexed by Rome.

Kings of the Bosphorus (first century BC)

Mithridates I	108–63	(Mithridates VI of Pontus)
Pharnaces	63–47	
Mithridates II	47–44	
Asander	47, 44–17	

Kings of Cappadocia (first century BC)

Ariarathes VIII	101–96
Ariarathes IX	95
Ariobarzanes I	95–c.63

Ariobarzanes II   c.63–51
Ariobarzanes III   51–42
Ariarathes X   42–36
Archelaus   36–AD 17

Kings of Commagene (first century BC)

Mithridates I   109–70
Antiochus I   70–38
Mithridates II   38–20
Mithridates III   20–12

Kings of Galatia (first century BC)

Deiotarus   63–40
Brogitarius   63–50
Castor   40–36
Amyntas   37–25

25 BC: Kingdom of Galatia Annexed by Rome.

Kings of Judea (first century BC)

Alexander Jannaeus   103–76
Salome Alexandra   76–67
Hyrcanus II   67–66, 63–40
Aristobulus II   66–63
Antigonus II   40–37
Aristobulus III   36
Herodes   37–4 (Herod the Great)

Kings of Media (first century BC)

Mithridates I   67–66
Darius I   c.65
Ariobarzanes I   65–56

Artavasdes I	56–31
Asinnalus	30–20s
Ariobarzanes II	20s

Kings of Nabataea (first century BC)

Aretas II	110s–96
Obodas I	c.96–85
Rabbel I	c.85/84
Aretas III	84–c.59
Obodas II	c.62–c.59
Malichus I	59–30
Obodas III	30–9

Kings of Pontus (first century BC)

Mithridates VI	120–63
Pharnaces II	63–47
Darius I	39–37
Arsaces I	37
Polemon I	37–8

Appendix II

Sources For Parthian History: An Introduction

W hen dealing with the Parthians, we need to be fully aware of the extent of our ignorance on the subject. Despite the fact that the Parthian Empire lasted for over 470 years, was one of the two great civilizations of the ancient world and spanned an area from Syria to India and Central Asia, we have a ridiculously small amount of surviving material about it. A brief survey of the sources will reveal how truly little we know about this fascinating civilization.

1. Native Sources

The first and main point to note is the almost total absence of any surviving Parthian documents. Not only was the Parthian civilization swept away by its successor, the Sassanid Persians, but they too were swept away by the Muslim invasions. This double blow has meant that virtually no literary material survives from Parthian sources. The only historical documents of any note from the Parthian period are the Babylonian Astronomical records, which as well as recording astronomical data, record some of the historical actions of that particular year.[1] Even in fragmentary form they provide an invaluable record for the Parthian control of Mesopotamia, in the period from 141 to the 90s BC. Nevertheless, despite their valuable insight into the Parthian control of Mesopotamia, their narrow remit still leaves us in the dark about wider matters. As seen earlier (Chapter One), this lack of native documents means that we are largely reliant upon non-Parthian sources, which leaves large gaps in Parthian internal history (such as their foundation) when these events do not impact upon the external world.

   With a lack of written sources, our only remaining native sources come from coins and archaeology. As can be seen from the modern works on the subject,[2] we have a considerable number of Parthian coins which survive and they can help us reconstruct the outline of a number of events, notably those surrounding the various Parthian kings' reigns. However, once again, they are limited in the scope of what they can tell us about the details of Parthian history. Archaeology is another possible field open to us, and notable digs have been carried out at Nisa and Dura-Europus.[3] However, given the relatively low awareness of the Parthian civilization, especially in comparison to the earlier First Persian Empire, and the fact that a number of these sites are all in politically sensitive parts of the world (the former Soviet Union, Iran, Iraq and Afghanistan), then we can understand why work on Parthian sites is not as advanced as on other periods of history. Nevertheless, given the poor state of our other sources, archaeology remains the best hope we have for gaining more knowledge of the Parthians.

2. Non-Native Sources – Surviving Greco-Roman Sources on Parthian History

As can be seen above, we are largely reliant on non-Parthian sources for the history of Parthia.[4] Again, we have to acknowledge the difference between those sources that survive and those that were in circulation in the ancient world. Throughout this analysis of the Romano-Parthian War, we have encountered a number of sources which contain sections on Parthian history. Although there were numerous works on Parthian history by Greeks or Romans, none of them have survived, which means that we are reliant on later works which incorporate some of their material.

Polybius – *Histories* (Mid-second century BC)

As well as being our earliest surviving source for Roman history, Polybius is our earliest source for Parthian history, with five chapters of Book 10 (numbers 27–31) devoted to the eastern campaigns of Antiochus III against the Parthians (see Chapter Two), campaigns that resulted in the temporary loss of Parthian independence. These chapters are intact in themselves, but we do not have the conclusion of the campaign. Nevertheless, they were written less than seventy years after the events occurred and were likely to have been based on eyewitness accounts. Not only does this shed light on the campaign itself, but it shows that the

Parthians were being dealt with by the Hellenistic historians (who again, unfortunately, do not survive). As well as Polybius showing us that the Parthians were being dealt with by the Hellenistic historians, he also reveals that they had entered the consciousness of Rome well before the two empires eventually clashed, which is unique amongst our surviving sources.

Diodorus – *Library of History* (Mid–Late first century BC)

Coming a century after Polybius, we have the history of Diodorus. He was a Greek Sicilian writing in the late Republic and composed a world history which covered a number of different ancient races, from the earliest times to c.60 BC. He made extensive use of a range of Hellenistic historians, all of which are now lost, and has a number of references to early Parthian history, notably during its role in the wars of succession following the death of Alexander the Great (see Chapter Two). Had more of his work survived, then we would undoubtedly have more detail on Parthian history. By the time he wrote his histories, Rome and Parthia would have just clashed, though the ancient world would not have yet been partitioned between the two.

Isidore of Charax – *Parthian Stations* (Late first century BC)

The *Parthian Stations* of Isidore was a short geographical work which detailed the trade routes across the Parthian Empire. Starting in Syria, the work lists the various towns and cities along the way until it reaches Parthia's eastern borders with China and India. The work only survives in fragments but is a fascinating account of the origins of the Silk Road.[5] It also provides us with the only reference to the invasion of Parthia by Tiridates in c.26 BC.

Strabo – *Geography* (Early first century AD)

As we have seen throughout this work, the *Geography* of Strabo provides us with a number of sections on Parthian history, geography and society, especially in Book 11. It is unfortunate that Strabo's other works do not survive, as at one point he states that:

'But since I have said much about the Parthians in the sixth book
of my historical Sketches and in the second book of my History of
events after Polybius, I shall omit discussion of that subject there,
lest I may seem to be repeating what I have already said.'[6]

If Strabo had shown less consideration for his reader and actually repeated
himself, we would know so much more about Parthia. For his Parthian
sections, he referred to the works of Apollodorus and Poseidonius (see
below).

Pliny – *Natural History* (first century AD)

The encyclopaedic *Natural History* of Pliny preserves a number of notes
on aspects of Parthian history, geography and culture. He was a Roman
Senator who wrote a wide-ranging work on various aspects of the ancient
world. The sources of his Parthian references are unknown. He was killed
whilst observing the famous eruption of Mount Vesuvius in AD 79.

Justin – *Epitome of Pompeius Trogus* (third century AD)

Justin's epitome of the works of Pompeius Trogus (see below), though
brief, provides us with our best source for Parthian history as a whole.
His narrative covers the whole period from the foundation to near the
end of Augustus' reign. His books on Parthian history (41 and 42) form
an indispensable starting point for Parthian history.

Eusebius and Jerome – *Chronicles* (fourth century AD)

The *Chronicles* of Eusebius and Jerome, both of whom were fourth-
century AD Christian chroniclers, provide us with some interesting
nuggets of information concerning Parthia (which by then no longer
existed). Eusebius is especially good at detailing the clashes between the
Parthians and the Seleucids over Mesopotamia in the second century BC,
whilst Jerome confirms the date of the foundation of the Arsacid dynasty
to 248 BC.[7]

Byzantine Sources

There are a number of Byzantine histories and chronicles which preserve fragments of earlier works on Parthian history, notably Arrian's *Parthica*. The Byzantine histories are on the whole neglected by ancient historians, but as shown with Synkellos, they can preserve accounts which throw fresh light on Parthian history. Other goods works include those by Zosimus and Photius.

3. Non-Native Sources – Original Greco-Roman Works on Parthian History

We know that there were a number of specialist histories written about Parthia, which now no longer exist but were available to the later writers.

Hellenistic Historians

Though we have no clearly attested fragments, given the role that Parthia played in eroding the power of the Seleucid Empire (including capturing two kings), then it is clear that there must have been a significant amount of material written on the Parthians in the late third- and second-century histories. We can see this in Polybius' account of the Seleucid-Parthian War of c.210 BC (Book 10.27–31), taken from an unnamed Hellenistic source.

Apollodorus – *Parthica* (Late second century BC/Early first century BC)

Apollodorus was a Greek historian who lived in the Mesopotamian city of Artemita. We are told that he wrote a history of the Parthians in four volumes.[8] Aside from one fragment, the work is totally lost, although we believe that it is the source for virtually all of Strabo's passages on Parthia. His work would have been an invaluable source, given the fact that it was written by someone who lived under Parthian rule and would therefore have avoided any pro-Roman bias. It has also been suggested that his work informed the histories of Pompeius Trogus (see below), though this is disputed.[9]

Poseidonius – *Histories* (Early first century BC)

Poseidonius was a philosopher, geographer and historian from Rhodes, who was ambassador to Rome in the late Republican period and counted a number of the leading Romans, such as Pompey and Cicero, amongst his friends. He wrote a history of Rome from 146–88 BC in fifty-two books, continuing from where Polybius left off, which heavily influenced Diodorus. Strabo (11.9.3) quotes him on the composition of the Parthian Council of Elders, so we can assume that he had a detailed account of the Parthians in his work at some point. Sadly, nothing of substance remains of his work.

Pompeius Trogus – *Historiae Philippicae* (Late first century BC/Early first century AD)

Pompeius Trogus was a contemporary of Livy who wrote a world history from the time of the Assyrians to c. AD 9, in forty-four books. The scope of his work complemented that of Livy, and his focus was on the East and away from domestic Roman politics. Given that the epitome of this work done by Justin in the third century is our best source for Parthian history (see above), we can only wonder what level of detail we would get from the original. His 41st and 42nd books dealt with Parthian history and would have given us a detailed narrative from the foundation onwards.

Arrian – *Parthica* (second century AD)

Arrian was a Greco-Roman writer most famous for his work on Alexander the Great (which is our best surviving source for him). He also composed a work on the Fourth Romano-Parthian War, under Emperor Trajan, in seventeen books.[10] As we have seen earlier (Chapter Two), Arrian's work digressed onto the subject of Parthian origins, as was much used by Byzantine writers (Zosimus, Synkellos and Photius). We do not know what other earlier Parthian topics he touched on, but again little of this work survives.

Appian – *History of the Parthian Wars*   (second century AD)

As stated above, on several occasions throughout his other works, Appian said that he would write a *History of the Parthian Wars*.[11] However, no trace of it remains, and many scholars have wondered, given the survival of his other material and the total absence of any of his Parthian fragments, whether it ever existed. We know that he certainly planned it, but whether he ever got around to writing it is another question.

Later Histories of Romano–Parthian Wars

We know that every Romano–Parthian War was accompanied by a flurry of literary works (not unlike the situation today). Although we have no clear details, it is possible that a number of them touched on Parthian history, though it is likely that if they did, then they would have used one of the above works.

Thus we can see once again that we only possess a small percentage of the works that were written on Parthian history by Greek and Roman authors. This loss has left us with an alarming lack of knowledge concerning one of the ancient world's great powers.

Notes

Chapter 1: The Rise of the New World Order; Rome and Parthia (to 50 BC)
1. Liv. 9.17–19.
2. For an overview of the wars, see J. Grainger (2010), *The Syrian Wars* (Leiden).
3. For an overview of Roman history up to this period, see T. Cornell (1995), *The Beginnings of Rome: Italy and Rome from the Bronze Age to the Punic War* (London).
4. See G. Sampson (2016), *Rome Spreads Her Wings: Territorial Expansion Between the Punic Wars* (Barnsley).
5. See J. Sheldon (2006), 'The Ethnic and Linguistic Identity of the Parthians: A Review of the Evidence from Central Asia', *Asian Ethnicity* 7, pp.5–17.
6. See F. Holt (1999), *Thundering Zeus: The Making of Hellenistic Bactria* (Berkeley).
7. See G. Assar (2004), 'Genealogy and Coinage of the Early Parthian Rulers I', *Parthica* 6, pp.69–93, and (2005), 'Genealogy and Coinage of the Early Parthian Rulers II. A Revised Stemma', *Parthica* 7, pp.29–63.
8. See J. Grainger (2010) and J. Lerner (1999), *The Impact of Seleucid Decline on the Eastern Iranian Plateau* (Stuttgart); N. Overtoom (2016), 'The Power-Transition Crisis of the 240s BC and the Creation of the Parthian State', *International History Review* 38, pp.984–1013; R. Strootman (2018), 'The coming of the Parthians: Crisis and Resilience in Seleukid Iran in the reign of Seleukos II', in: K. Erickson (ed.), *The Seleukid Empire, 281–222 BC: War Within the Family* (Swansea), pp.129–50.
9. For a full analysis, see J. Lerner (1999), pp.31–40.
10. See G. Assar (2008), 'The Proper Name of the 2nd Parthian Ruler', *Bulletin of Ancient Iranian History* 4, pp.1–7.
11. For more detail on the reign of Antiochus, see M. Taylor (2013), *Antiochus The Great* (Barnsley); and J. Grainger (2015), *The Seleukid Empire of Antiochus III (223–187 BC)* (Barnsley).
12. See J. Larsen (1935), 'Was Greece Free between 196 and 146 BC', *Classical Philology* 30, pp.193–214; and C. Champion (2017), 'Conquest, Liberation, Protectionism, or Enslavement? Mid-Republican Rome from a Greek Perspective', in T. Naco del Hoyo & F. Sanchez (eds), *War, Warlords, and Interstate Relations in the Ancient Mediterranean* (Leiden), pp.254–65.
13. J. Grainger (2002), *The Roman War of Antiochus the Great* (Leiden).

14. See E. Paltiel (1979), 'The Treaty of Apamea and the Later Seleucids', *Antichthon* 13, pp.30–41.
15. G. Assar (2004), p.81
16. Assar argues for an intervening Parthian king, Arsaces IV (c.176–175 BC), see G. Assar (2004), pp.82–87.
17. See E. Paltiel (1979), 'Antiochos IV and Demetrios I of Syria', *Antichthon* 13, pp.42–47.
18. See J. Wiesehöfer (1996), 'Kings of Kings and Philhellen; Kingship in Arsacid Iran', in P. Bilde (ed.), *Aspects of Hellenistic Kingship* (Aarhus), pp.55–56; E. Dabrowa (2006), 'The Conquests of Mithradates I and the Numismatic Evidence', *Parthica* 8, pp.37–40; and (2009), 'Mithradates I and the Beginning of the Ruler Cult in Parthia', *Electrum* 15, pp.41–51.
19. Polyb. 10.4.
20. See S. Mandell (1991), 'Did the Maccabees Believe that They Had a Valid Treaty with Rome?', *Catholic Biblical Quarterly* 53, pp.202–20.
21. See N. Debeviose (1938), *A Political History of Parthia* (Chicago), p.31.
22. See J. Nabel (2017), 'The Seleucids Imprisoned: Arsacid-Roman Hostage Submission and its Hellenistic Precedents', in J. Schlude & B. Rubin (eds), *Arsacids, Romans and Local Elites. Cross-Cultural Interactions of the Parthian Empire* (Oxford), pp.25–50.
23. John of Antioch, fr.66.2.
24. Assar argues for another intervening Parthian monarch between Phraates and Artabanus, named Bagasis, who ruled c.126 BC from the Tiridatian line of Arsacids. See G. Assar (2005), pp.47–48.
25. Assar again argues for another intervening Parthian monarch, who came to the throne ahead of Mithradates, known only as Arsaces X, who ruled c.122–121 BC and died. See G. Assar (2005), pp.49–51.
26. See G. Assar (2006), 'A Revised Parthian Chronology of the Period 165–91 BC', *Electrum* 11, pp.87–158; and M. Olbrycht (2010), 'The Early Reign of Mithradates II the Great in Parthia', *Anabasis* 1, pp.pp.144–58.
27. See G. Sampson (2010), *The Crisis of Rome. The Jugurthine and Northern Wars and the Rise of Marius* (Barnsley), pp.130–41.
28. See D. Glew (1977), 'Mithridates Eupator and Rome: A Study of the Background of the First Mithridatic War', *Athenaeum* 55, pp.380–405; and M. Olbrycht (2011), 'Subjects and Allies: The Black Sea Empire of Mithradates VI Eupator (120–63 BC) Reconsidered', in *PONTIKA 2008: Recent Research on the Northern and Eastern Black Sea in Ancient Times* (Krakow), pp.275–81.
29. See L. Ballesteros and L. Pastor (1999), 'Marius' Words to Mithridates Eupator (Plut. Mar. 31.3)', *Historia* 48, pp.506–08, and (2014), 'The Meeting between Marius and Mithridates and the Pontic Policy in Cappadocia', *Cedrus* 2, pp.225–39.
30. M. Olbrycht (2009), 'Mithradates VI Eupator and Iran', in J. Hoejte (ed.), *Mithridates VI and the Pontic Kingdom* (Aarhus), pp.163–90.

31. The date is disputed; being either 96 or 92 BC. See E. Badian (1959), 'Sulla's Cilician Command', *Athenaeum* 37, pp.279–303; A. Keaveney (1995), 'Sulla's Cilician Command: The Evidence of Apollinaris Sidonius', *Historia* 44, pp.29–36; P. Cagniart (1991), 'L. Cornelius Sulla in the Nineties: a Reassessment', *Latomus* 50, pp.285–303; and T. Brennan (1992), 'Sulla's Career in the Nineties', *Chiron* 22, pp.103–58.

32. See R. Sullivan (1990), *Near Eastern Royalty and Rome 100–30 BC* (Toronto).

33. Much is made in both the ancient and modern sources about the falling out between the two men, which led to a new phase of the Civil War in 88 BC. Yet there is nothing to say that they had fallen out by this early 90s period. Thus the probability is that Sulla was still acting under his mentor's guidance.

34. See A. Sherwin-White (1977), 'Ariobarzanes, Mithridates, and Sulla', *Classical Quarterly* 27, pp.173–83.

35. A. Keaveney (1981), 'Roman Treaties with Parthia circa 95 – circa 64 BC', *American Journal of Philology* 102, pp.195–212; and E. Wheeler (2002), 'Roman Treaties with Parthia: Völkerrecht or Power Politics', in P. Freeman (ed.), *Limes XVIII: Proceedings of the XVIIIth International Congress of Roman Frontier Studies held in Amman, Jordan* (Oxford), pp.287–92.

36. See A. Mayor (2014), 'Common Cause versus Rome: The Alliance between Mithradates VI of Pontus and Tigranes II of Armenia, 94–66 BC', in M. Metin (ed.), *Tarihte Turkler ve Ermeniler* (Ankara), pp.99–119.

37. See G. Sampson (2013), *The Collapse of Rome. Marius, Sulla and the First Civil War (91–70 BC)* (Barnsley), pp.56–75; and (2017), *Rome, Blood and Politics. Reform, Murder and Popular Politics 133–70 BC* (Barnsley), pp.159–79.

38. See A. Gatzke (2013), 'The Propaganda of Insurgency: Mithridates VI and the "Freeing of the Greeks" in 88 BC', *Ancient World* 44, pp.66–79.

39. See K. Dobbins (1975), 'Mithridates II and his Successors; A Study of the Parthian Crisis 90–70 BC', *Antichthon* 5, pp.63–79; and (1975), 'The Successors of Mithridates II of Parthia', *Numismatic Chronicle* 15, pp.19–45. G. Assar (2006), 'A Revised Parthian Chronology of the Period 91–55 BC', *Parthica* 8, pp.55–104.

40. See T. Rice Holmes (1917), 'Tigranocerta', *Journal of Roman Studies* 7, pp.120–38.

41. Also see G. Assar (2005), 'The Genealogy of the Parthian King Sinatruces (93/92–69/68 BC)', *Journal of the Classical and Medieval Numismatic Society* 6, pp.16–33.

42. See G. Assar (2005), pp.82–95.

43. See D. Glew (1981), 'Between the Wars: Mithridates Eupator and Rome, 85–73 BC', *Chiron* 11, pp.109–30.

44. See G. Sampson (forthcoming), *Rome's Great Eastern War. Lucullus, Pompey and the Conquest of the East 74–63 BC* (Barnsley).

45. B. McGing (1984), 'The Date and Outbreak of the Third Mithridatic War', *Phoenix* 38, pp.12–18.

46. See Sampson (2013), pp.197–211.
47. For more details on the career of Lucullus, see J. van Ooteghem (1959), *Lucius Licinius Lucullus* (Brussels); A. Keaveney (1992), *Lucullus. A Life* (London); and L. Fratantuono (2017), *Lucullus: The Life and and Campaigns of a Roman Conqueror* (Barnsley).
48. See G. Sampson (2019), Chapter One.
49. See J. Schlude (2013), 'Pompey and the Parthians', *Athenaeum* 101, pp.163–81.
50. See G. Downey (1951), 'The Occupation of Syria by the Romans', *Transactions and Proceedings of the American Philological Association* 82, pp.149–63.
51. See G. Sampson (2019), *Rome, Blood & Power. Reform, Murder and Popular Politics in the Late Republic 70–23 BC* (Barnsley).
52. See P. Freeman (1994), 'Pompey's Eastern Settlement: A Matter of Presentation?', *Studies in Latin Literature and Roman History* VII, pp.143–79; and T. Rising (2013), 'Senatorial Opposition to Pompey's Eastern Settlement. A Storm in a Teacup?', *Historia* 62, pp.196–221.
53. See G. Sampson (2008), *The Defeat of Rome, Crassus, Carrhae and the Invasion of the East* (Barnsley).
54. See G. Assar (2006).
55. Plut. *Ant*. 3.
56. Barnet has recently argued that Crassus was following Alexander the Great's invasion route of Mesopotamia, but there were solid tactical reasons to take that route and Crassus seldom strikes us as a figure prone to being governed by romantic notions of the past. See G. Barnet (2017), *Emulating Alexander. How Alexander the Great's Legacy Fuelled Rome's Wars with Persia* (Barnsley), p.26.
57. The first being the Marian general M. Aquillius (Cos. 101 BC) by Mithridates in 88 BC.

Chapter 2: The Cold War: Parthia and the Roman Civil War (50–44 BC)
1. See E. Dąbrowa (1986), 'L'attitude d'Orode II à l'égard de Rome de 49 à 42 av. n. è.', *Latomus* 45, pp.119–24; and J. Schlude (2012), 'The Parthian Response to the Campaign of Crassus', *Latomus* 71, pp.11–23.
2. Since the Battle of Arausio in 105 BC, where two Roman armies were defeated by the Cimbri and Teutones, migrating north European tribes, with casualties in excess of 100,000. See G. Sampson (2010), pp.130–41.
3. See G. Sampson (2008), p.97.
4. G. Sampson (2019). H. Appel (2012), 'Pompeius Magnus: his Third Consulate and the senatus consultum ultimum', *Biuletyn Polskiej Misji Historycznej* 7, pp.341–60.
5. Crassus' surviving son Marcus was serving with Caesar in Gaul.
6. Caes. *BG* 8.54.

7. Dio 65.2–66.1.
8. Dio 40.30.1.
9. Liv. *Per.* 108.
10. Cic. *Fam.* 12.18.
11. Cic. *Att.*7.2.6–7.
12. Dio 40.30.2.
13. During his governorship, his two eldest sons were murdered in Egypt by rogue Roman forces left behind by Gabinius. See Caes. BC 3.16.3, Cic. *Att.* 6.5.3, Val. Max. 4.1.15, Sen. *Dial.* 6.14.2. See M. Gray-Fow (1990), 'The Mental Breakdown of a Roman Senator: M. Calpurnius Bibulus', *Greece & Rome* 37, pp.179–90.
14. Elsewhere (Sampson, 2019) I have argued that the events of 63–62 BC constitute a Second Civil War, making the war between 49 and 27 BC the Third Roman Civil War.
15. *Ibid.*
16. Caes. BC 3.31–32.
17. Caes *BA* 3.82.4.
18. Dio 42.2.5.
19. See T. Hillman (1996), 'Pompeius ad Parthos?', *Klio* 78, pp.380–99.
20. Dio 42.2.5–6.
21. Caes. *BA* 34–41.
22. Caes. *BA* 34.
23. *Ibid.* 37.
24. *Ibid.* 39.
25. *Ibid.* 40.
26. Dio 42.47.2–3.
27. Caesar. *BA* 69–78.
28. In 67 BC against Lucullus' legate C. Valerius Triarius.
29. Caes. *BA* 74
30. *Ibid.* 75.
31. *Ibid.* 76.
32. App. *Mith.* 91, Plut. *Caes.* 50.3–4.
33. Caes. *BA* 77–78.
34. App. *Mith.* 90.
35. Dio 47.25.4–7.
36. Dio 47.27.1–4.
37. Cic. *Att.* 14.9.3.
38. See W. McDermott (1982/83), 'Caesar's Projected Dacian-Parthian Expedition', *Ancient Society* 13/14, pp.223–31; and J. Malitz (1984), 'Caesars Partherkrieg', *Historia* 33, pp.21–59.
39. App. BC 2.110.
40. Dio 43.51.
41. Suet. *Caes.* 44.3.
42. L. Caesetius Flavus and C. Epidius Marullus.

Chapter 3: Civil War and the Romano-Parthian Conquest of the East

1. See Joseph. *BJ* 1.217, *AJ* 14.270, App. *BC* 3.77.
2. App. *BC* 2.119.
3. *Ibid.* 3.77.
4. *Ibid.* 4.58.
5. *Ibid.* 3.7.
6. *Ibid.* 3.8.
7. Dio 47.28.
8. App. *BC* 4.58.1.
9. *Ibid.* 4.59.1.
10. Dio 47.28.4.
11. App. *BC* 4.26.
12. *Ibid.* 3.78.
13. *Ibid.* 4.62.
14. *Ibid.* 4.63.
15. *Ibid.*
16. Dio 48.24.5. Also see Vell. 2.78.1, Flor. 2.19.4, Iust. 42.4.7.
17. Plut. *Cat. Min.* 73.
18. App. *BC* 4.63.
19. See G. Sampson (2019).
20. App. *BC* 5.4–7.
21. *Ibid.* 5.2.
22. See G. Sampson (forthcoming).
23. See G. Barnet (2017).
24. Debevoise (1938, p.104) argues that a lack of surviving Parthian coins struck in this region from the 40s indicated that the Parthian court was focused on matters in the east of the empire.
25. App. *BC* 5.9.
26. *Ibid.* 5.10.
27. Dio 48.24–27.
28. Flor. 2.19.6.
29. Dio 48.24.6–8.
30. *Ibid.* 48.25.1–2.
31. *Ibid.* 48.25.3–4.
32. *Ibid.* 48.25.4.
33. *Ibid.* 48.26.3–4.
34. *Ibid.* 48.26.5.
35. See J. Curran (2007), 'The Ambitions of Quintus Labienus "Parthicus"', *Antichthon* 41, pp.33–53.
36. *Ibid.* 48.26.3–4.
37. Joseph. *BJ* 1.248–249.
38. App. *BC.* 5.65.
39. For a fuller account, see G. Sampson (2019).
40. See A. Powell (2002), *Sextus Pompeius* (Swansea).

Chapter 4: From the Ashes; Ventidius and the Roman Recovery (39 BC)

1. The Bassus cognomen may not be contemporary but may be a later addition.
2. J. Seaver (1952), 'Publius Ventidius. Neglected Roman Military Hero', *Classical Journal* 47, pp.275–80, 300; G. Wylie (1993), 'P. Ventidius – From Novus Homo to "Military Hero"', *Acta Classica* 36, pp.129–41.
3. Gell. 15.4.
4. App. *BC* 5.33.
5. Dio 48.39.3.
6. *Ibid.* 48.39.4.
7. *Ibid.* 48.40.1–3.
8. Front. *Strat.* 2.5.36.
9. Dio 48.40.4.
10. *Ibid.* 48.40.5.
11. *Ibid.* 48.40.6.
12. Liv. *Per.* 127, Plut. *Ant.* 33.4.
13. Dio 48.41.1.
14. *Ibid.* 48.41.1–4.
15. Front. *Str.* 2.5.36.
16. Dio 48.41.4.
17. Iust. 42.7.
18. See G. Sampson (forthcoming).
19. Dio 48.41.4.
20. *Ibid.* 48.41.6.
21. Plut. *Ant.* 33.4.
22. Dio 48.41.4–5.
23. Joseph. *BJ* 288–291, *AJ* 392–393.
24. Plut. *Ant.* 33.4.
25. Dio 48.41.5.

Chapter 5: The Battle of Gindarus and the Collapse of Parthia (38 BC)

1. Dio 49.19.1.
2. *Ibid.* 49.19.2–4.
3. Front. *Strat.* 1.1.6.
4. Strabo. 16.571.
5. Dio 49.20.1–3.
6. Flor. 2.19.5–7.
7. Iust. 42.8–10.
8. Front. *Strat.* 1.1.6.
9. *Ibid.* 2.2.5.
10. Plut. *Ant.* 34.1.
11. Strabo 16.571.
12. Eutrop. 7.5.1.
13. Fest. 18.2.

14. C. Cassius won the first Roman victory over a Parthian force in 51 BC.
15. See G. Sampson (2008), pp.114–36.
16. Iust. 42.8.
17. *Ibid*. 42.9–10.
18. Flo. 2.19.6.
19. Dio 49.20.3.
20. Dio 49.20.4.
21. Flor. 2.19.7.
22. Dio 49.20.5.
23. Plut. *Ant*. 34.2–3.
24. Dio 49.21.1.
25. Seaver (1952).
26. Gell. 15.4.4.
27. Plut. *Ant*. 34.3–4.
28. Dio 49.22.1–2.
29. Dio 49.22.2.
30. Plut. *Ant*. 34.5.
31. App. *BC* 5.92.
32. Iust. 42.4.11–5.1.
33. Dio 49.23.2–5.

Chapter 6: Roman Consolidation in the East; Judea and Armenia (38–37 BC)
1. Dio 49.22.3.
2. See J. Grainger (2011).
3. See S. Mandell (1991).
4. See C. Seeman (2013), *Rome and Judea in Transition: Hasmonean Relations with the Roman Republic and the Evolution of the High Priesthood*. S. Rocca (2014), 'The Late Roman Republic and Hasmonean Judea', *Athenaeum* 102, pp.47–78.
5. Joseph. *BJ* 290.
6. *Ibid*. 297.
7. *Ibid*. 299.
8. *Ibid*. 301–302.
9. *Ibid*. 309.
10. *Ibid*. 317.
11. No other names are recorded.
12. Joseph. *BJ* 319.
13. *Ibid*. 324.
14. *Ibid*. 327.
15. *Ibid*. 345–346.
16. Dio 49.23.1.
17. Joseph. *BJ* 351–352.
18. Hyrcanus II was still alive in Babylon, and was subsequently invited back to Judea by Herodes and then executed in 30 BC following Antonius' defeat at Actium.

19. Dio 49.22.6.
20. Plut. *Ant.* 36.2.
21. See L. Patterson (2015), 'Antony and Armenia', *Transactions of the American Philological Association* 145, pp.77–105.
22. Dio 49.24.1.
23. Plut. *Ant.* 34.6.
24. Strabo 11.501.
25. Dio 49.23.4–5.
26. Plut. *Ant.* 37.1.
27. Dio 49.24.2.
28. Plut. *Ant.* 37.2.

Chapter 7: The Roman Invasion of the Parthian Empire I (The Invasion)

1. Dio 49.24.3–5.
2. Plut. *Ant.* 37.3.
3. See G. Sampson (2008), pp.182–85.
4. See G. Sampson (2008), pp.94–110.
5. Dio 49.25.1.
6. Plut. *Ant.* 37.3.
7. Liv. *Per.* 130.
8. Vell. 2.82.
9. Iust. 42.5.
10. Iust.41.5–6.
11. See R. Syme (1989)' 'Janus and Parthia in Horace', in J. Diggle, J. Hall & H. Jocelyn (eds), *Studies in Latin Literature and its Tradition* (Cambridge), pp.113–21.
12. Hor. *Odes.* 3.6.9.
13. Plut. *Ant.* 38.1.
14. Strabo 11.524.
15. Dio 49.25.2.
16. Plut. *Ant.* 38.2.
17. Dio 49.25.3.
18. Plut. *Ant.* 38.3.
19. Dio 49.25.3–4.
20. Plut. *Ant.* 38.3.
21. Dio 49.25.5 – 26.1.
22. Plut. *Ant.* 39.1.
23. Dio 49.26.1.
24. Dio 49.26.2.
25. Plut. *Ant.* 39.2–5.
26. *Ibid.* 39.6.
27. *Ibid.*
28. Dio 49.26.3–27.1.

29. Plut. *Ant.* 40.1.
30. *Ibid.* 40.2–4.

Chapter 8: The Roman Invasion of the Parthian Empire II (The Retreat)

1. Dio 49.27.5–28.1.
2. Plut. *Ant.* 41.1–3.
3. *Ibid.* 41.3–5.
4. *Ibid.* 42.1.
5. *Ibid.* 42.2.
6. *Ibid.* 42.3–4.
7. *Ibid.* 43.1.
8. *Ibid.* 44.1–2.
9. *Ibid.* 45.1–3.
10. Dio 49.29.2–4.
11. *Ibid.* 49.30.1–4.
12. Plut. *Ant.* 45.3.
13. *Ibid.* 45.4–6.
14. *Ibid.* 46.1–2.
15. *Ibid.* 46.2–3.
16. *Ibid.* 47.1–2.
17. *Ibid.* 47.2.
18. *Ibid.* 47.4–48.1.
19. *Ibid.* 48.1–2.
20. *Ibid.* 48.2–3.
21. *Ibid.* 49.1–3.
22. *Ibid.* 49.3–4.
23. *Ibid.* 50.
24. *Ibid.* 51.1–2.
25. See K. Jones (2017), 'Marcus Antonius' Median War and the Dynastic Politics of the Near East', in J. Schlude & B. Rubin (eds), *Arsacids, Romans and Local Elites: Cross-Cultural Interactions of the Parthian Empire* (Oxford), pp.51–63.

Chapter 9: Consolidation and Civil War (36–35 BC)

1. Val. Max. 9.15, e2.
2. Dio 49.32.3.
3. App. *BC* 5.7.
4. See R. Syme (1939), *The Roman Revolution* (Oxford), pp.214, 260; (1995), *Anatolica: Studies in Strabo* (Oxford), pp.144, 148.
5. Dio 49.32.5.
6. *Ibid.*
7. See F. Romer (1985), 'A Case of Client-Kingship', *American Journal of Philology* 106, pp.75–100; and D. Jacobson (2001), 'Three Roman Client

Kings: Herod of Judaea, Archelaus of Cappadocia and Juba of Mauretania, *Palestine Exploration Quarterly* 133, pp.22–38.
8. Dio 49.32.1.
9. Plut. *Ant.* 53.2.
10. *Ibid.* 53.1. Also see 53.3–5.
11. App. BC 5.133.
12. *Ibid.* 5.134.
13. *Ibid.* 5.135, see 5.134–135 for the whole content.
14. *Ibid.* 5.137.
15. *Ibid.*
16. See G. Sampson (2019).
17. App. BC 138.
18. *Ibid.*
19. *Ibid.*
20. *Ibid.* 5.139.
21. *Ibid.*
22. *Ibid.*
23. *Ibid.* 5.140.
24. Dio 49.18.4.
25. *Ibid.*
26. App. BC 5.142.
27. *Ibid.*
28. *Ibid.* 5.144.
29. Plut. *Ant.* 52.1–2.
30. Dio 49.33.1–2.
31. *Ibid.* 49.33.2.

Chapter 10: The Rise and Fall of the Antonine Empire (34–30 BC)
1. See G. Sampson (2019).
2. Dio 49.39.4–5.
3. *Ibid.* 49.39.6–40.1.
4. *Ibid.* 49.40.2.
5. *Ibid.* 49.40.3.
6. *Ibid.* 49.41.1–3.
7. Plut. *Ant.* 52.3–6.
8. See R. Strootman (2010), 'Queen of Kings: Cleopatra VII and the Donations of Alexandria', in T. Kaizer & M. Facella (eds), *Kingdoms and Principalities in the Roman Near East* (Stuttgart), pp.139–57.
9. There may have been an earlier marriage ceremony, but it certainly was officially proclaimed this year.
10. Alexander and Selene were born c.40 BC, making them 5 or 6, whilst Ptolemy was born in 36, making him around 2 years old.
11. Dio 49.41.4–5.

12. Plut. *Ant.* 52.1–2.
13. Iustin. 42.4.
14. Plut. *Ant.* 53.6.
15. Dio 49.44.1–2.
16. *Ibid.* 49.44.3.
17. For his subsequent career, see L. Taylor (1936), 'M. Titius and the Syrian Command', *Journal of Roman Studies* 26, pp.161–73.
18. *Ibid.* 50.4.1–2.
19. *Ibid.* 50.4–5.
20. Dio 50.7.1–2.
21. *Ibid.* 50.13.8.
22. See Dio 50; C. Lange (2009), *Res Publica Constituta: Actium, Apollo and the Accomplishment of the Triumviral Assignment* (Leiden); and (2011), 'The Battle of Actium: A Reconsideration', *Classical Quarterly* 61, pp.608–23; L. Fratantuono (2016), *The Battle of Actium 31 BC: War for the World* (Barnsley).
23. Plut. *Ant.* 68.2 provides the figures.
24. Dio 51.2.1–3.
25. *Ibid.* 51.7.1–2.
26. *Ibid.* 51.9.2–4.
27. *Ibid.* 51.10.1–2.
28. Plut. *Ant.* 76.1–2.
29. Dio 51.15.5.
30. Q. Dellius, Cn. Domitius Ahenobarbus, C. Sosius.
31. The only known descendant of the Ovinius who held the Tribunate in the fourth century BC and passed the *lex Ovinia* on the composition of the Senate.
32. Oros. 6.19.20.
33. Dio 49.44.4.

Chapter 11: Waiting for Augustus (30–20 BC)
1. Dio 51.18.2.
2. Iustin. 42.6.
3. Hor. *Odes.* 3.18.
4. N. Debevoise (1938), p.135.
5. Dio 51.18.2–3.
6. Iust. 42.6–9.
7. Dio 51.18.3.
8. *Ibid.* 51.16.2.
9. *Ibid.* 51.2.
10. Joseph. *BJ* 396–397.
11. See G. Sampson (2019).
12. See J. Schlude (2015), 'The Early Parthian Policy of Augustus', *Anabasis* 6, pp.139–56.

13. Isidore. *Parthian Stations* 1.
14. See J. Nabel (2015), 'Horace and the Tiridates Episode', *Rheinisches Museum fur Philologie* 158, pp.304–25.
15. Iust. 42.6–9.
16. Dio 53.33.
17. See R. McLaughlin (2014), *The Roman Empire and the Indian Ocean. The Ancient World Economy & the Kingdoms of Africa, Arabia and India* (Barnsley); (2016), *The Roman Empire and the Silk Routes: The Ancient World Economy and the Empires of Parthia, Central Asia and Han China* (Barnsley); and K. Evers (2017), *Worlds Apart Trading Together: The organisation of long-distance trade between Rome and India in Antiquity* (Oxford).
18. R. McLaughlin (2014), pp.54–56.
19. See S. Jameson (1968), 'Chronology of the Campaigns of Aelius Gallus and C. Petronius', *Journal of Roman Studies* 58, pp.71–84.
20. Strabo 16.4.22.
21. *Ibid.* 16.4.23.
22. McLaughlin (2014), p.56.
23. *Ibid.* 16.4.24.
24. Now residing in the British Museum, though McLaughlin argues that it came from a later raid. R. McLaughlin (2014), p.67.
25. Strabo 17.1.54.
26. See S. Jameson (1968).
27. Strabo 17.1.54.
28. *Ibid.*
29. R. McLaughlin (2014), p.66.
30. R. McLaughlin (2014), pp.18–27.
31. Dio 53.26.3.
32. Suet. *Aug.* 21.
33. Oros. 6.21.19.
34. R. McLaughlin (2014), pp.157–59.
35. Dio 54.9.8.
36. Strabo 15.1.73.
37. R. McLaughlin (2014) p.157.
38. Vell. 2.92.2.
39. Dio. 53.32.1.
40. See D. Magie (1908), 'The Mission of Agrippa to the Orient in 23 BC', *Classical Philology* 3, p.147.
41. Joseph. *AJ* 15.10.2.
42. See D. Magie (1908), pp.149–51.
43. See G. Sampson (2019).
44. Dio 54.7.5–6.
45. See G. Sampson (2008), pp.182–85.
46. Prop. 4.1–19.

47. Dio 54.8.1–3.
48. Iust. 42.10–12.
49. Dio 54.9.4–5.
50. *Ibid*. 54.9.2–3.
51. See B. Campbell (1993), 'War and Diplomacy: Rome and Parthia, 31 BC–AD 235', in J. Rich & G. Shipley (eds), *War and Society in the Roman World* (London), pp.213–40.
52. See J. Rich (1998), 'Augustus' Parthian Honours, The Temple of Mars Ultor and the Arch in the Forum Romanum', *Papers of the British School of Rome* 66, pp.71–128; C. Rose (2005), 'The Parthians in Augustan Rome', *American Journal of Archaeology* 109, pp.21–75; T. Babnis (2017), 'Augustan Poets on the Roman-Parthian Treaty of 20 BC', *Classica Cracoviensia* 20, pp.5–44.
53. See P. Edwell (2013), 'The Euphrates as a boundary between Rome and Parthia in the late Republic and Early Empire', *Antichthon* 47, pp.191–206.

Appendix I: Rulers of the Eastern Kingdoms
1. N. Debevoise (1938), p.270.
2. G. Assar (2004), pp.69–93, and (2005), pp.29–63.

Appendix II: Sources For Parthian History: An Introduction
1. A. Sachs & H. Hunger (1996), *Astronomical Diaries and Related Texts from Babylonia Volume III* (Vienna).
2. See P. Garner (1968), *The Coinage of Parthia* (Chicago), and D. Sellwood (1980), *An Introduction to the Coinage of Parthia 2nd edition* (London). For more modern interpretations, see the works of G. Assar and E. Dabrowa.
3. See A. Invernizzi, 'Parthian Nisa, New Lines of Research', and F. Miller, 'Dura-Europos under Parthian Rule', in J. Wiesehöfer (ed.), *Das Partherreich und seine Zeugnisse* (Stuttgart, 1998), pp.45–59 & 473–92 respectively.
4. See S. Muller & J. Wiesehofer (eds), *Parthika. Greek and Roman Authors' Views of the Arsacid Empire* (Harrassowitz).
5. W. Schoff (1914), *The Parthian Stations of Isidore of Charax* (Philadelphia).
6. Strabo 11.9.3.
7. In the first year of the 133rd Olympiad.
8. Athenaeus *Deipnosophists* 15.29 and Strabo 11.7.3.
9. See W. Tarn (1938), *The Greeks in Bactria and India*, p.45.
10. See Photius' *Bibliotheca*.
11. App. *Syr.* 9.1.

Bibliography

Roman and Romano-Parthian

Adcock, F. (1937), 'Lesser Armenia and Galatia after Pompey's Settlement of the East', *Journal of Roman Studies* 27, pp.12–17.

Alexander, C. (2017), *The Second Triumvirate: Augustus, Marc Antony, Marcus Aemilius Lepidus, And The Founding Of An Empire* (London).

Altman, (2017), 'The Egyptian Question in Roman Politics (65–30 BC)', *Caliope* 33, pp.4–32.

Anderson, J. (1922), 'Pompey's Campaign against Mithridates', *Journal of Roman Studies* 12, pp.99–105.

Arnaud, P. (1991), 'Sylla, Tigrane et les Parthes. Un nouveau document pour la datation de la propréture de Sylla : Sidoine Apollinaire Paneg. Aviti, 79–82', *Revue des Études Anciennes* 93, pp.55–64.

—— (1998), 'Les Guerres Parthiques de Gabinius et de Crassus et la politique occidentale des Parthes Arsacides entre 70 et 53 av. J.-C.', in E. Dabrowa (ed.), *Ancient Iran and the Mediterranean World* (Krakow), pp.13–34.

Babnis, T. (2017), 'Augustan Poets on the Roman-Parthian Treaty of 20 BC', *Classica Cracoviensia* 20, pp.5–44.

Badian, E. (1956), 'Q. Mucius Scaevola and the Province of Asia', *Athenaeum* 34, pp.104–23.

—— (1959), 'Sulla's Cilician Command', *Athenaeum* 37, pp.279–303.

—— (1959), 'The Early Career of A. Gabinius (Cos. 58 BC)', *Philologus* 103, pp.87–99.

—— (1965), 'M. Porcius Cato and the Annexation and Early Administration of Cyprus', *Journal of Roman Studies* 55, pp.110–21.

—— (1976), 'Rome, Athens and Mithridates', *American Journal of Ancient History* 1, pp.105–28.

Ball, W. (2000), *Rome in the East* (London).

Ballesteros, Pastor L. (1999), 'Marius' Words to Mithridates Eupator (Plut. Mar. 31.3)', *Historia* 48, pp.506–08.

—— (2008), 'Cappadocia and Pontus, Client Kingdoms of the Roman Republic from the Peace of Apamea to the Beginning of the Mithridatic Wars (188–89 BC)', in A. Coskun (ed.), *Freundschaft und Gefolgschaft in den auswärtigen Beziehungen der Römer (2 Jh. v. Chr.-1 Jh. n. Chr.)* (Berlin), pp.45–63.

—— (2014), 'The Meeting between Marius and Mithridates and the Pontic Policy in Cappadocia', *Cedrus* 2, pp.225–39.

Barnet, G. (2017), *Emulating Alexander. How Alexander the Great's Legacy Fuelled Rome's Wars with Persia* (Barnsley).

Bellinger, A. (1949), 'The End of the Seleucids', *Connecticut Academy of Arts and Sciences* 38, pp.51–102.

Blanchard, B. (2009, unpublished), *Rome, Roman Generals, and the East: 53–36 BC* (California).

Braund, D. (1983), 'Gabinius, Caesar and the *publicani* of Judea', *Klio* 65, pp.241–44.

—— (1983), 'Royal Wills and Rome', *Papers of the British School at Rome* 51, pp.16–57.

—— (1984), *Rome and the Friendly King: The Character of the Client Kingship* (London).

Brennan, T. (1992), 'Sulla's Career in the Nineties', *Chiron* 22, pp.103–58.

Broughton, T. (1942), 'Cleopatra and the 'Treasure of the Ptolemies', *American Journal of Philology* 63, pp.328–32.

—— (1951/2), *The Magistrates of the Roman Republic Volume I & 2* (New York).

—— (1960), *Supplement to the Magistrates of the Roman Republic* (New York).

—— (1986), *Supplement to the Magistrates of the Roman Republic* (New York).

Brown, T. (1964), 'Polybius' Account of Antiochus III', *Phoenix* 18, pp.124–36.

Cagniart, P. (1991), 'L. Cornelius Sulla in the Nineties: a Reassessment', *Latomus* 50, pp.285–303.

Campbell, B. (1993), 'War and Diplomacy: Rome and Parthia, 31 BC–AD 235', in J. Rich & G. Shipley (eds), *War and Society in the Roman World* (London), pp.213–40.

Champion, C. (2017), 'Conquest, Liberation, Protectionism, or Enslavement? Mid-Republican Rome from a Greek Perspective', in T. Naco del Hoyo & F. Sanchez (eds), War, *Warlords, and Interstate Relations in the Ancient Mediterranean* (Leiden), pp.254–65.

Cornell, T. (1995), *The Beginnings of Rome: Italy and Rome from the Bronze Age to the Punic War* (London).

Coskun, A. & Engels, D. (eds) (2019), *Rome and the Seleukid East. Selected Papers from the Seleukid Study Day V, Brussels, 21–23 August 2015* (Brussels).

Curran, J. (2007), 'The Ambitions of Quintus Labienus "Parthicus"', *Antichthon* 41, pp.33–53.

Dabrowa, E. (ed.) (2003), *The Roman Near East and Armenia* (Krakow).

Derow, P. (1979), 'Polybius, Rome, and the East', *Journal of Roman Studies* 69, pp.1–15.

—— (2003), 'The Arrival of Rome; From the Illyrian Wars to the Fall of Macedon', in A. Erskine (ed.), *A Companion to the Hellenistic World* (London), pp.51–70.

—— (2014), *Rome, Polybius, and the East* (Oxford).

De Ruggiero, P. (2013), *Mark Antony. A Plain Blunt Man* (Barnsley).

Dmitriev, S. (2006), 'Cappadocian Dynastic Arrangements on the Eve of the First Mithridatic War', *Historia* 55, pp.285–97.

Dobiás, J. (1931). 'Les premiers rapports des romains avec les parthes et l'ocuptaion de la syria', *Archiv Orientalni* 3, pp.215–56.

Downey, G. (1951), 'The Occupation of Syria by the Romans', *Transactions and Proceedings of the American Philological Association* 82, pp.149–63.

Eckstein, A. (2006), *Mediterranean Anarchy, Interstate War and the Rise of Rome* (Berkeley).

—— (2008), *Rome Enters the Greek East. From Anarchy to Hierarchy in the Hellenistic Mediterranean, 230–170 BC* (London).

—— (2013), 'What is an empire and how do you know when you have one? Rome and the Greek States after 188 BC', in P. Burton (ed.), *Culture, Identity and Politics in the Ancient Mediterranean World. Papers from a Conference in Honour of Erich Gruen* (Canberra), pp.173–90.

—— (2017), 'Rome, Empire, and the Hellenistic State-system', in T. Naco del Hoyo & F. Sanchez (eds), *War, Warlords, and Interstate Relations in the Ancient Mediterranean* (Leiden), pp.231–53.

Edwell, P. (2008), *Between Rome and Persia. The Middle Euphrates, Mesopotamia and Palmyra under Roman Control* (Oxford).

—— (2013), 'The Euphrates as a boundary between Rome and Parthia in the late Republic and Early Empire', *Antichthon* 47, pp.191–206.

Errington, R. (1971), 'The Alleged Syro-Macedonian Pact and the Origins of the Second Macedonian War', *Athenaeum* 49, pp.336–54.

—— (1972), *Dawn of Empire: Rome's Rise to World Power* (London).

Evans, R. (2011), *Roman Conquests: Asia Minor, Syria and Armenia* (Barnsley).

Evers, K. (2017), *Worlds Apart Trading Together: The organisation of long-distance trade between Rome and India in Antiquity* (Oxford).

Facella, M. (2010), 'Advantages and Disadvantages of an Allied Kingdom; The Case of Commagene', in T. Kaizer. & M. Facella (eds), *Kingdoms and Principalities in the Roman Near East* (Stuttgart), pp.181–97.

Fantham, E. (1975), 'The Trials of Gabinius in 54 BC', *Historia* 24, pp.425–43.

Fratantuono, L. (2016), *The Battle of Actium 31 BC: War for the World* (Barnsley).

—— (2017), *Lucullus: The Life and and Campaigns of a Roman Conqueror* (Barnsley).

Freeman, P. (1994), 'Pompey's Eastern Settlement: A Matter of Presentation?', *Studies in Latin Literature and Roman History* VII, pp.143–79.

Gatzke, A. (2013), 'The Propaganda of Insurgency: Mithridates VI and the "Freeing of the Greeks" in 88 BC', *Ancient World* 44, pp.66–79.

Glew, D. (1977), 'Mithridates Eupator and Rome: A Study of the Background of the First Mithridatic War', *Athenaeum* 55, pp.380–405.

—— (1977a), 'The Selling of the King: A Note on Mithridates Eupator's Propaganda in 88 BC', *Hermes* 105, pp.253–56.

—— (1981), 'Between the Wars: Mithridates Eupator and Rome, 85–73 BC', *Chiron* 11, pp.109–30.

Goldsworthy, A. (2010), *Antony and Cleopatra* (London).

—— (2014), *Augustus: From Revolutionary to Emperor* (London).

Graham, D. (2013), *Rome and Parthia: Power, Politics and Profit* (North Charleston).

Grainger, J. (2002), *The Roman War of Antiochus the Great* (Leiden).

—— (2013), *Roman Conquests: Egypt and Judaea* (Barnsley).

—— (2013), *Rome, Parthia and India: The Violent Emergence of a New World Order 150–140 BC* (Barnsley).

Gray-Fow, M. (1990), 'The Mental Breakdown of a Roman Senator: M. Calpurnius Bibulus', *Greece & Rome* 37, pp.179–90.

Greenhalgh, P. (1980), *Pompey. The Roman Alexander* (London).

—— (1981), *Pompey. The Republican Prince* (London).

Grimal, P. (ed.) (1968), *Hellenism and the Rise of Rome* (London).

Gruen, E. (ed.) (1970), *Imperialism in the Roman Republic* (New York).

—— (1974), *The Last Generation of the Roman Republic* (Berkeley).

—— (1976), 'Rome and the Seleucids in the Aftermath of Pydna', *Chiron* 6, pp.73–94.

—— (1984), *The Hellenistic World and the Coming of Rome Volumes 1 & 2* (Berkeley).

Harl, K. (2007), 'The Roman Experience in Iraq', *Journal of the Historical Society* 7, pp.213–27.

Harris, W. (1979), *War and Imperialism in Republican Rome 327–70 BC* (Oxford).

—— (ed.) (1984), *The Imperialism of Mid-Republican Rome* (Rome).

Hillman, T. (1996), 'Pompeius ad Parthos?' *Klio* 78, pp.380–99.

Huzar, E. (1978), *Mark Antony; A Biography* (Minneapolis).

Jacobson, D. (2001), 'Three Roman Client Kings: Herod of Judaea, Archelaus of Cappadocia and Juba of Mauretania', *Palestine Exploration Quarterly* 133, pp.22–38.

Jameson, S. (1968), 'Chronology of the Campaigns of Aelius Gallus and C. Petronius', *Journal of Roman Studies* 58, pp.71–84.

Jones, A. (1970), *Augustus* (London).

Jones, K. (2017), 'Marcus Antonius' Median War and the Dynastic Politics of the Near East', in J. Schlude & B. Rubin (eds), *Arsacids, Romans and Local Elites: Cross-Cultural Interactions of the Parthian Empire* (Oxford), pp.51–63.

Kaizer, T. & Facella, M. (eds) (2010), *Kingdoms and Principalities in the Roman Near East* (Stuttgart).

Kallet-Marx, R. (1995), *Hegemony to Empire; The Development of the Roman Empire in the East from 148 to 62 BC* (Berkeley).

Keaveney, A. (1981), 'Roman Treaties with Parthia circa 95 – circa 64 BC', *American Journal of Philology* 102, pp.195–212.

—— (1982), 'The King and the War-Lords: Romano-Parthian Relations Circa 64–53 BC', *American Journal of Philology* 103, pp.412–28.

—— (1992), *Lucullus. A Life* (London).

—— (1995), 'Sulla's Cilician Command: The Evidence of Apollinaris Sidonius', *Historia* 44, pp.29–36.

Kennedy, D. (1996), 'Parthia and Rome; Eastern perspectives', in D. Kennedy (ed.), *The Roman Army in the East* (Michigan), pp.67–90.

Kryśkiewicz, H. (2017), 'The Parthians in the 1st century BC – a worthy enemy of Rome? Remarks on the issue of Roman-Parthian political conflict in the ending period of existence of the Roman Republic, and on its influence on Roman imperial ideology', *Shidnyj Svit* 3, pp.60–72.

Lander, J. (1975, unpublished), *Roman-Parthian relations in the time of Augustus with reference to Augustus' foreign policy* (Durham).

Lange, C. (2008), 'Civil War in the Res Gestae Divi Augusti: Conquering the World and Fighting a War at Home', in E. Bragg, L. Hau & E. Macaulay-Lewis (eds), *Beyond the Battlefields: New Perspectives on Warfare and Society in the Graeco-Roman World* (Newcastle), pp.185–204.

—— (2009), *Res Publica Constituta: Actium, Apollo and the Accomplishment of the Triumviral Assignment* (Leiden).

—— (2011), 'The Battle of Actium: A Reconsideration', *Classical Quarterly* 61, pp.608–23.

—— (2013), 'Triumph and Civil War in the Late Republic', *Papers of the British School at Rome* 81, pp.67–90.

Larsen, J. (1935), 'Was Greece Free between 196 and 146 BC?', *Classical Philology* 30, pp.193–214.

Magie, D. (1908), The Mission of Agrippa to the Orient in 23 BC', *Classical Philology* 3, pp.145–52.

—— (1939), 'The "Agreement" between Philip V and Antiochus III for the Partition of the Egyptian Empire', *Journal of Roman Studies* 29, pp.32–44.

—— (1950), *Roman Rule in Asia Minor Volumes I & II* (Princeton).

Malitz, J. (1984), 'Caesars Partherkrieg', *Historia* 33, pp.21–59.

Manandyan, H. (2007), *Tigranes II and Rome: A New Interpretation Based on Primary Sources* (Mazda).

Mandell, S. (1989), 'The Isthmian Proclamation and the Early Stages of Roman Imperialism in the Near East', *Classical Bulletin* 65, pp.89–94.

—— (1991), 'Did the Maccabees Believe that They Had a Valid Treaty with Rome?', *Catholic Biblical Quarterly* 53, pp.202–20.

Marshall, B. (1976), *Crassus: a political biography* (Amsterdam).

Mattern-Parkes, S. (2003), 'The Defeat of Crassus and the Just War', *Classical World* 96, pp.387–96.

Matyszak, P. (2008), *Mithridates the Great: Rome's Indomitable Enemy* (Barnsley).

—— (2009), *Roman Conquests: Macedonia and Greece* (Barnsley).

Mayor, A. (2011), *The Poison King: The Life and Legend of Mithradates, Rome's Deadliest Enemy* (Princeton).

—— (2014), 'Common Cause versus Rome: The Alliance between Mithradates VI of Pontus and Tigranes II of Armenia, 94–66 BC', in M. Metin (ed.), *Tarihte Turkler ve Ermeniler* (Ankara), pp.99–119.

McDermott, W. (1982/83), 'Caesar's Projected Dacian-Parthian Expedition', *Ancient Society* 13/14, pp.223–31.

McDonald, A. (1970), 'Rome and Greece 196–146 BC', in B. Harris (ed.), *Auckland Classical Essays* (Oxford).

McGing, B. (1984), 'The Date and Outbreak of the Third Mithridatic War', *Phoenix* 38, pp.12–18.

—— (1986), *The Foreign Policy of Mithridates VI Eupator King of Pontus* (Leiden).

McLaughlin, R. (2014), *The Roman Empire and the Indian Ocean. The Ancient World Economy & the Kingdoms of Africa, Arabia and India* (Barnsley).

—— (2016), *The Roman Empire and the Silk Routes: The Ancient World Economy and the Empires of Parthia, Central Asia and Han China* (Barnsley).

Mielczarek, M. (1993), *Cataphracti and Clibanarii; Studies on the Heavy Armoured Cavalry of the Ancient World* (Lodz).

Millar, F. (1973), 'Triumvirate and Principate', *Journal of Roman Studies* 63, pp.50–67.

—— (1993), *The Roman Near East (31 BC–AD 337)* (Harvard).

—— (2004), 'Emperors, Frontiers and Foreign Relations 31 BC to AD 378', in *Rome, the Greek World and the East Volume 2* (Chapel Hill), pp.160–94.

Morrell, K. (2017), *Pompey, Cato, and the Governance of the Roman Empire* (Oxford).

Moscovich, M. (1983), 'Hostage Princes and Roman Imperialism in the Second Century BC', *Echos du monde classique* 27, pp.297–309.

Nabel, J. (2015), 'Horace and the Tiridates Episode', *Rheinisches Museum fur Philologie* 158, pp.304–25.

Naco del Hoyo, T. & Sanchez, F. (eds) (2017), *War, Warlords, and Interstate Relations in the Ancient Mediterranean* (Leiden).

Orian, M. (2015), 'Hyrcanus II versus Aristobulus II and the Inviolability of Jerusalem', *Jewish Studies Quarterly* 22, pp.205–42.

Overtoom, N. (2016), 'The Rivalry of Rome and Parthia in the Sources from the Augustan Age to Late Antiquity', *Anabasis* 7, pp.137–74.

—— (2017), 'The Parthians' Unique Mode of Warfare: A Tradition of Parthian Militarism and the Battle of Carrhae', *Anabasis* 8, pp.95–122.

—— (2017a), 'The Parthian Rival and Rome's Failure in the East: Roman Propaganda and the Stain of Crassus', *Acta Antiqua Academiae Scientiarum Hungaricae* 57, pp.415–35.

Paltiel, E. (1979), 'The Treaty of Apamea and the Later Seleucids', *Antichthon* 13, pp.30–41.

Patterson, L. (2015), 'Antony and Armenia', *Transactions of the American Philological Association* 145, pp.77–105.

Powell, A. (2002), *Sextus Pompeius* (Swansea).

Powell, L. (2014), *Marcus Agrippa: Right-Hand Man of Caesar Augustus* (Barnsley).

—— (2016), *Augustus at War: The Struggle for the Pax Augusta Hardcover* (Barnsley).

Primo, A. (2010), 'The Client Kingdom of Pontus Between Mithridatism and Philoromanism', in T. Kaizer & M. Facella (eds), *Kingdoms and Principalities in the Roman Near East* (Stuttgart), pp.159–79.

Raaflaub, K. & Tohler, M. (1990), *Between Republic and Empire: Interpretations of Augustus and His Principate* (Berkeley).

Rea, C. (2014), *Leviathan vs. Behemoth: The Roman-Parthian Wars 66 BC–217 AD* (Milton Keynes).

Regling, K. (1907), 'Crassus' Partherkrieg', *Klio* 7, pp.357–94.

Rich, J. (1998), 'Augustus' Parthian Honours, The Temple of Mars Ultor and the Arch in the Forum Romanum', *Papers of the British School of Rome* 66, pp.71–128.

Ridley, R. (2006), 'Antiochus XIII, Pompeius Magnus and the Unessayed Coup', *Ancient Society* 36, pp.81–95.

Rising, T. (2013), Senatorial Opposition to Pompey's Eastern Settlement. A Storm in a Teacup?', *Historia* 62, pp.196–221.

Rocca, S. (2014), 'The Late Roman Republic and Hasmonean Judea', *Athenaeum* 102, pp.47–78

Romer, F. (1985), 'A Case of Client-Kingship', *American Journal of Philology* 106, pp.75–100.

Rose, C. (2005) 'The Parthians in Augustan Rome', *American Journal of Archaeology* 109, pp.21–75.

Sampson, G. (2008), *The Defeat of Rome, Crassus, Carrhae and the Invasion of the East* (Barnsley).

—— (2010), *The Crisis of Rome. The Jugurthine and Northern Wars and the Rise of Marius* (Barnsley).

—— (2013), *The Collapse of Rome. Marius, Sulla and the First Civil War (91–70 BC)* (Barnsley).

—— (2016), *Rome Spreads Her Wings: Territorial Expansion Between the Punic Wars* (Barnsley).

——— (2017), *Rome, Blood and Politics. Reform, Murder and Popular Politics in the Late Republic 133–70 BC* (Barnsley).

—— (2019), *Rome, Blood & Power. Reform, Murder and Popular Politics in the Late Republic 70–23 BC* (Barnsley).

—— (forthcoming), *Rome's Great Eastern War. Lucullus, Pompey and the Conquest of the East 74–63 BC* (Barnsley).

Sanford, E. (1939), 'The Career of Aulus Gabinius', *Transactions and Proceedings of the American Philological Association* 70, pp.64–92.

Sartre, M. (2005), *The Middle East under Rome* (London).

Scheiber, A. (1979), 'Antony and Parthia', *Rivista Storica dell'Antichita* 9, pp.105–24.

Schlude, J. (2009, unpublished), *Rome, Parthia and Empire: The First Century of Roman-Parthian Relations* (Berkeley).

—— (2012), 'The Parthian Response to the Campaign of Crassus', *Latomus* 71, pp.11–23.

—— (2013), 'Pompey and the Parthians', *Athenaeum* 101, pp.163–81.

—— (2015), 'The Early Parthian Policy of Augustus', *Anabasis* 6, pp.139–56.

Schlude, J. & Rubin, B. (eds) (2017), *Arsacids, Romans and Local Elites: Cross-Cultural Interactions of the Parthian Empire* (Oxford).

Scott, K. (1933), 'The Political Propaganda of 44–30 BC', *Memoirs of the American Academy in Rome* 11, pp.7–49.

Seager, R. (1977), 'The Return of the Standards in 20 BC', *Liverpool Classical Monthly* 2, pp.201–02.

Seaver, J. (1952), 'Publius Ventidius. Neglected Roman Military Hero', *Classical Journal* 47, pp.275–80, 300.

Seeman, C. (2013), *Rome and Judea in Transition: Hasmonean Relations with the Roman Republic and the Evolution of the High Priesthood* (New York).

Shatzman, I. (1971), 'The Egyptian Question in Roman Politics (59–54 BC)', *Latomus* 30, pp.363–69.

Sheldon, M. (2010), *Rome's Wars in Parthia: Blood in the Sand* (London).

Sherwin-White, A. (1976) 'Rome, Pamphylia and Cilicia, 133–70 BC', *Journal of Roman Studies* 66, pp.1–14.

—— (1977), 'Ariobarzanes, Mithridates, and Sulla', *Classical Quarterly* 27, pp.173–83.

—— (1977a), 'Roman Involvement in Anatolia, 167–88 BC', *Journal of Roman Studies* 67, pp.62–75.

—— (1984), *Roman Foreign Policy in the East 168 BC to AD 1* (Oklahoma).

Siani-Davies, M. (1997), 'Ptolemy XII Auletes and the Romans', *Historia* 46, pp.306–40.

Simpson, A. (1938), 'The Departure of Crassus for Parthia', *Transactions and Proceedings of the American Philological Association* 69 (1938), pp.532–41.

Southern, P. (1998), *Augustus* (Oxford).

—— (2002), *Pompey the Great* (Stroud).

Stark, F. (1966), *Rome on the Euphrates* (London).

Strootman, R. (2010), 'Queen of Kings: Cleopatra VII and the Donations of Alexandria', in T. Kaizer & M. Facella (eds), *Kingdoms and Principalities in the Roman Near East* (Stuttgart), pp.139–57.

Syme, R. (1939), *The Roman Revolution* (Oxford).

—— (1989), 'Janus and Parthia in Horace', in J. Diggle, J. Hall & H. Jocelyn (eds), *Studies in Latin Literature and its Tradition* (Cambridge), pp.113–21.

—— (1995), *Anatolica: Studies in Strabo* (Oxford).

Taylor, L. (1936), 'M. Titius and the Syrian Command', *Journal of Roman Studies* 26, pp.161–73.

Timpe, D. (1962), 'Die Bedeutung der Schlact von Carrhae', *Museum Helveticum* 19, pp.104–29.

Traina, G. (2010), *Carrhes, 9 juin 53 av. J.-C. Anatomie d'une défaite* (Paris).

van Ooteghem, J. (1959), *Lucius Licinius Lucullus* (Brussels).

Van-Wijlick, H. (2013, unpublished), *Rome and Near Eastern Kingdoms and Principalities, 44–31 BC: A Study of Political Relations During Civil War* (Durham).

Walbank. F. (1963), 'Polybius and Rome's Eastern Policy', *Journal of Roman Studies* 53, pp.1–13.

Wallace, R. & Harris, E. (eds) (1996), *Transitions to Empire. Essays in Greco-Roman History, 360–146 BC – In Honor of E. Badian* (Oklahoma).

Ward, A. (1977), *Marcus Crassus and the late Roman Republic* (Columbia).

Waterfield, R. (2014), *Taken at the Flood: The Roman Conquest of Greece* (Oxford).

Weigel, R. (1992), *Lepidus: The Tarnished Triumvir* (London).

Wheeler, E. (2002), 'Roman Treaties with Parthia: Völkerrecht or Power Politics', in P. Freeman (ed.), *Limes XVIII: Proceedings of the XVIIIth International Congress of Roman Frontier Studies held in Amman, Jordan* (Oxford), pp.287–92.

Williams, R. (1985), 'Rei Publicae Causa: Gabinius' Defence of His Restoration of Ptolemy Auletes', *Classical Journal* 81, pp.25–38.

Williams, R. & Williams, B. (1988), 'Cn. Pompeius Magnus and L. Afranius. Failure to Secure the Eastern Settlement', *Classical Journal* 83, pp.198–206.

Wylie, G. (1993), 'P. Ventidius – From Novus Homo to "Military Hero"', *Acta Classica* 36, pp.129–41.

Hellenistic and Parthian History

Allen, R (1983), *The Attalid Kingdom. A Constitutional History* (Oxford).

Arnaud, P. (1987), 'Les guerres des Parthes et de l'Arménie dans la première moitié du première siècle av. n. è. Problèmes de chronologie et d'extension territoriale (95 BC–70 BC)', *Mesopotamia* 22, pp.129–45.

Assar, G. (2000), 'Recent Studies in Parthian History I', *The Celator* 14, pp.6–22.

—— (2001), 'Recent Studies in Parthian History II', *The Celator* 15, pp.17–27, 41.

—— (2001a), 'Recent Studies in Parthian History III', *The Celator* 15, pp.17–22.

—— (2003), 'Parthian Calendars at Babylon and Seleucia on the Tigris', *Iran* 41, pp.171–91.

—— (2004), 'Genealogy and Coinage of the Early Parthian Rulers I', *Parthica* 6, pp.69–93.

—— (2005), 'Genealogy and Coinage of the Early Parthian Rulers II. A Revised Stemma, *Parthica* 7, pp.29–63.

—— (2005a), The Genealogy of the Parthian King Sinatruces (93/92–69/68 BC)', *Journal of the Classical and Medieval Numismatic Society* 6, pp.16–33.

—— (2006), 'Moses of Chorene and the Early Parthian Chronology', *Electrum* 11, pp.61–86

—— (2006a), 'A Revised Parthian Chronology of the Period 165–91 BC', *Electrum* 11, pp.87–158.

—— (2006b), 'A Revised Parthian Chronology of the Period 91–55 BC', *Parthica* 8, pp.55–104.

—— (2006/07), 'Arsaces IV (c.170–168 BC) the 1st "Missing" Parthian King', *Nāme-ye Irān-e Bāstān* 6/1&2, pp.3–14

—— (2007), 'The Inception and Terminal Dates of the Reigns of Seleucus II, Seleucus III and Antiochus III', *Nouvelles Assyriologiques Brèves et Utilitaires* 3, pp.49–53.

—— (2008), 'The Proper Name of the 2nd Parthian Ruler', *Bulletin of Ancient Iranian History* 4, pp.1–7.

—— (2009), 'Artabanus of Trogus Pompeius' 41st Prologue', *Electrum* 15, pp.119–40.

Bar-Kochva, B. (1976), *The Seleucid Army: Organization and Tactics in the Great Campaigns* (Cambridge).

Bennett, B. & Roberts, M. (2008), *The Wars of Alexander's Successors 323–281 BC: Commanders and Campaigns v.1* (Barnsley).

—— (2009), *The Wars of Alexander's Successors, 323–281 BC, Vol. 2: Battles and Tactics* (Barnsley).

—— (2011), *Twilight of the Hellenistic World* (Barnsley).

Bickermann, E. (1944), 'Notes on Seleucid and Parthian Chronology', *Berytus* 8, pp.73–83.

Bivar, A. (1983), 'The Political History of Iran under the Arsacids', in E. Yarshater (ed.), *The Cambridge History of Iran Volume 3.1; The Seleucid, Parthian and Sasanian Periods* (Cambridge), pp.21–99.

Boyce, M. (1994), 'The Sedentary Arsacids', *Iranica Antiqua* 29, pp.241–51.

Brodersen, K. (1986), 'The Date of the Secession of Parthia from the Seleucid Kingdom', *Historia* 35, pp.378–81.

Charlotte, L. (2005), 'Les guerres parthiques de Démétrios II et Antiochos VII dans les sources gréco-romaines, de Posidonios à Trogue/Justin', *Journal des Savants*, pp.217–52.

Chrubasik, B. (2016), *Kings and Usurpers in the Seleukid Empire: The Men who would be King* (Oxford).

Colledge, M. (1967), *The Parthians* (London).

—— (1977), *Parthian Art* (London).

Curtis, J. (2000), *Mesopotamia and Iran in the Parthian and Sasanian Periods: Rejection and Revival c.238 BC–AD 642* (London).

Curtis, V. & Stewart, S. (eds) (2007), *The Age of the Parthians* (London).

Dąbrowa, E. (1986), 'L'attitude d'Orode II à l'égard de Rome de 49 à 42 av. n. è.', *Latomus* 45, pp.119–24.

—— (1999), 'L'éxpedition de Démétrius II Nicator contre les Parthes (139–138 avant J-C.)', *Parthica* 1, pp.9–17.

—— (2005), 'Les aspects politiques et militaries de la conquête parthe de la Mésopotamie', *Electrum* 10, pp.73–88.

—— (2006), 'The Conquests of Mithridates I and the Numismatic Evidence', *Parthica* 8, pp.37–40.

—— (2008), 'The Political Propaganda of the First Arsacids and its Targets (From Arsaces I to Mithradates II)', *Parthica* 10, pp.25–31.

—— (ed.) (2009) *Orbis Parthicus: Studies in Memory of Professor Jozef Wolski* (Krakow).

—— (2009a), 'Mithradates I and the Beginning of the Ruler Cult in Parthia', *Electrum* 15, pp.41–51.

—— (2010), 'The Parthian Kingship', in Lanfranchi, G & Rollinger, R. (eds), *Concepts of Kingship in Antiquity* (Padova), pp.123–34.

—— (ed.) (2011), *Studia Graeco-Parthica: Political and Cultural Relations Between Greeks and Parthians* (Wiesbaden).

—— (ed.) (2011a), *New Studies on the Seleucids* (Krakow).

—— (2013), The Parthian Aristocracy: Its Social Position and Political Activity', *Parthica* 15, pp.53–62.

Debecq, J. (1951), 'Les Parthes et Rome', *Latomus* 10, pp.459–69.

Debeviose, N. (1931), 'Parthian Problems', *American Journal of Semitic Languages and Literatures* 47, pp.73–82.

—— (1938), *A Political History of Parthia* (Chicago).

Dilmaghani, J. (1986), 'Parthian Coins from Mithradates II to Orodes II, *Numismatic Chronicle* 146, pp.216–24.

Dobbins, K. (1975), 'Mithradates II and his Successors; A Study of the Parthian Crisis 90–70 BC', *Antichthon* 5, pp.63–79.

—— (1975a), 'The Successors of Mithradates II of Parthia', *Numismatic Chronicle* 15, pp.19–45

Drijvers, J. (1998), 'Strabo on Parthia and the Parthians', in J. Wiesehöfer (ed.), *Das Partherreich und seine Zeugnisse* (Stuttgart), pp.279–93.

Edson, C. (1958), 'Imperium Macedonicum: The Seleucid Empire and the Literary Evidence', *Classical Philology* 53, pp.153–70.

Engels, D. (2008), 'Cicéron comme proconsul en Cilicie et la guerre contre les Parthes', *Revue belge de philologie et d'histoire*, pp.23–45.

Erickson, K. (ed.) (2018), *The Seleukid Empire 281–222: War within the family* (Swansea).

Erickson, K. & Ramsey, G. (eds) (2011), *Seleucid Dissolution: The Sinking of the Anchor* (Harrassowitz).

Errington, A. (2008), *A History of the Hellenistic World. 323–30 BC* (Oxford).

Erskine, A. (ed.) (2003), *A Companion to the Hellenistic World* (Oxford).

Fyre, R. (2000), 'Parthian and Sasanian History of Iran', in J. Curtis (ed.), *Mesopotamia and Iran in the Parthian and Sasanian Periods; Rejection and Revival c.238 BC–AD 642* (London), pp.17–22.

Garner, P. (1968), *The Coinage of Parthia* (Chicago).

Grainger, P. (2010), *The Syrian Wars* (Leiden).

—— (2011), *The Wars of the Maccabees* (Barnsley).

—— (2014), *The Rise of the Seleukid Empire (323–223 BC): Seleukos I to Seleukos III* (Barnsley).

—— (2015), *The Seleukid Empire of Antiochus III (223–187 BC)* (Barnsley).

—— (2015a), *The Fall of the Seleukid Empire 187–75 BC* (Barnsley).

—— (2016), *Great Power Diplomacy in the Hellenistic World* (London).

—— (2017), *Kings and Kingship in the Hellenistic World 350–30 BC* (Barnsley).

Grajetzki, W. (2011), *Greeks and Parthians in Mesopotamia and Beyond 331 BC– 224 AD* (London).

Green, P. (1990), *From Alexander to Actium. The Historical Evolution of the Hellenistic Age* (Berkeley).

Hoejte, J. (ed.) (2009), *Mithridates VI and the Pontic Kingdom* (Aarhus).

Hölbl, G. (2000), *A History of the Ptolemaic Empire* (London).

Holt, F. (1999), *Thundering Zeus: The Making of Hellenistic Bactria* (Berkeley).

Hoover, O. (2007), 'A Revised Chronology for the Late Seleucids at Antioch, 121/0–64 BC', *Historia* 56, pp.280–301.

Keall, E. (1994), 'How many Kings did the Parthian King of Kings rule?', *Iranica Antiqua* 29, pp.253–72.

Koselenko, G. (1980), 'Les Cavaliers Parthes', *dialogues d'histoire ancienne* 6, pp.177–99.

Kosmin, P. (2014), *The Land of the Elephant Kings: Space, Territory, and Ideology in the Seleucid Empire* (Harvard).

—— (2019), *Time and Its Adversaries in the Seleucid Empire* (Harvard).

Kuhrt, A. & Sherwin-White, S. (1987), *Hellenism in the East: The Interaction of Greek and Non-Greek Civilizations from Syria to Central Asia After Alexander* (London).

—— (1993), *From Samarkhand to Sardis: A New Approach to the Seleucid Empire* (London).

Lerner, J. (1995/96), 'Seleucid Decline on the Eastern Iranian Plateau', *Berytus* 42, pp.103–12.

—— (1999), *The Impact of Seleucid Decline on the Eastern Iranian Plateau* (Stuttgart).

Lewis, T. (1728), *The history of the Parthian Empire, from the foundation of the monarchy by Arsaces, to its final overthrow by Artaxerxes the Persian; contained in a succession of twenty-nine kings* (London).

Lozinski, B. (1959), *The Original Homeland of the Parthians* (Hague).

Lozinski, P. (1984), 'The Parthian Dynasty', *Iranica Antiqua* 19, pp.119–39.

Matyszak, P. (2019), *The Rise of the Hellenistic Kingdoms 336–250 BC* (Barnsley).

McEwan, G. (1986), 'A Parthian Campaign Against Elymais in 77 BC', *Iran* 24, pp.91–97.

Morkholm, O. (1980), 'The Parthian Coinage of Seleucia on the Tigris, c.90– 55 BC', *The Numismatic Chronicle* 20, pp.33–47.

Muller, S. & Wiesehofer, J. (eds) (2017), *Parthika. Greek and Roman Authors' Views of the Arsacid Empire* (Harrassowitz).

Nabel, J. (2017), 'The Seleucids Imprisoned: Arsacid-Roman Hostage Submission and its Hellenistic Precedents', in J. Schlude & B. Rubin (eds), *Arsacids, Romans and Local Elites. Cross-Cultural Interactions of the Parthian Empire* (Oxford), pp.25–50.

Neusner, J. (1963), 'Parthian Political Ideology', *Iranica antique* 3, pp.40–59.

Newell, E. (1925), *Mithradates of Parthia and Hypaosines of Characene* (New York).

Olbrycht, M. (2009), 'Mithradates VI Eupator and Iran', in J. Hoejte (ed.), *Mithridates VI and the Pontic Kingdom* (Aarhus), pp.163–90.

—— (2010), 'The Early Reign of Mithradates II the Great in Parthia', *Anabasis* 1, pp.144–58.

—— (2011), 'Subjects and Allies: The Black Sea Empire of Mithradates VI Eupator (120–63 BC) Reconsidered', in *Pontika 2008: Recent Research on the Northern and Eastern Black Sea in Ancient Times* (Krakow), pp.275–81.

Overtoom, N. (2016), 'The Power-Transition Crisis of the 240s BC and the Creation of the Parthian State', *International History Review* 38, pp.984–1013.

Paltiel, E. (1979), 'Antiochos IV and Demetrios I of Syria', *Antichthon* 13, pp.42–47.

Rawlinson, G. (1873), *The Sixth Great Oriental Monarchy; or the Geography, History & Antiquities of Parthia* (London).

Rea, C. (2013), *The Rise of Parthia in the East. From the Seleucid Empire to the Arrival of Rome* (Milton Keynes).

Rice Holmes, T. (1917), 'Tigranocerta', *Journal of Roman Studies* 7, pp.120–38.

Sachs, A. & Hunger, H. (1996), *Astronomical Diaries and Related Texts from Babylonia Volume III* (Vienna).

Sarkhosh-Curtsi, V. & Stewart, S (eds) (2007), *The Age of the Parthians. The Idea of Iran Volume II* (London).

Schippman, K. (1980), *Grundzüge der Parthischen Geschichte* (Darmstadt).

Schoff, W. (1914), *The Parthian Stations of Isidore of Charax* (Philadelphia).

Sellwood, D. (1962), 'The Parthian Coins of Gotarzes I, Orodes I, and Sinatruces', *The Numismatic Chronicle and Journal of the Royal Numismatic Society* 2, pp.73–89.

—— (1965), 'Wroth's Unknown Parthian King', *The Numismatic Chronicle and Journal of the Royal Numismatic Society* 5, pp.112–35.

—— (1976), 'The Drachms of the Parthian "Dark Age"', *The Journal of the Royal Asiatic Society of Great Britain and Ireland* 1, pp.2–25.

—— (1980), *An Introduction to the Coinage of Parthia 2nd edition* (London).

Shayegan, M. (2003), 'On Demetrius II Nicator's Arsacid Captivity and Second Rule', *Bulletin of the Asia Institute* 17, pp.83–103.

—— (2011), *Arsacids and Sasanians: Political Ideology in Post-Hellenistic and Late Antique Persia* (Cambridge).

Sheldon, J. (2006), 'The Ethnic and Linguistic Identity of the Parthians: A Review of the Evidence from Central Asia', *Asian Ethnicity* 7, pp.5–17.

Simonetta, A. (1966), 'Some Remarks on the Arsacid Coinage of the Period 90–57 BC', *The Numismatic Chronicle* 6, pp.15–40.

——— (2001), 'A Proposed Revision of the Attributions of the Parthian Coins Struck During the So-called "Dark Age" and Its Historical Significance', *East and West* 51, pp.69–108.

Strootman, R. (2018), 'The coming of the Parthians: Crisis and resilience in Seleukid Iran in the reign of Seleukos II', in: K. Erickson (ed.), *The Seleukid Empire, 281–222 BC: War Within the Family* (Swansea), pp.129–50.

Sullivan. R. (1990), *Near Eastern Royalty and Rome 100–30 BC* (Toronto).

Tao, W. (2007), 'Parthia in China: a Re-examination of the Historical Records', in V. Curtis & S. Stewart (eds), *The Age of the Parthians: The Ideas of Iran* (London), pp.87–104.

Tarn, W. (1930), 'Seleucid–Parthian Studies', *Proceedings of the British Academy* 16, pp.105–35.

——— (1938), *The Greeks in Bactria and India* (Cambridge).

Taylor, M. (2013), *Antiochus The Great* (Barnsley).

Van der Spek, R. (1997/78), 'New Evidence from the Babylonian Astronomical Diaries Concerning Seleucid and Arsacid History', *Archiv für Orientforschung* 44–45, pp.167–75.

Waterfield, R. (2011), *Dividing the Spoils: The War for Alexander the Great's Empire* (Oxford).

Wiesehöfer, J. (1996), 'Kings of Kings and Philhellen; Kingship in Arsacid Iran', in P. Bilde (ed.), *Aspects of Hellenistic Kingship* (Aarhus), pp.55–66.

——— (ed.) (1998), *Das Partherreich und seine Zeugnisse* (Stuttgart).

——— (2006), 'Iran from Arsaces I to Artabanus IV; the Parthian Reign', in *Ancient Persia* (London), pp.115–49.

Wolski, J. (1956/58), 'The Decay of the Iranian Empire of the Seleucids and the Chronology
of the Parthian Beginnings', *Berytus* 12, pp.35–52.

——— (1980), L'Armenie dans la politique du Haut-Empire Parthe (env. 175–87 av. n.Ã".)', *Iranica Antiqua* 15, pp.251–67.

——— (1983), 'Les rapports romano-parthes et la question de l'Arménie', *Ktema* 8, pp.269–77

——— (1993), *L'Empire des Arsacides* (Lovanii).

——— (1999), *The Seleucids, The Decline and Fall of Their Empire* (Krakow).

——— (2003), *Seleucid and Arsacid Studies: A Progress Report on Developments in Source Research* (Krakow).

Ziegler, K. (1964), *Die Beziehungen Zwischen Rom und dem Partherreich* (Wiesbaden).

Index

Philip V (Macedonian King 221–179 BC),
7, 10
Philippi, Battles of (42 BC), 70–2, 83, 89,
156, 195, 243
Phoenicia, 20, 27, 78, 141, 218
Phraates I (Parthian King c.168–165 BC),
11
Phraates II (Parthian King c.132–126 BC),
14–15
Phraates III (Parthian King c.70/69–
58 BC), 21, 25–7, 29, 126
Phraates IV (Parthian King 37–2 BC),
127-8, 146–7, 149–50, 153–5, 159–60,
163, 167–70, 172–4, 178, 180–3, 186,
189, 193–4, 210–11, 223, 234, 237–8,
241–3, 245, 247–50, 254, 257–62,
264–6
Phriapatius (Parthian King c.185–170 BC),
10
Perperna, M., 24
Perseus (Macedonian King 179–167), 11
Perusia, 89
Petronius, C., 252–4
Pinarius Scarpus, L., 230–1
Polemon, 159–60
Pompaedius Silo, Q., 95
Pompeius Strabo, Cn. (Cos. 89 BC), 87–8,
124
Pompeius 'Magnus', Cn. (Cos. 70, 55,
52 BC), 23–30, 32–3, 36–9, 41–5, 49–50,
53–6, 58, 67, 70, 121, 123, 137, 144–5,
200, 208–209, 212, 227, 262
Pompeius, Sex., 71–2, 77, 84–6, 108,
125–6, 133, 136, 147, 149, 189,
199–209, 212, 216, 229
Pompeius Rufus, Q. (Cos. 88 BC), 20
Pontus, 17, 19–20, 23, 27–8, 46, 48, 50,
52, 56, 63, 72, 80, 83, 85–6, 95, 100,
126, 153, 160, 194, 200–202, 212, 221,
230, 246, 265
Popillius Laenas, C. (Cos. 172, 158 BC), 11
Porcius Cato, M., 40, 50, 53, 70–1
Porcius Cato, M., 70
Praaspa, 157–8, 162–6, 168, 170–2, 174,
197

Ptolemaic Empire, 5, 12–13, 28, 30, 45,
48–9, 80, 83, 86, 98, 135, 188, 199,
227–8, 230, 233, 242, 246, 250, 254,
258
Ptolemy I (Egyptian Pharaoh c.304–283 BC),
99
Ptolemy XII Auletes (Egyptian Pharaoh
80–58 & 55–51 BC), 30
Ptolemy XIII (Egyptian Pharaoh
51–47 BC), 44
Ptolemy XV Caesarion (Egyptian
Pharaoh 44–30), 218–20, 233–5, 244
Ptolemy Philadelphus (Antonine King
34–30 BC), 218–19, 221, 234
Pupius Piso Frugi Calpurnianus, M (Cos.
61 BC), 29
Pydna, Battle of (168 BC), 11
Pyrrhus (Epirote King 307–302,
297–272 BC), 6
Pythodoros, 235

Raudine Plain / Vercellae, Battle of
(101 BC), 16
Rhodes, 10, 71

Saka, 12, 15–16, 225–6
Salvidienus Rufus Salvius, Q., 89
Samosta, 122, 124, 140–1, 157
Scamandrian Plain, Battle of (36 BC),
203–204
Scythians, 242–3, 248, 250, 255
Seleucia, 31, 75, 151
Seleucid Empire, 5, 7–21, 26–8, 31, 35,
57, 74, 85, 121, 135–6, 219, 265
Seleucus II (Seleucid King 246-226 BC),
8–9
Sempronius Atratinus, L. (Cos. 34 BC),
213
Sertorius, Q., 23–4
Sicily, 6, 84–6, 108, 189, 199–200,
205–206
Sinatruces (Parthian King c.92–69 BC), 21
Sosius, C., 125–6, 133–5, 140–2, 144,
146, 222, 226
Sparta, 4, 187